Great-Uncle Harry

Michael Palin has written and starred in numerous TV programmes and films, from *Monty Python* and *Ripping Yarns* to *A Fish Called Wanda* and *The Death of Stalin*. He has also made several much-acclaimed travel documentaries, his journeys taking him to the North and South Poles, the Sahara Desert, the Himalayas, Eastern Europe, Brazil, North Korea and Iraq. His books include accounts of his journeys, novels (*Hemingway's Chair* and *The Truth*), several volumes of diaries and *Erebus: One Ship, Two Epic Voyages, and the Greatest Naval Mystery of All Time*. From 2009 to 2012 he was president of the Royal Geographical Society. He received a BAFTA fellowship in 2013 and a knighthood in the 2019 New Year Honours list. He lives in London, UK.

GREAT-UNCLE HARRY

A Tale of War and Empire

Michael Palin

VINTAGE CANADA

VINTAGE CANADA EDITION, 2024

Copyright © 2023 Michael Palin

Published by Vintage Canada, an imprint of Penguin Random House Canada
Limited, Toronto, in 2024, and simultaneously published in Great Britain by
Penguin Books, a division of Penguin Random House UK, London. Previously
published in hardcover by Random House Canada, a division of Penguin Random
House Canada Limited, Toronto, in 2023, and simultaneously in Great Britain
by Hutchinson Heinemann, a division of Penguin Random House UK, London.
Distributed in Canada and the United States of America by
Penguin Random House Canada Limited, Toronto.

Vintage Canada and colophon are registered trademarks.

www.penguinrandomhouse.ca

The excerpt from Cyprian Brereton's unpublished memoir
on pp. 165–6 is reproduced by kind permission of Annie Coster.

Library and Archives Canada Cataloguing in Publication
Title: Great-Uncle Harry : a tale of war and empire / Michael Palin.
Names: Palin, Michael, author.
Description: Previously published: Toronto: Random House Canada, 2023. |
Includes index.
Identifiers: Canadiana 20230225500 | ISBN 9781039002005 (softcover)
Subjects: LCSH: Palin, Harry, 1884-1916. | LCSH: Soldiers—
Great Britain—Biography. | LCSH: World War, 1914-1918—Great Britain. |
LCSH: Somme, 1st Battle of the, France, 1916.
Classification: LCC D545.S7 P34 2024 | DDC 940.4/272092—dc23

Cover design by Henry Petrides
Cover illustration by Chris Wormell
Maps by Darren Bennett (www.dkbcreative.com)
Typeset in 11.96/15pt Dante MT Std by Jouve (UK), Milton Keynes

Printed in Canada

2 4 6 8 9 7 5 3 1

Penguin
Random House
VINTAGE CANADA

For Helen

CONTENTS

MAPS

The statue of Sir Philip Sidney atop the Shrewsbury School war memorial.

THE SHORT LIFE OF MY GREAT-UNCLE

At the gates of Shrewsbury School, where three generations of Palins were educated, there is a war memorial on which stands an elegant likeness of Sir Philip Sidney, poet, courtier, scholar and personification of all the finest qualities of the first Elizabethan age.

He died at the Battle of Zutphen in 1586, at the age of thirty-one.

Listed below are the names of 329 other former pupils of the school who gave their lives for their country. Among them is H. W. B. Palin. He died in the Battle of the Somme in 1916, at the age of thirty-two.

Much has been written about the distinguished life of Sir Philip Sidney. Nothing has been written about the life of H. W. B. Palin. But he was my great-uncle, and I felt his story should be told.

Not – I have to confess – that I've always thought that. Throughout my childhood and early adult years I was more preoccupied with the present and the future than the past, more interested in making sense of the course of my own life than that of anyone else. So far as I was concerned, the past was something to be dealt with by people who had time on their hands. It was a luxury.

So when in November 1971 we received a batch of family documents, including a black leather-backed notebook which contained a travel diary kept by my great-grandfather, a detailed Palin family tree stretching back two centuries, and five barely legible diaries kept by a great-uncle, I'm afraid they seemed nowhere near as relevant to my life as trying to earn a living writing and recording material for a new Monty Python series. Oddly enough, my father and mother seemed equally incurious. The whole bundle of documents ended up being set aside in some dusty cupboard.

Six years later I recorded in my diary the arrival at my parents' cottage in Reydon, near Southwold, of an Austin 1100, driven by a late-middle-aged lady called Joyce Ashmore, an unmarried cousin of my father. She seemed to be the nearest we had to a custodian of family history, and it was she who had sent the first tranche of documents. Now she had more. 'A very capable lady with a brisk and confident well-bred manner,' I wrote. 'She has a rather heavy jaw, but seems exceedingly well and lively. She is down-to-earth and unsentimental about the family, but interested in and interesting about stories of the Palins.' It was from her that I first heard the extraordinary tales of the lives of my great-grandparents and how they had met.

Before Joyce left, she handed over, rather apologetically, a further stash of Paliniana, among which were some photographs. One of these caught my eye. It was of a young man in a military uniform wearing a wide-brimmed hat and throwing a guarded glance at the camera.

I asked Joyce who he was. She was dismissive. It was an unfortunate younger son, she said. Killed in the war. Not much known about him and, by implication, not much worth knowing.

Rather in the same way that being told not to laugh makes you laugh more, her dismissal of this mysterious young man piqued my curiosity. But before I had a chance to do any digging, along came *Life of Brian* and *A Fish Called Wanda* and eight televised journeys around the world, and my great-uncle slipped to the back of my mind.

Years later, in 2008, I came across his name again while I was working on a documentary about the last day of the First World War. It was on the wall of another war memorial, this time in one of the Somme battlefields. Just a name, not a grave. H. W. B. Palin. One of many thousands 'Known Only Unto God'.

I knew then that I had to know more.

The photograph that started it all: Great-Uncle Harry in the uniform of the 12th Nelson Regiment.

PRELUDE

Henry William Bourne Palin, known throughout his life as Harry, came into the world on Friday 19 September 1884.

Consulting the *On This Day* website I find that no one of particular note was born on that day, and that nothing worth recording happened in the wider world.

Harry was delivered in a spacious upper room at the rectory in the village of Linton in Herefordshire. It looks out across rolling hills towards the Welsh border to the west and the Forest of Dean and the Wye valley to the south. At the time of his birth, his mother, Brita, was forty-two. His father, Edward, the vicar of Linton, was two days short of his sixtieth birthday.

Counting all the servants, upwards of a dozen people would have been in the house to hear Henry's first cries, and in the mild, dry, early-autumn weather of that month the sounds would have wafted out through open windows to the men working on the home farm.

At that time husbands were kept well away from wives in labour, and as their seventh child was being thrust into the world, Edward would most likely have been down in his study mapping out Sunday's sermon or hearing tales of hardship from distressed parishioners. But like everyone else inside or outside the house, he would have been listening out for the sounds from the bedroom above. And not without some anxiety.

By the time Harry made his entrance Brita had had half a dozen children in ten years, the last one being born more than six years earlier. Bearing a child at the age of forty-two was not without risk in an era when so many mothers perished giving birth. For Brita, another pregnancy, so long after the previous one, might well have been something of an unwelcome shock. In any case, of course, she already had a substantial family.

But then, large families were common in those days. With contraception methods limited to abstinence, withdrawal or the rhythm method, it's not so surprising that the average number of children born to middle-class couples married in the 1860s was far above the two that it is now. Charles and Emma Darwin, for example, had ten.

The impressive stone-walled vicarage at Linton which was the infant's first home was built in the fashionable Gothic Revival style – part French chateau, part German schloss. It was no ordinary rural rectory, but then Brita and Edward Palin were no ordinary couple. The story of their life together was remarkable by any standards. It was one of achievement, sacrifice and an unrelenting sense of purpose. A Victorian success story of which Henry William Bourne was the latest manifestation.

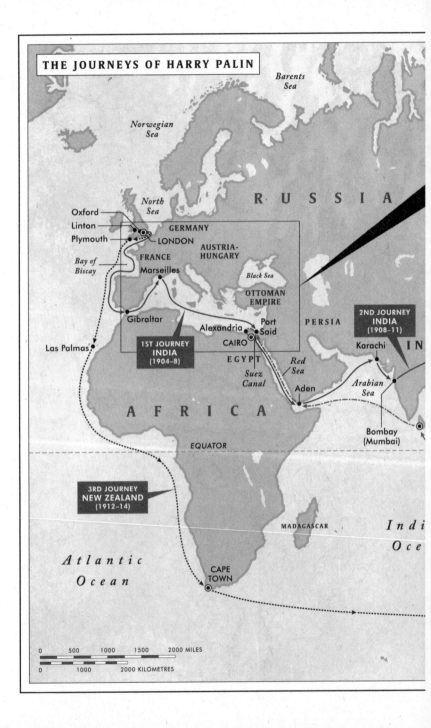

THE JOURNEYS OF HARRY PALIN

Barents Sea

Norwegian Sea

RUSSIA

North Sea

Oxford
Linton
Plymouth — LONDON
GERMANY
AUSTRIA-HUNGARY

Bay of Biscay
FRANCE
Marseilles
Black Sea
OTTOMAN EMPIRE

Gibraltar
Alexandria
Port Said
CAIRO
PERSIA

2ND JOURNEY
INDIA
(1908–11)

Karachi

IN

Las Palmas

1ST JOURNEY
INDIA
(1904–8)

EGYPT

Red Sea

Suez Canal

Aden

Arabian Sea

AFRICA

EQUATOR

Bombay
(Mumbai)

3RD JOURNEY
NEW ZEALAND
(1912–14)

MADAGASCAR

Ind
Oce

Atlantic Ocean

CAPE TOWN

| 0 | 500 | 1000 | 1500 | 2000 MILES |
| 0 | 1000 | | 2000 KILOMETRES |

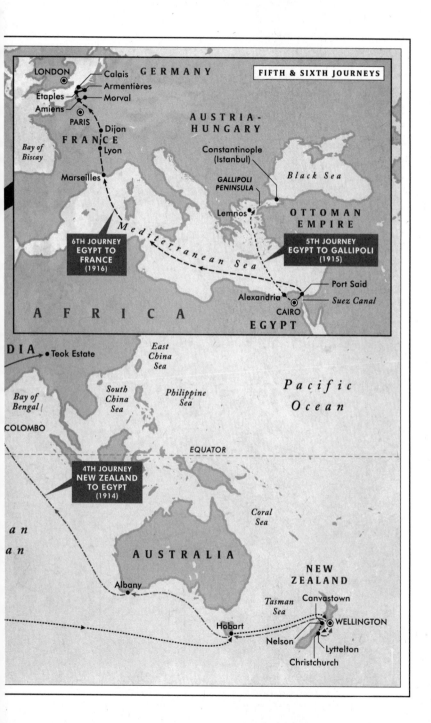

PART I

LINTON

St John's College, Oxford, where Edward Palin was an undergraduate and a Fellow. A watercolour of the St Giles' front by George Pyne, c.1870.

STAR PUPIL

IT IS THE SUMMER OF 1859 and Edward Palin, perpetual curate of St John the Baptist's, Summertown, and Fellow of St John's College, Oxford, is off on his summer holidays. He is thirty-three years old, a highly successful member of the college, recipient of any number of awards and exhibitions, a lecturer, preacher and since this last summer a Bachelor of Divinity. He takes his teaching seriously and is well respected.

Edward was the older of two children born to Richard Palin, a storehouse clerk from St Luke's in Middlesex, and Sophia Freeman. Edward's grandfather, another Richard, had come to London at the end of the eighteenth century. Previously the Palins had been a Cheshire family, and, thanks to Edward's exemplary record-keeping, I've been able to trace them back to a George Palyn of Wrenbury. Born in the reign of Henry VIII, he was a member of the Girdlers' Company who made enough money to endow exhibitions for 'poor scholars' at Brasenose

College in Oxford (something I didn't find out until after I'd left that establishment in 1965) and almshouses in Finsbury and Peckham in London. The Peckham properties were intended specifically 'for the relief and sustentation of six poor men'. They've since been rebuilt, but still bear the name Palyn's Almshouses, though you'd have to have around a million pounds to live in one of them now. George also bequeathed £500 for one of the bells at Bow, for which he was thanked with the accolade 'Cheshire made sweet Bow Bells chime'. His grandson, Thomas Paylin, was one of the three boys who, in 1651, helped hide the future King Charles II from Parliamentary forces after the Battle of Worcester.

For the next two hundred years the Palin family tree was a little less bushy, a little more obscure. Sadly, I've been unable to find out that much about Richard Palin – what, for example, his work as a storehouse clerk involved, or how much he earned – though I do know that he and Sophia had a house in Artillery Lane in Shoreditch and that they were listed as living there with four servants in the 1841 census. I have also discovered that he and Sophia were among the first to be buried in Highgate Cemetery, just around the corner from where I live. Their gravestone is next door to those of the family of Dante Gabriel Rossetti.

Whatever their precise circumstances may have been, it's clear that Richard and Sophia were determined to give their only son the best start in life. In the mid-nineteenth century it's estimated that no more than five to six thousand children a year were able to get an education that fitted them for university, but the couple managed to secure Edward a place at Merchant Taylors' School, which specialised in subsidised education for bright pupils from the trading – as opposed to the landed or military – classes. From there he proceeded, via a scholarship, to St John's College, Oxford. Founded within a few years of Merchant Taylors' in the mid-sixteenth century, and by the same man, St John's operated something of a closed shop with the school: thirty-seven out of fifty of the scholarships offered by the college were reserved for Merchant Taylors' pupils (a situation that would change in the light of the report of a Royal Commission in 1852). Edward began his academic studies at Oxford on 26 June 1843. Around the time his future wife was born.

Edward worked hard and did so well in his exams – which would have been both written and oral (the *viva voces*) – that he secured an exhibition, ensuring that most of his undergraduate studies were paid for by the college. He then went on, in the Easter term of 1848, to secure a first-class degree in *Literae Humaniores* – 'Lit Hum', or 'Greats', as it was colloquially known; Classics as we'd call it now. He was clearly a talented and assiduous student.

A heavy leather-bound, brass-clasped ledger book, in which from November 1849 onwards he began to record his thoughts, ideas and general jottings, offers a treasure trove of clues as to his character and aspirations at this time. There are passages admiringly and laboriously copied out from Scott, Wordsworth, Shelley and Coleridge, which reveal Edward's interest in and empathy with nature – for example, he has highlighted Coleridge's line, 'O Nature! Healest thy wandering and distemper'd child'. There are odd statistics that clearly caught his fancy: 'A clergyman writes that a pair of sparrows have been known during the time they were feeding their young, to destroy every week 3360 caterpillars.' There are jokes he enjoyed: 'An undergraduate with a cigar in his mouth is accosted by the Proctor [the university police] and stammers out that "he was only just finishing a cigar". "Oblige me, sir," said the Proctor, "by informing me who began it".' And there are oddities he appreciated, such as the inscription he'd seen on a barber's shopfront: 'Hair scientifically cut, and mathematically arranged.'

For someone like Edward, who so clearly relished his studies and college life generally, the logical next step, once he had graduated, was to become a Fellow. This would entail making a binding commitment: in an age when higher learning and religion were still intertwined, any undergraduate who sought a Fellowship was required to take Holy Orders within ten years of their graduation. It comes as no surprise, therefore, that in his ledger book Edward should have transcribed ruminations on the nature of God ('A God understood would be no God at all'), and that he should have included paragraphs with headings such as 'Preaching and Praying', 'Pantheism', 'Scepticism' and 'Reflections on Anglican and Roman Catholic Differences', and made notes on the use of wax lights in ritual, and meditations on faith, superstition and immortality.

But there was also another, more intrusive condition for a prospective Fellow. He had to commit to a vow of celibacy. Up until several decades later, only the President of the college was permitted to marry.

Which makes it intriguing, in view of the future course of his life, that I find Edward has taken the trouble to copy out a poem by the Scottish poet Thomas Campbell, entitled 'The Maid's Remonstrance'.

> *Never wedding, ever wooing,*
> *Still a love-lorn heart pursuing,*
> *Read you not the wrong you're doing*
> *In my cheek's pale hue?*
> *All my life with sorrow strewing,*
> *Wed, or cease to woo.*

Had Edward got himself into a similar situation?

Another poem that is constantly revisited in his notebook is 'The Princess', a lesser-known work by Alfred Tennyson. Its overall themes are the underestimated strength of women, and the poor provision for their education. But the two passages he's picked out, about love and loss, suggest that celibacy is not going to be an easy path for Edward.

> *Dear as remembered kisses after death,*
> *And sweet as those by hopeless fancy feigned*
> *On lips that are for others; deep as love,*
> *Deep as first love, and wild with all regret;*
> *O Death in Life, the days that are no more.*

And later:

> *She ended with such passion that the tear*
> *She sang of, shook and fell, an erring pearl*
> *Lost in her bosom.*

This esoteric collection of his thoughts on politics, history, literature, as well as theology, put together between 1849 and 1853, paints a portrait of a young man with a broad mind and wide-ranging curiosity, but also suggests the temptations that he knew he had to overcome as he prepared to dedicate himself and the rest of his life to God and the college.

They show, in addition, that even as he prepared to commit himself wholly to the donnish life, he was still considering other avenues. Reproduced towards the end of the ledger are some twenty references he assembled to help him procure the headmastership of Durham School. Dr Wynter, the President of St John's, talks of 'the high opinion I entertain of Mr Palin's merits as a gentleman and a scholar'. The Revd Warburton, Assistant Inspector of Schools, has 'high esteem for him as a teacher, which is shared by all those who have come under his influence as his pupils'. Mr Neate, a Senior Fellow of Oriel, has 'formed a very high opinion of his disposition, principle, and more especially of his great aptitude for gaining the respect and affection of the young'. The Revd Bellamy, his old headmaster at Merchant Taylors' School, recommends his 'scholarship, temper, industry and facility for communicating knowledge', while the Revd Mansel notes the 'zealous discharge of his sound but not extreme theological opinions'.

Despite this avalanche of academic support he failed to get the job. And that decided him: he would take Holy Orders and remain with the college. The same year, 1853, he was ordained a deacon of the church by Samuel Wilberforce (son of the anti-slavery campaigner William), and two years later, after undertaking the Rites of Ordination, he was admitted to the priesthood.

Privately, though, he admitted in his ledger book that it had not been an easy decision and that he had doubts as to his suitability for the role he had now elected to take on. Contrasting himself with 'the spotless ones', he wrote, 'I have to thank God who has counted me faithful, putting me into the Ministry who before was a blasphemer and a persecutor and injurious.' 'From my youth up,' he went on, 'the mercy of God has never left me quite to myself, but in my most distant wanderings has been over me.' He touched cryptically on a three-week stay the previous year at the Ehrenbreitstein Hotel in Koblenz when 'reflection was forced upon me in moments of an unavoidable seclusion'. He noted, equally mysteriously, that 'illness at Amsterdam threw me upon myself and impressions deepened and resolutions were taken'.

Now, though, Edward had set his course as a churchman and a Fellow. He had committed himself to a future at Oxford. He acquired a reputation as a tough examiner, earning the nickname 'Plough Palin' – a reference to his merciless sinking of the hopes of those who didn't come

up to standard (*palin* being the Greek word for 'again').
And he threw himself enthusiastically into the life of the
college and of the university.

A search of Edward's battels, the accounts of college expenses, reveals that he lived on the premises right
through until 1865. This was probably because he was a
more active participant in college affairs than many of his
colleagues, lecturing and overseeing exams and taking
on for a while the administrative duties of Senior Bursar.
To this end he would have had a 'set' of rooms, consisting of a bedroom as well as a study for conducting tutorials and entertaining fellow dons. It would have been a
congenial existence in what was in many ways more a
glorified club than a strict and sheltered community.
Among his colleagues would have been tennis players,
bridge players, debaters, musicians, card players, actors
and, doubtless, a few cads. In a revealing photograph of
Edward at Oxford, in which he is shown standing with a
group of Fellows in an Oxfordshire garden, he – smaller
than most of them and with thick dark hair – looks trim,
neat, somehow contained. His dress, and that of those
around him, however, is quite informal, with no sign of
the long gowns and mortar boards more usually associ-
ated with college life.

In 1859, with six celibate years at the heart of college life
behind him, Edward set out on his annual walking holiday in Switzerland. He kept an account of his travels in a
black leather-covered notebook. From the very first page

it's clear that he couldn't help noticing what he was not allowed to have.

He'd barely left Oxford before noting that 'at dinner off Southend' he 'made acquaintance with two young German ladies'. One was a Miss Gebhard, off to stay with her aunt in Worms. Edward wrote in his diary that she was a very nice person, and spoke English. He didn't catch the name of her companion, which I think he would have liked to have done, as 'she was a tall beautiful girl', a governess with a family called Preston, from Lowestoft. Both girls, it seems, were the nineteenth-century equivalent of au pairs.

'The sea,' he reports, 'was delightfully calm, and everybody seemed to enjoy themselves. I did, I know.' After he had 'slept like a top', he went up on deck at 5.30 in the morning to an unexpected bonus. 'I found my young lady no. 2 already there.' Fog – fortuitously for him, perhaps – delayed the arrival of the ferry. However, eventually the skies cleared and 'another roastingly hot day' began. Even so, they were almost twelve hours late docking at Rotterdam.

Edward had booked his passage on a riverboat down the Rhine, as far as Mannheim, but, when he found out how long this might take, 'I tore up my ticket and left the boat for the Rail.' This, coincidentally, allowed him time to escort 'my two fair German friends' to their accommodation at the New Bath Hotel (previous guests included the architect Sir John Soane, who has left us a sketch of the room he and his wife occupied when they stayed at the hotel in 1835). Having seen them safely installed, Edward set off, on foot, for the railway station.

Soon another young lady crossed his path. 'Found a young person going some distance same way as myself named Goodman – travelled together, she had been a governess in a family at St. Petersburg and was going into the household of an Amsterdam banker with a country house at Ede, two stations from Arnhem.' He took a paternal interest in Miss Goodman. 'Poor young thing!' he noted. 'She was in an utterly strange country and seemed badly cast down.' When they reached Ede, she was met by what Edward surmised might be her future mistress. 'A woman with a loud voice, but not, I hope for poor little Miss Goodman's sake, a hard heart.'

On Edward went, constantly falling in with strangers as he did so. At 'Brugg' he met an Englishman, travelling with his daughter ('such a charming little maiden'). As he made his way further into Switzerland he met a young gentleman in the hardware business at St Gall who 'expressed a great desire to see Sheffield'. At St Gall, a group of schoolchildren embarked and 'kept up all the way the celebrated Appenzell musical howl'. Rather than cover his ears, he described it most approvingly: 'Besides being singular it was very melodious.'

The further he travelled from his academic responsibilities, the sunnier his mood became. One doesn't have to look far for one source of his rising spirits. At Ragatz, for example, where his lodgings were 'picturesquely situated' opposite some flour and sawmills, he was delighted by 'a bouncing Swiss damsel by the name of Francisca' who 'carries my tub full of water as easily as if it were a feather'. At other times he drew pleasure from long,

adventurous walks: steep climbs alternating with peril-
ous slides down unstable slopes.

He revelled in the beauty of the landscape, the Alpine
flowers and the goat-filled meadows. Nor was he averse
to stripping off for a dip in a mountain stream: 'Off with
my toggery and in I was in a jiffy.' As his youthful admiration for Wordsworth suggested, he was an early envir-
onmentalist, it seems, writing with frosty disapproval
when he came across some woodcutters 'indiscrimin-
ately laying waste swathes of pine and oak for timber'.
He called them wood butchers. 'To watch the fall of
creatures full of life is like watching a field of battle.'
I wonder if he was familiar with the work of his near-
contemporary, Henry Thoreau, who, in his famous book
Walden, described the activities of loggers in America as
'making the earth bald before her time'.

As the holiday progressed, Edward became increasingly absorbed in nature. Physical descriptions of a
sublime landscape dot a diary punctuated with such sub-
headings as 'My First Long Walk' and 'My First Walk up
an Alp'. Occasionally, less poetic thoughts struck him.
He was, for example, critical of the flowers he saw in
Roman Catholic churches, contrasting their 'tawdry, arti-
ficial, dirty' appearance unfavourably with those to be
found at home in England: 'Our beautiful fresh, choice
flowers at Summertown – never stale – genuine offer-
ings from genuine hearts (I trust).' And, as ever, ladies
were never far from his mind. Describing a dinner where
he became 'acquainted with an evidently newly married couple on their honeymoon trip' he immediately

'thought of Maule who brought his pretty little wife the same route and was probably here not far from this time last year'.

He returned to Oxford, physically and mentally refreshed.

So much did he enjoy his holiday that two years later he decided to return to the Alps – this time with consequences that would change his life.

A view of Stachelberg in Switzerland, where Edward Palin first met his future wife, Brita Gallagher.

2

AMERICAN FRIENDS

O N 12 JULY 1861, EDWARD PALIN, now thirty-five years old, set out for the Continent from London Bridge station, detailing his progress in the same diary he used for his previous foreign excursion. The tone of the entries this time, however, is different. There's a sense of time running out, of opportunities that may not come again. An account of a meal at 'His Lordship's Larder' in the Rue Royale in Paris, for example, includes the cryptic afterthought that it was 'underneath a Boarding House where last year I had enjoyed many pleasant hours in company which I fear I shall never meet again'. There are some uncharacteristically minor chords, too. His hotel, the Hotel Dieppe, is described with some asperity as 'a vile hole'.

His attraction to the ladies he met remained undiminished, though he appears to have shaken off any longings through increasingly arduous physical activity – nine-hour walks up to and across glaciers, soakings in thunderstorms and vigorous rowing across lakes. 'I never had harder work in my life,' he reported. He seems to have been a perfect example of the Victorian concept of 'Muscular Christianity' – of a healthy mind in a healthy body – popularised by Thomas Arnold, the headmaster of Rugby, a few years earlier.

Edward ascended and descended the mountain paths of central Switzerland with such fierce determination that it's no surprise that he ended up in the Hotel Jungfrau at 'Aggischorn' [Eggishorn] 'unable to set foot in shoe for a fortnight'. He found the hotel to which he was unwillingly confined badly built with 'no partitions worth speaking of between the rooms', noting wryly, and probably speculatively, that 'honeymoon couples generally find fault with the accommodation'. But there were compensations. One night, he recorded, 'my stay was enlivened by a party of young ladies. What with these, the daily Times and a good collection of English novels . . . my time passed pleasantly enough.' So far as novels went, he would have had plenty of choice for these were golden days for English-language fiction. *The Mill on the Floss*, *A Tale of Two Cities* and *Barchester Towers* had all been recently published.

His blisters healed, he resumed his assault on various glaciers. And, as ever, he discovered comforts along the way, including 'milk and hospitality in Schachen-hauser [Schachenhaus] at the hands of a very pretty maiden who gave the name of Rosaline'. But it's clear that looking but not touching was something that Edward Palin BD, perpetual curate of St John the Baptist's, Summertown, and Fellow and Tutor at St John's College, Oxford, was finding increasingly difficult. He slipped and slid down the rocky slopes both physically and emotionally, and eventually body and mind combined to bring him a life-changing encounter.

It happened in the small mountain village of Stachelberg. 'I refreshed myself on arrival with a bath (not mineral – the smell of the water was enough for me),' he wrote, 'and after dinner went to bed.' And then: 'The next morning showed me the beauties of Stachelberg.'

It's forty years too early to talk of a Freudian slip, but it was more than the beauty of the landscape that impressed him, as his diary goes on to make clear. 'Made the acquaintance of an American lady (Miss Watson) and her adopted daughter Beda (Callagher?) of whom I was destined to see much more. Arranged to accompany them next day over the Klausen [Pass] to Altorf [Altdorf]'.

They left early next morning, 'taking a bottle of Beaujolais and some meat. We had a very merry party . . . lunching on the Col. The descent is as steep a zigzag as I ever met with'. 'Down it the ladies walked,' he added, approvingly.

At Altdorf, Edward wrote, 'our Miss Beda was . . . taken poorly at supper and left me to finish without her bright and sunny little presence'. However, she was well enough to join them when they returned to Lucerne by steamer the next day. Once there, the ladies went off to stay at Madame Orchmann's, while Edward headed to the Swan. 'The season was on the wane . . .

the weather breaking,' he noted. But there were compensations. 'I became very intimate with my American
fair friends, seeing a great deal of them every day. In fact
we seemed to find one another's company so mutually
agreeable that we became inseparable. In particular one
day I rowed them over our part of the lake and enjoyed
the trip much. I became a pretty constant visitor chez
Madame "Orchmann", and if Miss B had only been a
little older I don't know what might have come of it.'
Her age at this time,' he recorded, 'was 17.6 months' – in
other words, she was exactly half his age.

Another entry for his time in Lucerne seems to
reinforce just how remorselessly the attractions of bach-
elorhood were being tested:

> I must also mention one other friendship (I will call it)
> with an extremely excellent, modest and pretty young
> person named Josephine Kaufmann at Danniker's Bib-
> liotek [*sic*]. Often going to the shop for books I could
> not help being struck by her appearance and deport-
> ment and we used to have many chats together in a
> simple way, and if ever I return this way I am to re-
> member to pay her a call, whether she is still in the
> shop or married or whatever she may be. She requested
> it all in pure faith and I shall certainly remember her
> among the most interesting friends I know, and pay her
> the visit in the spirit in which the invitation was given.

Edward's life had reached a watershed. Whether or
not my great-grandfather could see it himself, a career of

celibate sufficiency was no longer the right fit for a man who liked women this much.

Edward came from a background where the written word was an essential part of life – letters were written and diaries kept, addresses noted and family trees compiled. Bright and sunny Beda came from a very different world – a world where little was recorded. Even her infatuated admirer consistently got her name wrong. Beda was in fact Brita, and her surname was not Callagher but Gallagher.

I don't know the names of Brita's parents. My great-great-grandmother and great-great-grandfather were too poor to be remembered. All I do know is that Brita was born in rural Ireland around 1843, and that she was therefore just an infant when the Potato Famine hit the country, causing starvation on such an appalling scale that it led to the deaths of a million people and left a further two million, who had previously scratched a livelihood from the soil, with no choice but to emigrate. I can only assume that Brita's parents were among the victims and that Brita was to all intents and purposes an orphan, no more than seven years old, when someone put her aboard one of the overcrowded, insanitary and often barely seaworthy 'coffin ships' bound for America.

Many who tried to make the Atlantic crossing died of disease or malnutrition en route. Brita Gallagher, blessed with a strong constitution, was one of the lucky ones. Her good fortune continued to hold when she arrived in Philadelphia, for here she was met by a philanthropist called Miss Caroline Watson, who proceeded to adopt her. The first written mention of the object of Edward's romantic interest is in the New Jersey census of August 1850, where Brita (misspelled this time as 'Bridget') is recorded as being a member of the Watson household. On the same census form the value of her guardian's estate is given as $18,000, a substantial sum at the time and the equivalent of over $500,000 today.

It seems likely that Caroline Watson's adoption of Brita was not an entirely chance affair. Caroline herself had Irish ancestry, her father John Watson being part of the eighteenth-century diaspora when large numbers of non-Catholic Irish, mainly from Ulster, left their impoverished homeland to seek their fortune across the water. They settled in what were known before the War of Independence as the Thirteen Colonies, of which New Jersey was one. John Watson set up a successful shoemaking business, from whose proceeds Caroline inherited enough to make her an independently wealthy woman.

She was also independently minded. Content to remain single, and a stalwart of the Quaker community, she campaigned tirelessly to provide girls with the classical education that boys received as a matter of course. To that end she became involved in the establishment of America's first academic boarding school for girls – St Mary's Hall, founded by the Right Revd George Washington Doane and situated in the village in which Caroline lived and which was now young Brita's new home:

Green Bank, New Jersey, on the banks of the Delaware River.

Thanks to Caroline, Brita received the best education possible. When Brita turned seventeen, Caroline decided to cap it all off with a Grand Tour of Europe. Which is how, a few weeks later, Miss Watson and her adopted daughter found themselves guests in a hotel in a small Swiss village and the objects of a polite and well-read Englishman's attention.

His holiday over, Edward Palin returned to Oxford for the Michaelmas term. Almost immediately he rather unexpectedly resigned as perpetual curate of the church in Summertown, much to the regret of his parishioners. To show their esteem and their gratitude for his five years' service as their vicar, during which time the church had been renovated and a programme of lectures introduced during the winter months, they presented him with an envelope case, a book-slide made of walnut, and a silver inkstand 'supplied by Mr. Rowell, silversmith of the city'. The inkstand has pride of place on my desk as I write, fitting snugly beside my computer.

Soon to be Senior Bursar at St John's, and a leading candidate to be next college President, Edward Palin threw himself into his work with the same energy and enthusiasm with which he had walked the Alps. But it's hard not to think that he had undergone a sea change. Once the lectures and tutorials and the dinners and the ceremonial processions were over, more worldly thoughts must surely have distracted him – thoughts of the 'bright and sunny' Irish girl he'd rowed onto Lake Lucerne only months earlier and who had moved him to confide in his diary that, had she only been a little older, 'how different things might have been'. After all, he must have acknowledged to himself, she was getting older all the time.

I'm into a tantalising area of supposition here. I know that Edward and Brita were married in 1867, but precious little about what happened in the years in between. When writing the film script for *American Friends* – my reimagining of their courtship – I played with the idea that not one but both women were after the Tutor. After all, Caroline was a single woman and he was a handsome bachelor and the generation gap between the two of them would have seemed considerably less than that between middle-aged Edward and young Brita. In the film I had Caroline and Brita visit Oxford, strolling into the quad at St John's, turning heads and causing the Tutor considerable embarrassment. I doubt this would have actually happened. What we know of Caroline Watson suggests she was too well bred to be impetuous, though Brita was perhaps less so.

More likely, I now think, is that the well-educated, school-founding Miss Watson saw Edward's attraction to Brita as a golden opportunity for her ward. For ten years Brita has enjoyed the benefits of one of the finest educations in America. Then, to cap it all, she meets, on her first visit to Europe, one of Oxford University's most respected scholars, who clearly falls for her. To turn a holiday flirtation into a proposal of marriage promises to be the crowning achievement of Caroline's life: it will give her much-loved adopted daughter a secure future and show that the money she has lavished on Brita's education has been well spent, helping to secure her a highly intelligent, highly suitable husband.

Of course, Edward was wedded already: to the college he'd served for nearly two decades. But Caroline was an American and a smart, wealthy and persistent one at that. The Oxford don's enforced celibacy was simply a challenge to be overcome.

As for Edward, I can't help thinking that his enthusiasm for academic life was beginning to wane. That he should have opted to give up the church in Summertown may have been due to his increased workload as Senior Bursar at St John's. It's equally possible, though, that he had decided to start cutting the ties that bound him to Oxford. I suspect, too, that he was not the sort of man who would have tried to hide his acquaintance with the attractive young lady he'd met on holiday under a mask of 'business as usual'. He was too direct and honest for that. Such an attempt would probably have been doomed to failure in the gossipy world of Common Room and High Table, where sexual activity among the unmarried was by no means uncommon.

In 1864, three years after he had first met Brita, Edward's father Richard died. Shortly afterwards the health of his close friend and fellow tutor at St John's, Henry Mansel, declined to the point where an extended convalescence away from Oxford became necessary. Mansel was one of the brightest lights during Edward's time at Oxford, who not only took a double first but, in 1855, was elected Waynflete Reader in Moral and Metaphysical Philosophy (a position sufficiently distinguished to allow him to marry whilst still retaining his college fellowship). He would ultimately become Dean of St Paul's Cathedral. Henry Herbert, 4th Earl of Carnarvon, a contemporary of Mansel and Palin's at Oxford, known as Twitters to his friends because of his nervous tics and twitchy behaviour, described Mansel as 'the centre of conversation, full of anecdote, humour and wit, applying the resources of a prodigious memory and keen intellect to the genial intercourse of society'. Edward Palin was thought by all to be his favourite pupil, and must have found his enforced leave of absence difficult to bear.

These twin ruptures seem to have finally prompted Edward to decide where his future should lie. In 1865 he made the most momentous choice of his life. After twenty-two years of loyal service to St John's College he chose Brita Gallagher.

Once the decision had been made, he and the college moved swiftly to a separation. He applied for nomination to the living of St Mary's in Linton, a church in the gift of St John's College, and on 13 October his successful application was confirmed by Dr Wynter, the man who at one time Edward might well have succeeded as President.

Linton is a small village in Herefordshire, a few miles east of Ross-on-Wye. Old enough to be mentioned in the Domesday Book, under the name Lintune, it has an ancient church, outside which stands an even more ancient yew tree, estimated by some to have stood for a thousand years and believed to be one of the oldest in the country (its location on church property having spared it the fate of most yews in the Middle Ages, which were routinely felled to make longbows.) Linton also has a pub called the Alma, almost certainly after the Crimean War battle, whose pub sign now bears the likeness of Florence Nightingale, and a mobile post office, serving – as in Edward's day – a predominantly agricultural community. When he took over as vicar there was one big local landowner, Lord Ashburton (a member of the Barings banking family), and a scattering of small farms producing wheat, barley, beets and supporting a few cattle. This poor and unspectacular farming community in a quiet corner of the West Country could hardly have offered a greater contrast to the demanding, high-achieving world of Oxford University, although at £675 a year Edward's parson's salary was a considerable improvement on the £250 he would have been pulling in at St John's.

His first act was to commission a new vicarage. The existing building had been described by a firm of Worcester land agents, in characteristically impenetrable property waffle, as 'scarcely sufficient for the residence of an incumbent of such a living' and 'exceedingly difficult' to 'improve by any outlay and from the peculiar situation of the different rooms'. In other words, it was too small. For his purposes, Edward needed something on a much larger and more ambitious scale. Demolition and replacement seemed the logical course of action.

It had been a little over four years since he'd first met Brita. Since then the 'bright and sunny little presence' had grown into a partner with her own ambitions for their future together. On 6 September of that year, it was Brita who stood by Edward's side as the builders, Pearson & Sons of Ross, laid the first stone for their new home. She was not yet twenty-two, and ready to start a family. Edward, two weeks away from his fortieth birthday, had no time to waste if they were going to fill all those rooms.

The key figure in all this was the third of the Stachelberg trio, Caroline Watson. Without her money I can't see how they could have contemplated building a new vicarage from scratch, let alone one on a scale way beyond the means of most country parsons. They were even able to go so far as to employ as their architect the highly fashionable William Wilkinson, the man responsible for the big villas of North Oxford and Oxford's most famous hotel, the Randolph.

Wilkinson proceeded to design Linton Vicarage with all the elan of his trademark Gothic Revival style. Built with red and grey stone quarried on the glebe (the 68 acres of land that went with the church) and lined with brick, its steep gables, circular towers, turrets and lancet windows gave it the appearance of a small German castle. It was, however, far from ascetic. There was a conservatory, lots of bedrooms, separate cellars for beer and wine, and such fashionable decorative flourishes as stained glass, polychrome tiling, carved newel posts and painted fireplaces. The total cost came in at £2,150, a considerable

sum at a time when the average house cost under £500
to build. St John's arranged a mortgage for £1,600, and
Caroline presumably helped out with the balance, but
Brita must have acquired some of her guardian's self-
confidence, for she became quite intimately involved in
the design, construction and scale of the new house.

Edward's predecessor at Linton, the Revd Curties, had
died in post, so on Sunday 11 February 1866 Edward 'read
himself in' at morning service, confirming his appoint-
ment as the new vicar of Linton. To escape the disrup-
tion as work began on tearing down the old vicarage and
replacing it with the new, he and Brita, with Caroline
Watson as companion and chaperone, then took
themselves off to Europe. They stopped in Lausanne for
a while before moving to Paris, lodging first in the rue
des Batailles and finally settling in the rue de Vaugirard.

In the early 1860s the French capital had become a
haven for rich, well-educated American expatriates who
could afford to escape the convulsions of the Civil War
back home. Caroline and Brita, both expensively educated Irish-Americans, would therefore have felt entirely
comfortable there. Their previous travels had, in any case,
accustomed them to a cosmopolitan way of life. And
with the Exposition Universelle, or World Fair, taking
place on the Champ de Mars, Paris would no doubt have
seemed to them the centre of the civilised world.

Edward, fluent in German and French, was also a
comfortable traveller in Europe. Even so, in the year he,
Brita and Caroline spent as international transients he
never quite turned his back on Oxford. In November

1866 he returned briefly to the university to deliver a lecture entitled *Distinctiveness of Character Consistent with Unity of Faith*. Deemed worthy of a wider audience, it was published by James Parker of Oxford, which is how I was able to trace a copy to the British Library.

Taking as his text the words from Paul's Epistle to the Corinthians, 'to every seed his own body. All flesh is not the same flesh', Edward essentially put forward the argument that people are not made alike, that nature never repeats itself. It's a theme that bears some resemblance to 'You're all individuals' in *Monty Python's Life of Brian*. In making his point he contrasted the tolerant unity of Anglicanism with the authoritarian bickering of the Catholic Church as it tries to frame unifying doctrinal imperatives. Despite its forbidding title, I was glad to see that my great-grandfather's sermon was a defence of cosmopolitanism and diversity.

Once Edward was back in Paris, he and Brita were finally married. Their wedding certificate shows that they were formally joined together on 2 October 1867 at the English Episcopal chapel at the British Embassy 'with the consent of the ambassador' and in the presence of Caroline Watson, Henry Palin Gurney and Archer Gurney. The presence of Archer Gurney almost certainly explains the slightly unusual venue. Chaplain of the Court Church in Paris, he also happened to be the brother of Henry Archer who had married Edward Palin's only sibling, Eleanor. Henry Palin Gurney, their son, was Edward's much-loved nephew, who he looked after almost as his own son. If Edward and Brita wanted to marry without fuss the discreet environment of the Embassy was ideal.

By the end of 1867 the newly wedded Revd and Mrs Palin were back in Linton, moving into the recently completed vicarage, and starting the family that was to fill it. Edward, by now, was forty-two and, by the standards of the time, would definitely have been regarded as getting on a bit.

After the distracted last years at Oxford this small West Country parish turned out to be what Edward needed and what the adopted Irish orphan and the rich American spinster needed, too. All the disparate elements in their background were now bound together in an orderly and, above all, respectable fashion. They had become that most sacred of Victorian institutions, a family.

Their first child, also called Edward, was born on 26 July the following year. As a reminder of how much a part of the family Caroline had become and of the debt they owed her, he was given the second name Watson. The debt was further repaid a year later when a new addition to the family, a daughter, was christened Brita Emily Watson. Eighteen months after that, a second son was born and christened Richard Mansel, after Edward's mentor and best friend at St John's. In all, in the first eleven years of their marriage, Brita bore Edward six children – two boys and four girls, each one well and healthy – no small feat at a time and in an area of the country where the infant mortality rate was one in ten.

I have the feeling that the vicarage was a happy place to grow up. All the children, apart from Mary, were known by affectionately shortened names: Edward was always 'Eddy', Brita was 'Tissie', Richard 'Richie', Edith 'Edie', Eleanor 'Nellie'. It was a busy and sociable place, too, playing host to a constant stream of visitors and parishioners and accommodating not just the family but a small army of domestic staff. The census of 1871 lists Edward and Brita as having four servants living on the premises. That of 1881, three years before Harry's birth, shows their numbers had swelled. Alongside Caroline, Edward, Brita and five of the couple's six children, there were James Noel, aged twenty, described as a 'scholar', who was perhaps the family's private tutor; Wilhelmina Press, a governess from Dessau in Germany; Anne Davies, a domestic servant from Radnorshire; Ellen Marshall, a parlourmaid; Mary Preece, a housemaid; Mary Hawkins, a nurse; and Eliza Marshall, an under-nurse. The last two were presumably there to look after Caroline who would by that time have been eighty-three and frail. The eldest boy, Edward Watson, then aged twelve, was not present when the census was taken, as he had just started as a boarder at Shrewsbury School, 70 miles away to the north.

In February 1882 Caroline Watson died at the age of eighty-four. Joyce Ashmore, Edith's daughter and Harry's niece, who originally brought me the documents which prompted this book, once told me that when Caroline Watson was on the point of death at Linton, she wanted to make a last-minute change in her will in favour of the

Palins. But my grandfather wouldn't let the lawyers see her as their presence would have sullied Miss Watson's last hours. So, harrumphed Joyce, the Palins missed out on being very rich.

With Caroline's passing an era ended. Two decades before, she had been instrumental in turning a relationship between a middle-aged Oxford don and a young Irish orphan into a great Victorian success story. She had then become an integral part of that couple's married life. She died in the bosom of a large and happy family, knowing that all her hopes and ambitions for her adopted daughter had been achieved. Her death must have been a great loss, even if it didn't come as a surprise.

A surprise, however, was on its way. Brita fell pregnant again, and two years after her guardian's death gave birth to a seventh child and third son – her lastborn. When he was six weeks old he was christened Henry William Bourne Palin at St Mary's Church, Linton. To his family he would always be known as Harry.

The western aspect of the vicarage at Linton, from William Wilkin-son's book English Country Houses: Sixty-one Views and Plans of Recently Erected Mansions, Private Residences, Parsonage-houses, Farm-houses, Lodges and Cottages.

3

THE LASTBORN

I READ RECENTLY IN *Psychologies* magazine:

> Lastborns are the most likely to make breakthroughs in
> creativity and science – they are the innovators. They
> are most likely to test the limits. They are charming,
> and if it's taken too far they can be manipulative be-
> cause they are used to being cute to get things done for
> them. The downside of that is that they can give up too
> easily later on in life because there is no one stepping in
> to fix whatever's wrong. They can also be very con-
> fused about whether they should grow up.

I was the lastborn of two, entering the world in May
1943, nearly a decade after my sister Angela (and fifty-
nine years after Harry). The raising of our little family
could hardly have been more different from that of the
Linton Palins. My father displayed none of the procre-
ative enthusiasm of his grandfather. In fact, it took him

so long to make up his mind about a second child that my mother, by her own admission, took the matter into her own hands. She told me, just before she died, that my conception was entirely orchestrated by her non-installation of a contraceptive device. She seemed anxious to let me know the circumstances in graphic detail: 'I know exactly which night it happened. I even remember what was on top of the wardrobe.'

To be fair to both my parents my late addition to the family could be put down to the state of the world at the time. Even as my mother squinted up at the top of the wardrobe, the future looked very bleak indeed. We were in the middle of a world war, the second in my parents' lifetime. Bombs were falling on British cities, tens of thousands of people were being liquidated in concentration camps, the German army was racing into Russia, and U-boats were picking off our supply ships in the Atlantic on an unprecedented scale. To conceive a child at such a time was an act of hope, defiance and, in my mother's case, of desperation.

Edward and Brita, by comparison, propagated their lastborn in a much less menacing time. There had been no major conflicts since the Crimean War of the 1850s. Queen Victoria was in the fifth decade of her reign. Her Empire stretched across the globe. Stability seemed assured. Britons were enjoying the benefits of ever more spectacular technological advances – in medicine and photography, electric light and transport – and world war was the stuff of science fiction. There could hardly have been a more comfortable time to be born. Unless, of course, you were an Irish patriot or an agricultural worker or a factory hand in the dark Satanic mills of the north. None of which the Palins were. Henry William Bourne came into a middle-class family, with two well-educated parents who had shown themselves to be pillars of the local community, and had already raised six children.

My sister Angela and I were born too far apart to be playmates and, as the years passed, the age gap between us seemed unbridgeable. By the time I was ten and becoming aware of things like age difference, she was nineteen and a grown-up woman wrestling with grown-up problems, and not the slightest bit interested in trainspotting.

I wanted to understand and even be part of her world, but it was impossible. The contexts of our lives were so different. I was a busy schoolboy, listening to *The Goon Show*, doing extra maths prep and being driven up to our school football pitch in the headmaster's Standard Eight into which he frequently squeezed a dozen boys rather than pay for a coach. Angela, in her teenage years, was locked in tensions with my father over her choice of job. The atmosphere at home was not always a happy one. She loved the theatre, and if she'd been a little more self-confident, she might have been an actress. But he saw the theatre as a career cul-de-sac and insisted that she learn what he saw as more useful skills. Though brighter than me, she was, as far as I know, never offered a chance to go to university. Instead my father pushed her to embark on a career that would ensure her financial independence from him. She gave in, took a typing course and disappeared to London. She never quite gave up on the theatre. Her life was a drama of different boyfriends and different flats, and she ended up as a studio manager at the BBC doing all sorts of things like slicing cabbages to create the sound of someone being beheaded.

The age gap between Harry and most of his siblings was even wider than that between my sister and me. When he was ten his eldest brother, Edward, would have been twenty-six, his eldest sister, Brita, twenty-five and Mary, twenty-one. Even his two younger sisters were teenagers by then, Edith being nineteen and Eleanor sixteen; on another planet, physically and emotionally. His only other male sibling, Richard, would have been away at school at Shrewsbury for most of Harry's early life. And his father would have been nearly seventy. More the age of a grandfather.

Harry would have been brought up almost exclusively in the company of women. In addition to his sisters, who, whatever their own preoccupations, must have lavished a fair amount of attention on their little brother, there were the five domestic servants – Anne, Mary Hawkins, Ellen, Mary Preece and Eliza – and it's likely that amongst them there would have been some competition for Harry's affections. The chances are that he would have been spoiled rotten.

I have stayed in the room in which Harry came into the world. It stretches across the west-facing side of the house. Immediately below it is a stone-flagged terrace with three flights of shallow steps converging from different directions, leading down to the field which was occupied, when I was there, by three elderly geese and Hilda, a Jacob sheep, chewing her way slowly through the day. The land slopes down to a narrow valley, then rises again in a patchwork of fields, with colourful names like Gilbert's Horn, Pear Tree Piece, Eight Acres and Cows' Land.

Across the landing, looking out on the other side of the house, is a much smaller, quite snug room which became Harry's bedroom. He would have had a very different view of the world from there. If the western aspect was a sea of green rolling away to the horizon, the east was much more confined. Fringed from the road by a tall stand of trees, it was the livelier side of the house. From his window Harry could see both the front door and, twenty yards further on, the kitchen entrance. The front door, solid oak beneath a pointed Gothic arch, gave on to a porch with a black-and-white tiled floor and stained-glass windows, patterned with plants and animals. This is where the more important visitors would be admitted – churchmen, local landowners, magistrates and other worthies. My hunch is that Harry would have been much more interested in the kitchen entrance – the door for tradesmen, domestic servants and all concerned with the running of the house. Here deliveries would be taken in by the housekeeper from a constant stream of fishmongers, bakers, and farmers bearing freshly shot birds. This was where the maids gathered to gossip and where cats and dogs would have sniffed around. In short, a lot for a young boy to see and hear, and plenty of life to join in with.

His father's study was on the ground floor looking out to the west. Oak-panelled walls gave it a sense of tasteful gravity, and for Edward it must have conveyed a reassuring sense of continuity with his rooms at Oxford. He wrote his sermons here and even tried his hand at poetry. Looking out from his window he was moved to reflect on the higher things of life, like Linton Hill:

> *Daily a landscape spreads beneath your feet,*
> *Wider and vaster than the eye can scan,*
> *Ah! strange how littleness and greatness meet,*
> *Greatness of Nature, littleness of Man.*
>
> *'Tis not the scene without, can make us great,*
> *Unless our vision take in Heaven as well;*
> *Faith can alone the spirit elevate,*
> *Whether on hill top or in vales we dwell.*

Edward was never a recluse and his study would have been one of the busiest rooms in the house. Here he would have discussed church business and chatted with his more elevated parishioners. Here, too, he would have hatched his ambitious plans to improve the welfare of the lowlier members of his parish.

One of those plans was to provide the village with its own school. Spurred on in part by the 1870 Education Act that sought to provide schooling for all children between the ages of five and twelve, Edward persuaded the bishopric of Hereford and his old college, St John's, who owned the land that came with the vicarage, to allow him to build a school on part of it 'for the education of children . . . of the labouring, manufacturing and other poorer classes in the parish', on the condition (probably insisted on by the landowners) that the master or mistress of the school was a member of the Church of England and that he or she could be dismissed for 'any defective or unsound instruction of the children in religion'. The project's most generous benefactor was the local, absentee landowner Lord Ashburton, who put in £160 to help set the school up. St John's College provided a further £90 and a government grant of £156 was also secured. Edward himself contributed £70 and raised a further £754. The school, designed around a single room 40 foot long and 25 high, which could accommodate thirty boys and twenty-four girls, opened in 1872 with fifty-two pupils. A teacher's house was completed a year later. In 1881 an infant classroom was added, paid for by Edward himself.

Another project that had absorbed Edward since he and Brita came to Linton was the provision of a freshwater supply for the village. After several surveys a spring 'eligible for domestic use' was discovered 200 yards below the new vicarage; and in 1880 a hydraulic ram pump was installed to raise the water from it up to the vicarage at the rate of a gallon a minute. An overflow from the tank was fed to a fountain, providing running water for the public, and making the need to carry pails of water to and from the two village wells a thing of the

LINTON & THE BORDER COUNTIES, *c.*1900

STAFF.

DEN.

Oswestry

Wem

Perry

Roden

Shrewsbury

Welshpool

MONT.

Severn

S H R O P S H I R E

Much
Wenlock

Church
Stretton

Bridgnorth

Onny

Corve

Severn

Bishop's
Castle

Clun

Clun

Bromfield

Cleobury
Mortimer

Ludlow

Tenbury

Teme

WORCESTERSHIRE

Lugg

RADNORSHIRE

Teme

Severn

Kington

Leominster

WORCS.

Worcester

Bromyard

Weobley

Lug

H E R E F O R D S H I R E

Arrow

Hay-
on-Wye

Wye

Credenhill

Withington

Great
Malvern

Clehonger

Lugwardine

Frome

Leadon

Ledbury

Hereford

Monnow

BRECK.

HEREFORD-
SHIRE

Ewyas
Harold

Wye

LINTON
SEE INSET

Severn

Ross-on-Wye

Gorsley

Gloucester

| 0 | | 10 MILES |
| 0 | | 10 KILOMETRES |

MON.

GLOS.

Railways

LINTON, 1901 (inset)

Alma Inn

St Mary's
Church

School

Vicarage

past. It remained the chief supply to the village for the next eighty-two years.

All the while Edward was busying himself with a steady programme of church restoration. The beamed roof was opened up, some windows replaced and stone-work stripped of layers of plaster and whitewash. The old box pews, where the wealthier families had their own private space, were dispensed with, and in their place new, more comfortable pitch-pine pews were installed. A new reredos was a personal gift to the parish from Brita (which suggests that her private income from Caroline Watson was still trickling down), and a handsome new font carved from Painswick stone by a Mr Hards of Ross was fixed in the western tower.

In 1888, Edward oversaw the installation of a new organ for the church, built by Mr Eustace Ingram of Here-ford, and inaugurated just in time for Christmas, with a concert given by Brita Emily Palin, the church organist since she was fourteen.

Harry, just four at the time, would have sat by his mother's side and watched his father in the pulpit and his sister at the organ and looked along the rows of pews and seen elder brothers and sisters looking confident and comfortable. Later he would have been led amongst the crowd of fellow worshippers, and craned his neck upwards to watch hands being shaken, congratulations given, and Christmas kisses exchanged. He would have seen the warm glow of family success.

Many of those present that day would have thought Harry fortunate to have been born into a family that looked like a blueprint for late-Victorian energy and achievement. Sociable, philanthropic and energetic. Edward – 'Eddy' – the eldest, having distinguished himself in sport and study at Shrewsbury School, had gone on to get a First at Christchurch, Oxford, and was on his way to qualifying as a doctor at St Thomas's Hospital in London. Brita – 'Tissie' – the precociously gifted church organist, would marry in style at the age of twenty-five. Richard – 'Richie' – was making his mark at Shrewsbury as a runner and footballer. Edith – 'Edie' – ran the Sunday School and succeeded her sister as church organist. Both she and Eleanor – 'Nellie' – would ultimately make sound and respectable marriages.

And then there's Harry, the lastborn, just starting out on a life that will never fit the straight line of advancement, that takes twists and turns, defies convention and goes up blind alleys and in unexpected directions. It isn't always an easy route to follow, but it's different, often very different.

Harry's life may turn out to be the least conventional of the Palins of Linton, and to me, that's what makes it worth following.

In the summer of 1889, quite out of the blue, tragedy hit this apparently invincible family from the most unexpected direction.

On 15 June Harry's brother Richard died at the vicarage at the age of just eighteen. His death certificate shows the cause of death as 'Blood Poison. Typhoid'.

Though it was still common enough in the nineteenth century – Queen Victoria's beloved Prince Albert died of it – it was generally regarded as a disease that could be eliminated by improved hygiene and sanitation. Considering that Edward and Brita had spent so much on bringing a fresh-water supply to the village and testing its content for purity, it seems a cruel irony that their own son should fall victim to such a disease. However, from the evidence I've been able to unearth it would seem that the source of his infection was not home, but quite possibly the school he attended. Shrewsbury School, founded in 1552, had recently moved from the centre of town to a new and spacious site at Kingsland on the banks of the River Severn. Proximity to the river offered an exciting new opportunity for Shrewsbury to match other public schools, like Eton and Westminster, in the fashionable sport of competitive rowing. Unfortunately, the river was scandalously polluted at the time. Richard, a keen sportsman, would not have been the only one to have succumbed to the effects of untreated waste.

The progress of the disease would have been wretched: abdominal pain, high fever, nausea, lesions on the skin, constipation and diarrhoea and difficulty in breathing, before death by blood poisoning or intestinal haemorrhage. Throughout his ordeal Richie was looked after at home in the vicarage, where the atmosphere must have been strained to breaking point. Harry may have been protected from the worst of the ordeal, but he must have heard Richard's cries of pain and seen the

impact of his suffering on his parents and those minis-
tering to him.

When, after three or four weeks, it was all over, Harry
had lost the brother who was closest to him, the brother
he must have looked up to, perhaps even hero-worshipped.
The only one of his siblings he could play boys' games
with had been taken away long before his time. Harry
would have felt his own sense of loss, but how much
he was able to communicate it is another matter. Meanwhile the happy home, so suddenly transformed into a
place of suffering, was now going through weeks, maybe
months of mourning. His mother and father must have
been inconsolable. And everyone would have been talk-
ing of Richie.

Once the shadow of Richard's loss had retreated a
little, the routine of a busy house would have returned.
Brita would be busy managing domestic affairs, as well
as helping with parish business and the upkeep of the
church. Her daughters would be assisting in the school
Edward had founded, and in the musical life of the
church. And while Harry was playing or studying, he
would never be far from the openings and shuttings and
knockings and occasional slammings of the strong oak
door of his father's study as Edward, juggling the spirit-
ual and the material in his roles as vicar and magistrate,
attended to local grievances and the personal crises of
others. Two particular issues occupied him at this time.
One was competition from a new church set up by Baptist dissenters at nearby Gorsley, which locals loyal to
Edward and St Mary's now took to calling 'Heathen's

Heath'. The other was the calamitous agricultural reces-
sion that Linton, in common with the rest of the country, suffered in the last decades of the century. Largely
caused by the import of cheap wheat from across the
Atlantic, it led to plummeting prices and a mass exodus
from the land. Linton's population declined from 927 to
608 in just twenty years.

Harry must have needed some refuge from the whirlwind of activity around him, and I think the most likely
place he would have found it was on the farm attached
to the glebe land that came with the vicarage. Here
amongst the geese, chickens, even a cow or two, Harry,
like any young boy of his age, must have felt most at
home. He would have helped out at harvest, looked after
the animals, learnt to ride the horses and at the same
time been taught all sorts of skills like hedging, fencing
and wall building.

There's little evidence of his forming close friendships with other boys. And it's unlikely he went to the
local school. Despite it being founded and supported
by his father, it was largely for the children of agricultural workers in the area. When it came to his education, therefore, he would probably have followed the
middle-class path of both his brothers: a private tutor
at home, with the prospect of boarding school a little
later on and, given his father's academic background, the
hope of university at Oxford or Cambridge. His home-
schooling would have been partly provided by his father
and mother, but largely by a governess, presumably the
Wilhelmina Press from Dessau listed in the 1881 census.

Edward had gained a familiarity and respect for the language and culture of Germany from his holiday travels, so it comes as no particular surprise that he should have engaged a German governess. The irony is that Harry almost certainly received his early education at the hands of someone whose countrymen he would one day fight to the death.

In later life Harry showed no aptitude for public service or higher learning. Indeed, it looks as though he deliberately turned his back on that side of his father's life – the poems in Latin, the little jokes in classical Greek, the scholarly Oxford connections meant nothing to him. Perhaps the force of his father's personality was just too hard an act to follow. Harry's preference was for the practical rather than the administrative.

Whether he liked it or not, though, formal schooling could not ultimately be avoided. When he was fifteen he was sent away to Shrewsbury School to begin the conditioning that would deliver another fine, respectable, hard-working son of Empire.

A key Palin family trait is stubbornness. Often misunderstood as a negative quality, I know from my own life that it can make the difference between fulfilment and frustration. My guess is that it was at around the time that Harry was sent to Shrewsbury that the stubbornness that would shape his destiny started to show itself. Ultimately, it would yield a degree of fulfilment.

First, though, the frustration.

The main school building at Shrewsbury School, c.1890. It had, at various times, been an orphanage, a prison and a workhouse for the destitute. Harry was a pupil here for barely two years.

4

SCHOOLDAYS

—◆—

I N SENDING HARRY TO SHREWSBURY the Revd Palin
was maintaining a family tradition that had begun
with Eddy and Richard and would be carried on by
his grandson, my father (though not by me: all my children went to schools just five minutes' walk from our
house). But there were significant differences between
Harry's experience of Shrewsbury and that of his two
brothers. Rather than staying for the usual four years, he
remained there for just over two, joining in the summer
term of 1899 and leaving in July 1901. And while Eddy
and Richard both enjoyed distinguished school careers,
there's no evidence that Harry's time at Shrewsbury was
exactly overburdened with achievement.

Sporting competition is one of the main engines of the
public-school system and here both his brothers excelled.
In the school records Eddy is mentioned as Captain of
Football, member of the school rowing crew, and Senior
Whip in the RSSH (Royal Shrewsbury School Hunt,

aka the cross-country running team). In his last term, he also became a Praepostor, or school monitor – as high up the pecking order as it's possible to get. For his part, brother Richie made the school Football XI and was a Junior Whip.

Harry would have needed to have acquitted himself well to measure up to his brothers. But a thorough scouring of the school archives reveals no more than a brief mention as No. 7 in the trial Rowing VIII. Nor does his name appear on any honours boards, or on the School Wall, on which both his brothers were allowed to inscribe their initials, a privilege granted to those who excelled at sport.

I was fourteen when, in May 1957, and with my parents in tow, I arrived at Shrewsbury for the first time. If my own experience is anything to go by, I guess that the moment Harry crossed the Kingsland toll-bridge over the River Severn and carried on up the hill to the school for the beginning of the Lent term of 1899 he would have been aware of an increasing tightness in the stomach. Once through the school gates this would have intensified as the weight of authority and three hundred years of tradition bore down upon him. His eye would have been drawn to the imposing bulk of a long, four-storey red-brick building, dominated by a handsome verdigris clock tower. Here the classrooms awaited a new term's intake.

In my case, I'm bound to say that my first emotion at arriving at this ancient place of learning was embarrassment. As my parents unloaded my things from the car boot, including the same wooden 'tuck box' that my father's own parents had carried into the school forty-five years earlier, their old Austin Cambridge, the family's pride and joy, seemed no match for the Rovers and Jaguars that surrounded it. My parents, like Harry's, were at the older end of the spectrum and my father had a stammer which got worse when he met my housemaster. Young teenagers are always embarrassed by their parents, but I clearly remember that my feelings were conflicted. Faced with a twelve-week term ahead, I wanted them to stay and I wanted them to go. With equal intensity.

Whether or not Edward or Brita accompanied Harry on that first occasion is unknown. Either way, there rapidly came a point when he was on his own, and expected to fend for himself. As I know from my own experience, the first two years at a traditional boarding school are hard going. And made deliberately so. You are at the bottom of the pile, expected to deal with daily humiliations and setbacks before you can hope to reap any of the benefits and privileges that come with seniority. In my time they called it character building. Harry's comparatively short stay at the school would have ensured that he saw more of the worst and enjoyed less of the best that Shrewsbury had to offer.

There is a novel about life at Shrewsbury written shortly after Harry's time there, which follows a boy through his years at the school. It was written by Desmond Coke and its title, *The Bending of a Twig*, gives some idea of the theme of the ensuing story. It captures, through the eyes of a boy called Marsh, the effect of the arcane rules and customs of an ancient institution on a boy who, up until now, has been protectively home-schooled. Unfortunately named Lycidas by his artistic parents – his father's a poet – the story revolves around the boy's struggle to accept the hard knocks of life at Shrewsbury and his subsequent hard-won success in making friends and fitting in.

I wonder to what extent Harry's experiences paralleled those of Lycidas: if he too, having been spoiled by the comfortable, cosseted life at Linton, found it difficult to adjust to being on the bottom rung of a very long ladder. How well did he deal with the challenges of this new and hierarchical world in which he was always Palin, never Harry? Were his mother's anxieties the same as those which Lycidas Marsh's mother turns over in her mind on the night before her child leaves home for the first time? 'How would he fare at Shrewsbury? Would his ignorance of boys and their ways, of school and its life, make matters hideously hard for him?'

As a new arrival Harry would have been tested for any hint of weakness by a series of indignities. New boys were known as 'scum', and, under threat of a beating, were required to sing in the dormitory or wash older boys' football boots. There was a whole new language to learn. Work was 'sap', praying was 'digging', showers were 'swills', running was 'towing', paper was 'penal', and expressing any opinion of one's own was seen as 'being lifty'. Sporting prowess was admired, intellectual prowess mistrusted. New boys would be expected to prove themselves in Hall Boxing, cross-country runs like The Tucks and on the river.

The days were long, strictly measured out and, rather like life on board ship, ordered by the sounding of bells. After a cold shower in his boarding house at the crack of dawn Harry would have had to get very smartly across to the school chapel for morning prayers, over to the school buildings for his first lesson, and only then back to the house for breakfast. His progress would be monitored by regular takings of the register, known as 'call-overs', from which there was no hiding. Latin, French, English, history, elementary mathematics and scripture would be the bedrock of the school curriculum he was expected to master. Shrewsbury had, however, recently built a science block, known as the Stinks Room, and there were additional facilities for carpentry and a darkroom for budding photographers.

As I remember it, the two most important tools for survival in those first weeks at Shrewsbury were a sense of humour and a friend. The sense of humour enabled you to weather difficulties and deflect criticism. The friend was not necessarily someone with whom you had much in common, or in some cases even liked, but they were there to share the complications and confusions and to help you avoid displaying any suspicion of loneliness or self-pity.

Harry might well have been bold and gregarious and quite untouched by these emotions – but he would have had to get used to being ordered around, and because he left the school early would not have been given the opportunity to do the ordering around himself. There would undoubtedly have been hard and hurtful words spoken at Shrewsbury. That's part of the process. But in Harry's case there was the added pressure of a failure to achieve, a failure to win, a failure to come up to the high standards set by his older brothers. Such failure must have disappointed his parents. For Harry I suspect it resulted in yet more disillusion with privilege and the traditional trappings of success. And yet more discomfort with the world he was being forced into.

What other influences might there have been on Harry as he entered his teenage years? The novels of G. A. Henty, who prided himself on historical fidelity and manly sentiment, would almost certainly have found favour at Shrewsbury, along with the recently launched *Union Jack* magazine. Designed to promote 'high-class fiction' to counter the influence of the penny dreadfuls, its most popular creation was the detective Sexton Blake.

The *Boy's Own Paper*, launched in 1879, was also widely read. In it was a Correspondence Column that gives an interesting insight, often unintentional, into the concerns and anxieties of boys of Harry's age. Spots, masturbation and fear of weediness seemed to predominate.

The boys who wrote in mostly used pseudonyms, and since their letters were never published, their content had to be guessed at from the answers. This made for some bizarre reading. 'Fred L', for example, is advised, 'By all means remove your moustache if you are only five feet high.' 'Young Taxidermist' is told briskly, 'Why not boil the rabbit, eat the meat, preserve the bones and then prepare the skeleton? There is no better way for a beginner.' Then there are the frankly bizarre queries, for which the editor clearly has little patience. 'Arthur' is severely reprimanded: 'We do not understand you. You cannot get photographs of people who lived before photography was invented.'

The column is haunted by the ever-present spectre of Evil Habits. 'Swallow' is urged to 'have a cold bath every morning and wash yourself all over'. An anonymous correspondent is taken to task: 'Are you not constantly told that such practices ruin the life of thousands?'

I only hope Harry had a sense of humour.

The earliest photograph I have of Harry was taken as he approached the end of his time at Shrewsbury. The occasion was the wedding of his sister Edith at Linton in April 1901. At the time, the country was in mourning for Queen Victoria, who had died barely two months earlier. She had been on the throne for nearly sixty-four years, and was the only monarch most Britons had ever known.

In one carefully posed group photo, the Revd Edward Palin stands, holding his topper, with the inner circle of his family around him, and the roofs of the school he'd endowed as well as the vicarage he and Brita had built looming over the wall behind them. What's left of his hair is snow white, but he's kept his good looks and, despite all he's been through in his seventy-five years, his eyes still pierce the camera. The group around him, centred on the newly-weds, is bookended by two seated figures. On the left is Dr Edward Watson Palin, looking very much the son and heir. He sits comfortably at a slight angle to the rest of the group; legs crossed, revealing immaculately pressed trousers, clutching an impressive topper and wearing the hint of a smile. A recently qualified doctor, he's been married for two and a half years to Agnes, née Buckley, who stands, hat bursting with organza, beside him. They have one child, Edward. My father.

At the other end of the group sits Henry William Bourne, the youngest of Edward and Brita's children. Sixteen years old and nearing the end of his formal education, his appearance could hardly be in greater contrast to that of his elder brother. The two of them put me in mind of the figures in a weather house, one that comes out when the sun shines and one that comes out when rain is on the way. Edward exudes relaxed confidence. Harry sits bolt upright, staring hard as if challenging the camera.

What strikes me most about him is not so much his stiff pose – he was, after all, sitting the way public schoolboys were taught to sit – nor his scowl – he was a teenager and teenagers don't take well to being made to dress up – but something else, something more disconcerting.

As they pose together on the croquet lawn to one side of the vicarage, the family look assured. Everyone seems to have some role, some purpose. They are all playing their part in a successful story. Except for Harry. Sitting at the very edge of the group, his hard stare looks out from a world of his own. This is not the expression of someone at ease with himself or what's going on around him. There is no confidence, only world wariness.

There is another sight of Harry in a bigger group photo, taken on the same day. He's a slight figure, standing in one of the back rows, stiff and literally buttoned up, next to a markedly more relaxed companion. His expression hasn't changed. The same guarded glower. It's the look of someone who wants to be somewhere else, someone who doesn't fit the role he's being made to play.

I think that may be the key to Harry at this point. He's a boy brought up amongst women, growing up in a world run by men. A world whose role models, whether they be generals or governors, explorers, storytellers, adventurers, politicians or leaders of industry, are almost exclusively male. Harry is learning that the purpose of his education and upbringing is to earn him his rightful place at the heart of a male establishment that is in its heyday. At this time of imperial power and influence it is a fine time to be a young Englishman. But Harry is having none of it.

At a family level, he is only too aware of his father's reputation, his sisters' social ease, his brother's success at all he touches. For whatever reason, he has been unable to emulate any of it. So he deals with all this display by staring it down. He may have already decided his course. He will live his life his own way.

How he tries to steer a way between what he wants and what others expect of him is, I submit, the story of his short life. Right now, he's a work in progress, glaring out at us over the top hats, fine dresses, knowing laughter and confident smiles. His family are close and caring and are not going to give up on the lastborn. There are still avenues to explore. Maybe less academic and more practical.

And, of course, there is one great training ground to which they are lucky enough to have access. Memorably described by the historian Jan Morris as 'these immense possessions in the sunshine', the British Empire covers a quarter of the world and holds sway over more than 400 million people. And it's the British Empire that now beckons.

Port Said, c.1910, where 'the East' began.

5

TRAVELLING TO WORK

I N NOVEMBER 1903 EDWARD, THE patriarch of the family, died at the then considerable age of seventy-eight. His death certificate, signed by A. Curtfield MRCS, offers a bleak picture of his health at the end. 'Cause of Death' is given as 'Atheroma of Arteries, Senile gangrene left leg 16 days, Amputation 4 days, Congestion of lungs 24hrs'. The life-threatening gangrene, caused by hardening of the arteries, required the removal of one of his legs below the knee. He died soon after the procedure. His amputated leg was later retrieved and buried with him. A Nurse Nash 'who attended the deceased' was present at the funeral. Harry was one of the pallbearers who helped carry his father's coffin the short distance from the vicarage, across the road, past the ancient yew tree and into the church. A journey his father must have made almost daily for thirty-six years. The *Ross Gazette* reported the funeral as a solemn and ritualised affair. 'The remains were arrayed for burial in surplice and stole, and were enclosed in a St Alban's casket of polished oak.' 'O God, Our Help in Ages Past' was sung after the reading of the lesson, and the 'Dead March' from *Saul* was played on the organ as the body was brought into the chancel. The grave was lined with ivy, 'this being the work of Mr. Jones, gardener at the Vicarage'.

Harry must have had mixed feelings as he watched the coffin being lowered into the grave. One of the central figures – perhaps the central figure – in his life was gone. And his personality had left a very long shadow, from which Harry now had to step away. It wasn't going to be easy. The pathway his father had so confidently trodden was not one his youngest son could follow. He had been unable to seize the opportunities his eldest brother had made so much of, and he quite likely felt that any affection his father had for him could not match the affection his father had for Richie, the son he lost, and alongside whom he had requested to be buried.

To this day, the remains of Richard Palin and his father and mother lie side by side beneath a well-kept tomb in the well-kept graveyard of St Mary's, Linton.

The minutes of the vestry meeting of 5 April 1904 record a 'deep sense of loss' and also contain a warm appreciation of Edward's thirty-six years of service to the church and the parish. He is described as 'one of the greatest vicars the Parish had ever had', the minutes noting 'how entirely he had always cherished the interests of the Parish and . . . in all his actions been animated by a desire to . . . forward the welfare of the Parish as a whole and all who lived in it.'

Not surprisingly, there were those in Linton who hoped that the new incumbent at the vicarage would be another Edward Palin. Shortly after the funeral, William Webb, one of Edward's long-serving churchwardens, wrote to the Bishop of Hereford, requesting that he appoint as Edward's successor 'a clergyman of moderate views'. 'Our late vicar,' he wrote, 'had an aversion to ritualistic performances and we hope his successor may be of the same principles.' Confirmation, if any were needed, that Edward Palin, while socially enlightened, was in many ways a traditionalist who had no time for the High Church practices championed in his years at Oxford by Cardinal Newman and the reforming Tractarian movement. And when a new vicar, the Revd Box, was appointed, he was swiftly reminded of the pedigree of his predecessor and the size of the shoes he was expected to fill. In a letter to the fresh incumbent, Compton Reade, an Oxonian and old friend of Edward's, spoke of the legacy of 'genial "plough-Palin", the most rigorous of examiners, the most indulgent of friends', and went on, rather intimidatingly, 'I wish you may find in Linton as congenial a home for as many years as your brilliant predecessor, who might have been almost anything had he not deserted Oxford for Arcadia.'

The Revd Box, however, was not another Edward, and swiftly ruffled a few feathers when he declared his decision to call himself rector. Brita, for one, was unimpressed. In a letter of protest to the churchwarden she wrote, 'Mr Box has a perfect right to take the name of Rector, if he wishes to change the old traditions, a mistake to my thinking, but I am a great conservative, as my dear husband was.' She went on, 'Mr Palin would as soon of thought of taking down the Bells from the Church, as to have changed the fine old English title of Vicar . . . It is such a real English title, as there are Rectors all over the world, but not Vicars.'

The switch from vicar to rector was not the only change that Brita had to contend with. Just a few months before Edward died, Balfour's Education Act of 1902 removed the administration of church schools from local vicars, so depriving Edward and now his widow of any control over the village school they had brought into being at the start of their marriage. As the ties binding her to Linton were severed and as the winter deepened, Brita had to make swift plans to leave the vicarage which she and Edward had built and which St John's College had moved smartly to re-allocate. Along with Mary, Eleanor and Harry, Brita spent the first Christmas in thirty-six years away from Linton, at their eldest son Edward's recently acquired house at Great Ryburgh, near Fakenham in Norfolk.

The future must have seemed bleak. Luckily, though, Edward and Brita had planned ahead, and had the money to do so. In the same year that Edward died, he and Brita acquired, under Brita's name, a newly built house, 7 Staverton Road, North Oxford. This was very much Edward's old stamping ground. A two-minute walk from St John the Baptist's, Summertown, the church of which he had been the curate and from which he had resigned after meeting Brita. I realise that during my last year at Oxford I must have walked past the house many times when in student digs in nearby Woodstock Road. Very much in the North Oxford style of the Linton vicarage, it's a big, gabled affair, decorated with red brickwork, complete with a sitting room, family room, study, two cloakrooms and a kitchen on the ground floor, seven bedrooms on the top two floors, and a large garden. As I write, in early 2023, it has just been sold for £1.3 million, despite needing 'total renovation throughout'. The plot thickens when I discover, with a trace of reassuring familiarity, a Linton Road running parallel with Staverton Road. This was to be Brita's new home, and the start of a new life without Edward.

Finding work for her youngest son was her most pressing problem. As Harry approached his twentieth birthday, Brita must have looked round anxiously for something to occupy his time and start him out on his adult life. She couldn't rely on his adopting the same career path as her oldest son, nor could she pull strings for him via old college connections. Harry might be Edward Palin's son, but those clever Oxonian friends who could still remember his father would look down their noses at someone so clearly non-academic.

Fortunately, the family were on hand to help. Almost ten years earlier Harry's eldest sister Brita had married a vicar's son from the town nearest to Linton, Ross-on-Wye, and shortly afterwards had moved with him to India. Brita, or, rather, 'Tissie', was a tall, handsome woman, described by the local paper at the time of her wedding as 'A Herefordshire Beauty'. Her husband, Henry Ralph Cobbold, worked for a cloth manufacturer by the name of Mitchell Bardsley & Company. He must have been quite successful, because the couple were able to live on Middleton Street, off Chowringhee, an affluent area in the centre of Calcutta (now Kolkata). Their daughter, yet another Brita, had just turned seven when the couple stepped in to help Harry on his way.

India at that time was the workhorse of the British Empire, exporting cloth, tea and timber, and providing jobs in its administration for engineers, architects and civil servants. Lawyers were needed to interpret the law, judges to impose it and policemen to enforce it. The Indian army, large and formidably run by Lord Kitchener, was a big attraction for young Britons. In some ways, the subcontinent was so familiar to the British that it resembled more an extension of the Home Counties than an exotic foreign world.

Given the presence of Brita and her husband in Calcutta, and the wealth of opportunities for jobs of all kinds, it's not so surprising that a year after his father's death, Harry was persuaded to leave home and seek his fortune abroad. On 29 December 1904 he was listed as one of forty-eight second-class passengers on *Egypt*, a 4,100-ton vessel bound for Karachi and Bombay (now Mumbai).

He had just turned twenty. And he was on his own.

It must have been quite a shock for a vicar's son from the Herefordshire hills.

Before leaving London, Harry signed a three-page contract, with an impressive red seal on the top and a stamped price of sixpence, to become a Traffic Probationer with one of the biggest of the eight railway enterprises operating in India – the Great Indian Peninsula Railway Company. The post of Traffic Probationer was at the very bottom of the managerial hierarchy, and the fact that that was the best Harry could do suggests that he had no particular qualifications for the job other than a helpful sister and brother-in-law living on the other side of the country.

He saw in the New Year as they crossed the stormy and wave-tossed Bay of Biscay. After that came a quieter time in the Mediterranean – a welcome break from the midwinter weather he'd left behind in England. At the mouth of the Suez Canal, Harry inhaled the hot, dusty scent of Africa. His first taste of the exotic.

At Port Said, where the conventional West was viewed as giving way to the mysterious East, the cold-weather gear was labelled 'Cabin baggage' and stowed away. Now passengers brought out their full tropical clothing, and Harry would doubtless have been nudged by peer pressure to part with a few shillings for the traditional purchase of a sola topi. He was doubtless also warned about what were regarded as the dodgier aspects of the city. Passengers who went ashore were advised, among other things, to 'be very careful of men who want to sell or show you "French photographs"'.

East of Aden the heat increased relentlessly. Harry would most likely have slept on deck at night to stay cool. During the day he'd have watched the dolphins and the flying fish dart and dive around the ship and prepared himself for his new life in Bombay by learning a bit of Urdu.

In the 1920s my father, then aged twenty-two, followed in his uncle's footsteps as he set out for India to work as an engineer on the construction of one of the longest dams in the world. The Sukkur Barrage (or, as it was originally called, the Lloyd Barrage) runs for almost a mile and, though designed to last only seventy years, still holds back the powerful flow of the Indus River as it feeds one of the world's largest irrigation systems.

Frustratingly, my father never told me much about his time in India, but after he died I found among his possessions two phrase books from his time there which say as much about the colonial mentality as any E. M. Forster novel. One is the *Europeans' Guide to Hindustani*. The other is *Hindustani Simplified* by S. B. Syed, first published in 1909. Though compiled by an Indian, the tone of this latter work is uncompromisingly imperial, as can be seen from a brief glance at the phrases in Lesson One. They are written almost entirely in the imperative. 'Bring water. Bring bread. Bring Dinner. Come here. Go There. Go Out. Do This. Write this.' In Part Two, 'Sentences', there is an exercise which reads like an instruction sheet from Basil Fawlty to Manuel:

Write a letter. Call him here. Do this for me. Do not come near. Open this box. Do not sit here. Wait downstairs. Speak clearly. Bring all the books. Burn this. Come after dinner. Don't make a noise. Get down from there. Come here at once. Speak easy Hindustani. Go away. Hold your tongue. Bring three cups of tea. Sit here. Wash your face. Clean the table. Ask him his name. Put the gun there. Shut the box. Do not forget me. Prepare dinner for eight men. Read good books. Sit on the ground. Mend this pen. Don't come to me. Don't laugh.

These were the words of command that were felt necessary to keep the Empire together. They came from an assumption that the only way to govern the subcontinent, regarded by its occupiers as productive but unruly and divided, was to impose Western values and Western 'order' on it. Such attitudes led to a very partial view of Indians and their history. Harry would doubtless have been taught about the horrors of the Black Hole of Calcutta, when a number of British prisoners of war died from suffocation and heat exhaustion following their incarceration in 1756 by the Nawab of Bengal. He would certainly have known about the massacres of British women and children during the Indian Mutiny just over a century later. No one would have told him about the persecutions and massacres meted out by the British in the course of their years of occupation, or that the Indians regarded the Mutiny as the Great Rebellion.

Morally bolstered by this one-sided view of history, the subcontinent was considered not only a safe, but a prestigious place for young Englishmen to visit. And a playground, too, where they might enjoy themselves away from the prying eyes of friends and family back home in Britain.

There is nothing in his subsequent career in India to show that Harry approached his new life with any degree of excitement or anticipation, which leads me to wonder if his attitude to all things colonial was rather different from that of most of his fellow Brits. If that is so, the politics of his mother and father might account for it. His mother might have been too young to have fully understood the responsibility of the British government for the Great Famine that separated her from her parents, but once in America she would have been among Irish emigrants who would probably have talked of little else. Her American stepmother, Caroline, was a social progressive. Edward Palin had liberal instincts and a strong social conscience that manifested itself in the community projects he undertook in Linton.

Bearing in mind this background, I can understand why Harry would never have fitted comfortably into the ruling establishment in India. I do know that he bought himself a dress suit, as my grandmother remembered his doing so in a letter to my father, dated 28 August 1925: 'Uncle Harry was in Bombay and I have still his dress suit, bought in Bombay!' Somehow, though, I can't see him mixing uncritically with the army officers and their wives, the colonial administrators, the third sons of feckless aristocrats, the self-confident public schoolboys who, unlike Harry, hadn't left their educational establishments after only two years. The early twentieth-century photographs of the British Raj sum up an air of languid confidence, whether it's men in pith helmets off to a tiger shoot or couples draped around dining tables with servants waiting behind each chair. Harry wasn't part of that world. And we know what he thought of group photographs.

After four weeks at sea, the *Egypt* reached Bombay at the end of January 1905. It was midwinter, the best time of year to be in India, with low humidity and day-time temperatures dipping to 75 degrees Fahrenheit (24 degrees C). As the passengers disembarked they were met by what one arrival described as 'a difference in the air or in the atmosphere, or in the heat, or in the way the wind blew or possibly even the smell . . . difficult to pinpoint, partly the populace, partly the different vegetation, partly the very rapid fall of dusk and the cooling off which leads to a most lovely scent after sundown'.

PART 2

INDIA AND
NEW ZEALAND

The tea plantations of Assam: a Victorian view.

6

INDIAN SUNSET

COMING FROM THE BUCOLIC PEACEFULNESS of a village on the Welsh borders, Harry must have found the pace of life in Bombay quite bewildering. Judging from my own first encounter with the raucous streets of the city, he would always have found someone at his side, offering attentions of various kinds. Street vendors, bag carriers, shoe cleaners, shavers, hairdressers and, in my case, when we were filming *Around the World in 80 Days*, providers of more dubious items of bodily comfort, including men and women – even donkeys.

Harry would have made a lowly start in his new job, and in fairly lowly conditions. The railway company was not legally obliged to provide accommodation for its employees, so they had to squash in where they could – and pay for the privilege. Harry most likely ended up staying in a chummery, a bungalow or other accommodation shared with fellow Probationers. By contrast, his workplace was one of the grandest buildings in the city – the Victoria terminus, headquarters of the Great Indian Peninsula Railway, a station masquerading as a Gothic cathedral. Opened in 1887, the year of the Queen's Golden Jubilee, it was one of the most imperious examples of Victorian confidence. A reminder, for all to see, of the resources of the Raj and a celebration of the essential role of the railway in binding this jewel of the Empire together. Financed largely by British capital, the Indian railway had expanded from a single line in the early 1850s to some 30,000 miles of track by 1905. It was a colossal undertaking, pushing through mountains and bridging rivers, and having to contend with intense heat and monsoon rains. Running it smoothly required a massive native labour force, overseen by a cohort of managers and overseers, both Western and Indian.

Harry's starting salary was 200 rupees a month (then about £41) for the first two years. Not much by the standards of what many British people in India would have been paid, but the same as an indentured native railway worker would have earned in a year. Harry would have begun at the bottom of the pile and would almost certainly have had to tolerate some bossing around by his superiors. The British presence in India was dominated by the upper class, and one only needs to read Rudyard Kipling's poem 'The Law of the Jungle' to understand the vital importance of knowing one's place within the hierarchy of the Raj:

> *Now these are the Laws of the Jungle, and many and mighty*
> *are they;*

> *But the head and the hoof of the Law and the haunch and*
> *the hump is – Obey!*

The best course of action for Harry and his fellow Probationers was to keep their heads down and not rock any boats. They were expected to spend two years learning the ropes, which might involve anything from accompanying superintendents or DLOs (District Locomotive Officers) on rounds of inspection, to doing duty as train guards or sitting in the office signing passes. After that they could take an examination and, if they reached the minimum 60 per cent required to pass, then, and only then, would they start moving up the ranks. Their salary would rise, too – initially by 50 rupees a month. For Harry it must have felt like public school all over again, with the additional burden of knowing that his family expected him to move quickly off the bottom rung of the ladder, climb up the hierarchy as briskly as possible, and, in the process, enhance his financial and marital prospects.

When he arrived in Bombay there were signs of change in the highest echelons of the Raj. Back home the Conservatives had been replaced by a Liberal government and the Viceroy of India, Lord Curzon, every inch the imperial grandee, had been replaced by the less tub-thumping Lord Minto. The native leaders and politicians expected great things from the new Viceroy. He was clearly an instinctive unifier, less wedded to the might and majesty of office than his predecessor. Even so, on arrival he still allowed himself to be whisked off on tiger shoots and bear hunts, causing his private secretary, Sir James Dunlop-Smith, to note, 'The Native Press are loudly complaining that their Excellencies are being shown only the splendours of India and none of its poverty and suffering.'

Harry, stuck in Bombay on a very modest wage, was much closer to the poverty and suffering than most of his fellow expats.

Making assumptions from what I've learnt about him, from his later career path, and from his still-later diaries, I feel pretty sure that his heart was not altogether in the work – certainly not enough to seek promotion or to make the sort of friends in Bombay who might help him get ahead in life. The office side of things, even at such an impressive base as the Victoria terminus, must, I suspect, have bored him rigid. The boy on the farm at Linton was now the restless adult, still preferring physical over mental activity, distraction over concentration. I imagine him looking forward to the time when his job would take him away from his desk in Bombay, out onto the Permanent Way, perhaps being pushed on an inspection trolley with the Engineer Sahib alongside, sitting beneath a sunshade as they scrutinised the line. That said, I know that he was serious about learning Urdu and that he acquired a good working knowledge of the language. It was an accomplishment of which he was understandably proud and one that would subsequently prove very useful.

As things stood, I feel that the days would have passed slowly for him, stuck in a job for which he felt no particular affinity. The evenings, though, would have been a different matter. From later photos we know he was a smoker and likely to have enjoyed a night out with the lads, in whose uncomplicated company he would have felt free and unjudged, released from the weight of expectation which had brought him to India. His salary might have been relatively meagre by the standards of most of his fellow Englishmen, but it would have gone a long way in the poorer parts of Bombay. He could have a drink or two and a good meal. Perhaps, now that he was enjoying adult independence for the first time, he sought pleasure of a different variety among the ladies of Grant Road. It's clear from his later diaries that he had an eye for women and that he greatly enjoyed their company. Bombay would certainly have had temptations aplenty for him. The historian David Gilmour quotes a young soldier as finding on Sutlej Street 'European women of every nationality, except British, displaying themselves, seated on low chairs and clad only in semi-transparent chemises and stockings, loudly proclaiming their charms', and Japanese women, by contrast, 'demurely seated on the forecourt patiently sewing or knitting'.

This is all supposition on my part. It's possible that Harry wasn't tempted. It's also possible that – aware of the prevalence of venereal disease in the red-light districts – he was careful not to run the risk of 'copping a packet'. Of course, I'd like to think that my great-uncle had firm religious beliefs and healthy sporting activities that would have served to curb any sexual temptations. Sadly, there's no evidence of either.

There is little first-hand information about how he spent his years on the Indian railways. All we really know

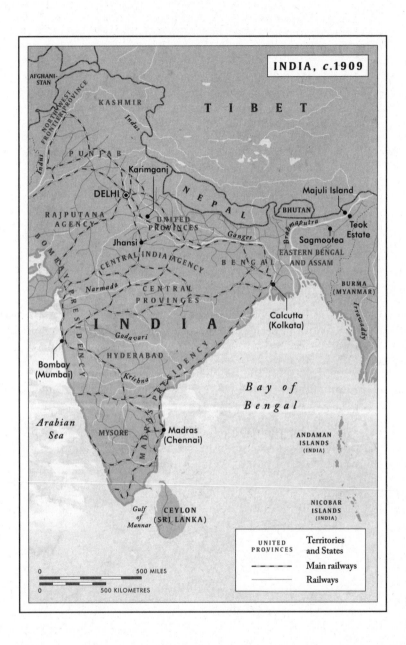

INDIA, *c*.1909

AFGHANI-
STAN

KASHMIR

TIBET

NORTHWEST FRONTIER PROVINCE

Indus

Indus

P U N J A B

Karimganj

DELHI

N E P A L

Majuli Island

BHUTAN

Teok
Estate

RAJPUTANA
AGENCY

UNITED
PROVINCES

Ganges

Brahmaputra

Sagmootea

Jhansi

CENTRAL INDIA AGENCY

B E N G A L

EASTERN BENGAL
AND ASSAM

BURMA
(MYANMAR)

BOMBAY

Narmada

C E N T R A L
P R O V I N C E S

Irrawaddy

I N D I A

Godavari

Calcutta
(Kolkata)

PRESIDENCY

HYDERABAD

Krishna

Bombay
(Mumbai)

*Arabian
Sea*

MYSORE

MADRAS PRESIDENCY

Madras
(Chennai)

*Bay of
Bengal*

ANDAMAN
ISLANDS
(INDIA)

*Gulf
of
Mannar*

CEYLON
(SRI LANKA)

NICOBAR
ISLANDS
(INDIA)

UNITED
PROVINCES

Territories
and States

Main railways

Railways

0   500 MILES

0   500 KILOMETRES

is that after two years he was still listed in *Thacker's Indian Directory*, the comprehensive list of all the British working in India, as a Traffic Probationer, and that he had been transferred to Jhansi in the United Provinces (now Uttar Pradesh). The first nugget of information suggests he had not been successful in his exams; the second that he had been – quite literally – sidelined. Bombay was a big, bustling city. Jhansi was a railway town in the hot heartlands of central India. For Harry it must have seemed the equivalent of a transfer from King's Cross to Crewe.

Jhansi had a history of resistance to the British stretching back to the Indian Mutiny fifty years earlier when the Rani, or Queen, of the area – Lakshmi Bai – had seized the strategic Jhansi Fort that dominates the town. Undeterred by an initial defeat, she had fought tirelessly to take back Jhansi, before being killed in action in June 1858, 'dressed like a man', according to the historian Christopher Hibbert, '. . . holding her sword two-handed and the reins of her horse in her teeth'. I can't imagine the people of Jhansi being particularly welcoming to the young Englishman who arrived in their midst in 1907.

A year later, still unpromoted, Harry resigned from the railway company and returned home. By this time his once close-knit family were widely dispersed. His older brother was now based in Norfolk, settling into life as a country doctor with his wife and two children. His sister Eleanor – 'Nellie' – had, a year earlier, married the well-to-do Revd Paul Jerome Kirkby, a Fellow of New College. With no ties to Linton any more, I can only assume that Harry went back to live with his mother, now in her sixties, who was sharing the house at 7 Staverton Road, Summertown, Oxford with her only unmarried daughter, Mary. He was back in the city where his father, had he not met Brita that summer in Switzerland, would probably have spent the rest of his life.

He was not destined to remain there for long, though. I get the impression that his family worried that he was not making enough of himself. They certainly seem to have wanted him off their hands again as quickly as possible. Once more, therefore, Brita Cobbold stepped forward to organise her younger brother's life, securing him, with the help of her husband Ralph, a job with James Finlay & Co., the Glasgow-based tea producers, to work on one of their estates in Assam. On 11 August 1908, a few weeks short of his twenty-fourth birthday, Harry signed an agreement of employment and the family doubtless breathed a collective sigh of relief. The new job might return him to the country he had only recently left in less than glorious circumstances, but at least this time he would be on the other side of the subcontinent, in the rolling hills of the north-east, and so not too far from the capital, Calcutta, where Brita and Ralph, and their young daughter, lived and worked.

Unlike his time on the railways, we have, thanks to a well-kept archive at Finlay's head office in Glasgow, a record of Harry's employment on the tea plantations. We know that he landed back in India on 5 November 1908, at the start of the cool season. A week later, after a cross-country train journey from Bombay, he arrived at the Teok Estate in the Noakachari Division of the Kanan Devan Hills Plantations Company. He was given a medical by a Dr Baddry, who reported favourably, 'I have just examined Mr Palin and find him in good health and fit for duty on any garden. His height is 5ft 11 and a half inches and his weight is twelve stone.' Both numbers being exactly the same as mine at that age.

Ninety-five years later, whilst shooting in Assam for the BBC's *Himalaya* series I passed very near the Teok Estate (now the Teok Tea Estate), which is a few miles from Majuli Island on the Brahmaputra River where we stayed and filmed. It's an unforgettably beautiful area, with a soft, warm air of drowsiness about the place. I was captured inexpertly playing a ceremonial drum at one of the Satras, or small monasteries, on the island, and nearby, at a small lake, we struck documentary gold when we encountered a group of local women on a fishing expedition. Amid jolly laughter, any fish they caught were slipped down the fronts of their dresses. It was a rare example of piscine eroticism, much trimmed by the BBC.

A less surreal memory of Assam, more touching, and more relevant to Harry's experience, was of meeting Anne, an Englishwoman, on the train to Dibrugarh. She was the product of a relationship between an English tea planter and one of the women from what they called 'the lines' (where the tea pickers lived). Such liaisons were strictly forbidden and Anne's father died in Singapore in the Second World War without ever being able to publicly acknowledge Anne as his daughter. Anne's mother, meanwhile, desperately wanted to find out what had become of the planter with whom she had had a child. But she was uneducated and illiterate, and didn't even know how he spelled his name. The two of them never saw each other again.

Anne, feeling herself neither English nor Indian, told me that she never really fitted in with the tea-planting set, who, embarrassed by her background, shut her out. Enquiries about her father were stonewalled. That was in the 1930s. I can't imagine planters were any more tolerant when Harry joined their ranks thirty years earlier.

Harry officially began his new job on 5 December 1908, with the company records confirming that 'Mr. Palin has been placed at Teok under Mr. Smart'. On Christmas Day, the neatly handwritten verdict of a Mr Mann is that 'Mr. Palin just arrived seems a likely man to turn out well.'

In switching from the railways to the tea plantations of the subcontinent Harry was moving from one manifestation of the Raj to another. The British had started growing tea in Assam in the 1830s, in a bid to break the traditional Chinese monopoly on the beverage, and within a few decades Indian tea had become big business. Supplemented with a drop or two of milk and a teaspoon or so of sugar imported from Britain's colonies in the West Indies, it had also become something of a national drink. By the time that Harry arrived at the Teok Estate the average person back home was getting through nearly six pounds of leaf tea a year.

Harry's professional duties are unrecorded, but they would presumably have involved ensuring that the tea bushes were properly cared for and irrigated, that an eye was kept out for blight and infestation by red spiders, and that at harvest time the leaves were picked, weighed, 'withered', rolled, fermented, 'fired' and finally packed in the approved manner. The actual hard work was done by Indian labourers, known pejoratively as 'coolies'.

At the end of a long day in the gardens, Harry, along with other new arrivals, would probably have met up with the more senior managers for a chota peg – a shot of whisky – before being served curry, washed down with the local beer. It was, in many ways, a circumscribed, lonely life, in which the main social distractions were limited to the local gymkhana club and polo. Many people's principal preoccupation was the drinks cabinet. David Gilmour, after quoting various contemporary descriptions of 'great drunken binges' and 'rough, rowdy bachelors, hardly fit society for ladies and gentlemen', suggests, 'Hospitality and heavy drinking were perhaps inherent in the lives of planters of all sorts, an essential antidote to the routine and monotony, a reward for missing out on what people in Britain might take for granted – friendships, a social life, a visit to the pub and the music hall.' In fact, everything I see Harry as enjoying.

Away from his colleagues Harry would have spent much of his time in his living quarters. On my visit to the tea gardens of Assam I stayed in a rather comfortable changa, a bungalow on stilts, whose polished darkwood floors reflected the white and cream-painted walls.

They also ensured that the sound from any room could be heard by all. A wide verandah ran around the house, full of easy chairs on which the children of the Empire once reclined and pulled on their cigars as the cicadas rattled in the night. Harry, I suspect, was not as fortunate. As a very junior employee, he probably had to make do with the less comfortable accommodation of one of the shared brick bungalows on the estate.

The world beyond the bungalow doors is evocatively described by Iris Macfarlane, in her memoir of her life and times in the British Raj. In a chapter rather Pythonically titled 'Twenty Years in Tea' (she was the wife of a plantation manager), she remembered 'wetness' as being her first memory of Assam: 'The whole country was awash and half the population seemed to be sitting on their roofs waiting for the floods to subside.' Every year, without fail, she recalled, the bamboo bridge that connected their house with the club was washed away by the monsoon. Each month had its own distinctive character:

> March was when the eyeflies started . . . ticks appeared on the dogs' ears and hibiscus flowers on the bushes . . . In April the tea bushes burst into precious leaf and girls danced in spring festivals with orchids behind their ears. May was mosquitoes and mini-cyclones . . . cassias and laburnums standing like gold and scarlet umbrellas around us and butterflies the size of birds. In June purple clouds massed every day, thunder rumbled . . . and at last came wind and the driving wall of wetness . . . Roofs dripped, rivers gushed, frogs croaked and the

temperature dropped a blessed ten degrees . . . and women moved like swans through the green sea of tea, plucking and plucking.

Then in early October 'there was a new smell and we walked out into a thick white mist and knew that the cold weather had begun'. In the autumn the tea was pruned and manufacturing stopped, 'leaving plenty of free time for managers and their assistants'. This period of leisure, she wrote, was filled with 'Sprees': day-long celebrations where everything from chicken and ham to soufflés and trifles was served and at which people became 'exhaustedly drunk'.

These jollities disguise the fact that those doing the hard work in the tea plantations would have been very badly paid recruits from poverty-stricken provinces like Bihar and Orissa (now Odisha). The conditions in the lines where they lived were basic, with leaky accommodation and very poor sanitation. Iris Macfarlane, a compassionate and honest woman, was not unaware of the squalor they were forced to endure or of the inequality and injustice that lay at the heart of a colonial life. 'Occasionally,' she writes, 'I marvelled that my servants could emerge from such surroundings and become the crisp, efficient bearers of trays around my polished rooms.' She tried to imagine 'what they felt handing round the six-course meals at my dinner parties, they, who lived on one meal of rice and lentils a day'.

The old colonial ways which Anne described to me on the train would probably have been more entrenched in the confined world of the tea gardens than in the more politically active urban areas in which Harry had stayed on his first visit to India. However, the minutes of an address to a plantation management meeting in 1910 give an early hint that the wind – or, at least, the breeze – of change was beginning to blow even here in rural Assam. 'We had not all paid sufficient attention in the past years to the housing of coolies,' the chairman was reported as saying. 'Sanitary arrangements were bad and the surroundings of most Lines very dirty. We want to find out what the Cooly prefers in the way of Lines and as far as possible give it him and so make him as comfortable and contented as we can.' This statement was followed by the telling observation from the chairman that 'He knew this was the desire of the people at home.'

Any honeymoon period Harry might have enjoyed appears to have been short-lived. In a report sent back to Finlay's head office on 22 May 1909, less than six months after Harry's arrival at Teok, a Mr Levick reported, 'Mr. Palin is learning under a good teacher.' But he swiftly moved on to express reservations. 'He is rather a self-satisfied young man and somewhat of a handful to Mr. Smart but is settling down to his work and I find it best for him to be kept at it.'

The handful of clues contained here would seem to confirm my hunches about Harry's character. 'Somewhat of a handful' is not a judgement one would make about a passive or even a lazy person. That slightly prissy phrasing suggests that Harry, stuck with what he regarded as a dull job, was doing his best to liven things up a bit. That the 'young man' appeared 'self-satisfied' implies that he had a touch of chippy self-confidence, which didn't fit easily into any hierarchical organisation. The fact that he spent three years on the railways without ever rising above the lowest rank of Traffic Probationer seems to bear out this likelihood. Or maybe he just wasn't very bright, which, given his parental pedigree, sounds less plausible.

And here's another thought about Harry. Brought up in a small village by correct, respectable and conventionally dutiful parents, and, apart from a short time at boarding school, only occasionally rubbing shoulders with men his own age, he had spent most of his life up until now with people who were concerned with upholding the rules rather than testing them. Suddenly, barely into his twenties and 5,000 miles from church and vicarage, he found himself let off the leash, first in Bombay, now on the Teok Estate. Life in India was a potential crash-course in finding out what life could offer beyond the protective walls of home. The sense of a whole new world out there to be experienced and enjoyed would have confirmed in his mind that his interests – and his skills – were not those that his studious father had doubtless hoped he would inherit.

Maybe because of his time with gardeners and farm-hands back at home Harry had a talent for uncomplicated companionship and an attraction to the informal life, away from the competitive world of exams and qualifications and polite social appearances. At the same time, while opportunities for sexual activity would have been fewer in rural Assam than they were in the busier cities of Bombay and the west, Anne's sad story highlights the fact that there were always the 'garden girls' to go with and possibly the bored wives or daughters of the company managers, happy to bend the rules. All this is speculation, but I am more and more convinced that Harry grew up fast in India. And as he grew up he seemed more and more to be opting out of the establishment into which he had been born.

Arguably Harry was on the side of history here. He was twelve at the time of Queen Victoria's Diamond Jubilee in 1897, which most agree was the high-water mark of imperial Britain. But now the tide was beginning to ebb. Victoria was dead. The Germans and Americans were challenging Britain economically and militarily. Socialism was beginning to tap away at the roots of entitlement. Women were demanding equal votes, and in India, as Harry trudged through the endless rows of green tea bushes or endured the heat of the factory and the endless management meetings, the process of transferring power to the Indians themselves was slowly but surely in train. The era of toeing the imperial line was beginning to pass.

In his rejection of the rules and norms of the Raj, one might see Harry as a prophet. But, of course, it wouldn't have seemed that way at the time. Viewed through the lens of British imperial might, Harry was doubtless regarded by many of his contemporaries as a failure.

At the end of his first year in the job it seems that Harry had briefly taken to heart the criticisms made of him and was knuckling under. On 9 December 1909, Mr Levick reported that 'he has stuck to his work well under Mr. Smart's good training and has proved useful'. Three days later, this was followed up with another note from Mr Levick, stating that 'I have sanctioned Mr. Palin's taking 14 days leave to enable him to spend Xmas with friends in Calcutta'.

This seems a generous gesture, prompted possibly by the status of Harry's 'friends in Calcutta' who were most likely Ralph Cobbold, Brita and the affluent circle of people who surrounded them in one of the most sought-after areas of the teeming city. After a year in the relative seclusion of the hills, time in Calcutta would see Harry looked after both financially and socially, whilst also offering him the diversions and distractions that came with big city life.

At the same time there must have been discussion of his future prospects, and with his sister Brita fifteen years his senior, they would have been cautionary. I sense that his return to the plantations was a deal struck between them for the good of the family. Harry's last chance to try and play the role of hard-working, socially responsible vicar's son.

And it does seem that he tried. On his arrival back at Teok he was given an approving commendation from Mr Mann: Mr Palin is 'well reported on', he wrote. This was followed almost immediately by a transfer to Sag-mootea, another part of the Noakachari Division, which could be construed as a promotion. Sagmootea Estate, still very much thriving, looks an idyllic place. Streams and lakes and waterfalls break up the lush, low carpet of tea bushes, which stretch like a great green blanket over rocky bluffs and low hills. Nearby, the wide Brahmaputra River threads its way between sandbanks and islands, slowly and lethargically, as if having no particular place to go.

Unfortunately, Harry's relationship with Finlay's now began to resemble the Brahmaputra River. Before the end of the 1910 monsoon system, Finlay's head office in Glasgow received a tersely unflattering missive from its north India operation. 'The most unsatisfactory report,' the local manager wrote, 'is perhaps that on Mr. H. W. B. Palin who, we regret to say, does not appear to be exerting himself to any great extent.'

As Harry's third Christmas in Assam comes round, there is no mention of allowing him leave in Calcutta. Worse is to come. Mr Mann's end-of-year report on Harry's time at Sagmootea is one of unreserved disapproval. 'I am not at all favourably impressed with Mr. Palin,' he writes, adding wearily, 'and I saw a good deal of him at this visit.' And then come two sentences that are damning in their brevity. 'He seems to be lacking in intelligence. Recommend transfer.'

On 2 February 1911 Finlay's Calcutta office responded to the latest report with a terse plan of action: 'We have discussed with Mr Mann the question of retaining this assistant's services and it has been arranged to give him another trial under a stronger manager.' To my relief, there's no mention here of his having a bit to spare in the intelligence department. It's an insinuation that I resist in any case, not simply because Harry is family and I want to give him the benefit of the doubt, but because Mr Mann offers no evidence to back up an assertion that has never previously been made. That reference to a 'stronger manager' seems to me to be closer to the mark. It's not that Harry is stupid; it's that he's tricky to handle. In fairness, he's only just turned twenty-six and he's in an alien environment doing a job he clearly doesn't enjoy. The fact remains, though, that after two years in the tea gardens Harry is once again in the last-chance saloon. Finlay's final proposal comes with an ultimatum: 'If he is not better reported on at the end of the season his services will be dispensed with.'

His next posting with the company took him some 70 miles west into the hills around Karimganj. There he was placed under the care of a Mr Mackintosh at the Goombira Estate, opened in 1843 and one of the oldest established of Finlay's plantations. It was also quite probably one of the most rule-bound and conservative, where Harry's commitment to tea-growing would be put to the test once and for all. The management at Goombira didn't take long to make their assessment of his usefulness, nor did they mince their words. In the heat of the summer, just four months after his arrival, and at the height of the tea-plucking season, they sent word to head office. 'We regret there appears to be no improvement in his work and fear it will be necessary to dispense with his services.'

The final act was, perhaps generously, described by the company as resignation rather than dismissal. On 17 August 1911, in a final note on his employment in India, head office was informed that 'We have granted this gentleman a passage home.' More generosity – or perhaps they couldn't wait to get rid of him.

Harry left India just as the monsoons waned and the best months of the year were beginning. Perhaps he had moments of regret as his steamer drew away from her shores. If it was the petty officialdom of company and colonial life that he rejected, the other attractions of India might well have appealed and suited him. The bustle, the throng, the mysterious energy of the place. The chance to lose himself in a world so different from the socially restricted one in which he had grown up. Whatever the truth of the matter, I can't help thinking of Great-Uncle Harry as one of those people who, for some reason or another, cannot find a place to settle. They may be running away from something, or they may still be looking for something. With Harry, the lastborn, it was a bit of both.

India may have been finished with Harry Palin, but it wasn't yet finished with the British. At some point in Harry's last voyage home, he may well have passed a much grander vessel going the other way. It would have been carrying the new king, George V, and Mary, his queen, on their way to the Delhi Durbar. A durbar was a gathering of all the princes of India, a time for great pomp, splendour and celebration. There had been three such spectacular gatherings since Queen Victoria took the title Empress of India, but George V was the only British monarch personally to attend, and indeed, at that point, the only British monarch ever to have set foot on Indian soil.

The clamour and confidence of the tremendous display in Delhi could not have offered a bigger contrast to Harry's dismal failure to make it in this corner of the Empire. But in fact the Grand Durbar heralded a far grander failure. The Indian princes who lined up to kneel before the King and Queen on their golden thrones that December day in Delhi would not do so again. This image of British ascendancy in India would never be equalled. A little over a generation later it would be entirely swept away.

Many of those who knew Harry no doubt thought he had let the Empire down. Ironically, though, he would ultimately ride to its rescue at its hour of greatest danger.

An early photograph of Wilderness Farm, just outside Canvastown in New Zealand's South Island. The forest that once stood here has been reduced to a few tree stumps.

7

THE CALL OF THE WILD

I T's NOT HARD TO GUESS the reaction of the family
when Harry arrived back in England in the late
autumn of 1911. The problem that they had hoped
six years in India would have been able to solve was
now back on their doorstep. Once Christmas had passed
and a new year dawned, that problem would have to be
resolved yet again.

It's entirely possible that Harry spent his twenty-
seventh Christmas at 7 Staverton Road, but it's not a
given. His mother certainly still owned the house then,
but if the 1911 census is anything to go by she wasn't
always there. On the night of 11 April, when the census
was taken, she was actually staying with an eighty-three-
year-old Major General called Henry Maclean and his
fifty-seven-year-old American-born wife Frances at an
eleven-room house in Hayne Road, Beckenham, in Kent,
leaving 7 Staverton Road in the care of a skeleton staff
of three. There was Rose Rudge, age thirty-two, 'Single,

Parlour Maid, Domestic' (the word 'Domestic' is crossed through and 'Head' written in, so clearly the parlour-maid was the senior of the three and head of the household, at least for that day); Emma Beal, twenty-nine, 'Single, Cook'; and Alice Hawkins, thirty-five, 'Single, Sewing Maid'. A Mary Hawkins was listed as living at Linton rectory in 1881. This 'Oxford' Alice must have been her daughter, who would have been eight years old when Harry was born – one of the group of women with whom he had grown up and whom he would have known well.

The suggestion in the 1911 census that Brita no longer felt particularly wedded to the city that had been so central to her husband's life is confirmed by her decision less than two years later to move away altogether. In February 1913 she put No. 7 up for auction with Buckle, Son & Ballard at the Golden Cross Hotel in Cornmarket Street, Oxford. The following year she purchased a substantial six-bedroom house in Dry Hill Road, Tonbridge, a market town on the River Medway in Kent. Money was clearly not a problem for her as she approached seventy. Mary, now thirty-eight, and the only unmarried one of the four daughters, stayed with her mother and looked after her. As to why Brita should have chosen Tonbridge, there's a hint in *Kelly's Directory* for 1914, which shows a Mrs Cobbold living at nearby 44 Dry Hill Park Road. Cobbold happens to be the surname of Eleanor Palin's mother-in-law, and while that could just be a coincidence, it fits in with my hunch that Brita wanted to be closer to people she knew. Her house in Tonbridge was also not too far from Camp Hill, Chiddingstone, where her daughter Edith and son-in-law Geoffrey Ashmore farmed. With her eldest daughter and her husband out in India, it feels like a circling of the wagons by the remaining family.

Apart from Tissie in Calcutta, Edward was now the only one of the Palin children living outside the Home Counties. With his wife Agnes (née Buckley) and their two children Edward and Katherine, he had settled happily into the life of a rural doctor, healing the sick at Fakenham in Norfolk. In all the photos of him, my grandfather Eddy radiates a benign pipe-smoking affability. Despite his medical qualifications and first-class degree from Oxford, he seems, in a way, no more ambitious than Harry. But he has none of Harry's restlessness. As far as I know, he rarely left Norfolk until the time came for him to retire, and even then he moved only as far as Chalford in Gloucestershire, 30 miles from where he was born. He was a keen gardener and photographer and left behind some carefully composed photos of his Fakenham garden with its distinctive brick wall built in a series of sinuous, wavy curves, known locally as a crinkle-crankle wall. Though I later saw and marvelled at the wall, I sadly never met Grandfather Eddy, as he died in 1937, six years before I was born. But by a strange chance, our lives did touch briefly. In the 1990s I had a very happy correspondence with a retired policeman and Python fan from Norwich called Ben Bray who told me that his father remembered my grandfather taking children's tonsils out, free of charge, on his kitchen table, after church on Sundays. I wouldn't let just anyone take *my* tonsils out on their kitchen table, but looking at the reassuring, kindly likenesses of Eddy, I can understand why many would have trusted him.

To this close-knit, reasonably well-off family, enjoying the benefits of a secure and settled life in one of the most prosperous and advanced countries in the world, Harry's rootlessness would have been regarded as increasingly vexing, perhaps even a little shaming. His record of employment in India had shown him to be neither ambitious nor qualified, and those closest to him must have been wondering just what else he might have to offer.

In the end, they were spared any further agonising. Harry, now twenty-eight, having accumulated at least some experience of life in the wider world, opted to take his fate into his own hands. Though his next move was radical, it was entirely in character. He decided to emigrate.

His chosen destination was New Zealand.

There was a good practical reason for Harry's decision. Emigration from Britain to this far-flung outpost of Empire might have fallen back after the boom times of the 1850s gold rush and the withdrawal of the generous assisted passage scheme introduced in the 1870s, but it had picked up again as New Zealand's fortunes revived in the early 1900s. In 1904 the scheme was reintroduced, and by the time Harry had resolved to leave England for the third time, some 30,000 British and Irish were taking advantage of it annually. For Harry, as for his fellow emigrants, New Zealand must have seemed a welcoming place: a land of promise where he could escape and start all over again.

As with his move to India, though, his decision to try his luck in yet another corner of the Empire may have had a family dimension to it. A cousin of his father's – Christopher Dampier-Crossley – was a lawyer for the Land Company in Christchurch, and it could well be that he promised to help, or even encouraged, his errant relative to make the long journey to the other side of the world. Of course, it's equally possible that Harry – by now wary of well-intentioned advice from his family – made the momentous decision unprompted. We will never know for sure. What is certain is that on 9 May 1912, just five months after he had returned home from India, Harry boarded the slim, single-funnelled SS *Rotorua*, bound for New Zealand.

On the ship's manifest Harry is described as a 'clerk', which is suitably neutral, and implies greater status than 'farmhand', which is what he eventually signed up for. 'Clerk' might just have been a cover of respectability, or a way of reassuring his family that he was still treading a middle-class path. For their part, they must have advanced him some money to keep him away from the riff-raff, as he was one of only 72 passengers enjoying the comforts of a second-class cabin. Below him were 156 in third class and 280 in emigrant class. The ship itself, all 11,130 tons of it, was a smart new cargo steamer, operated by the New Zealand Shipping Company and built at William Denny's shipyard on the north bank of the Clyde in 1910. Equipped with state-of-the-art refrigerated storage, a facility that had hugely increased the export potential of New Zealand's agricultural produce, *Rotorua* could carry 170,000 carcasses of lamb. She would be sunk just a few years later, in 1917, by a German U-boat in Lyme Bay on her way from Auckland to Plymouth, with the loss of one life.

On 2 June 1912 Harry sent a postcard to my father from Tasmania. Addressing it to 'Master Ted Palin' at The Oaks, Fakenham, Norfolk, he wrote in a clear, elegant hand:

> Here we are at Hobart and stay 24 hours a very pleasant rest after 18 days at sea out of sight of land. We had a rough time of it these last 3 days, there were various accidents such as broken arms and concussions. Two babies arrived in the steerage between Capetown and here, a record!
>
> Love to all, Uncle Harry

At 10.15 a.m. on 30 June 1912, after more than fifty days at sea, Harry arrived in Lyttelton, the port for Christchurch on the South Island of New Zealand. It was the depths of a Southern Hemisphere winter, just three days after the solstice. *Rotorua* had already disembarked passengers in Wellington, on the North Island, so Harry would have had a tantalising glimpse of red roofs and hillsides, before the ship turned out into the Pacific Ocean and ran down the coast prior to swinging starboard into the sheltering arm of the Banks Peninsula. As the *Rotorua* approached port Harry would have experienced a sense of being drawn in, of being embraced by the semicircle of towering peaks which form the rim of an ancient volcanic core. The tall mountain walls offer natural protection and a fine deep-water harbour, but keep the town in Stygian gloom for most of a winter's day.

Contemporary photos show two curving breakwaters, enclosing the harbour in a crab-like grip. The jetties look busy, with at least eight big cargo ships loading and unloading at any given time. The one unmissable building in Lyttelton would have been the Timeball Tower, erected in 1876, on top of which there is a large red-painted metal ball that drops at a certain precise time to enable incoming ships to coordinate their chronometers with Greenwich Mean Time. Around it, small residential buildings in a variety of colonial architectural styles were closely strung together along the hillside, rising up in terraces until the houses ran out and all you could see through the smoke from a thousand coal fires was rocky hillside covered with a thin skin of tight, tawny grass. Unlike green-girdled Wellington, Lyttelton must have felt more like an outpost than a welcoming town.

Coming from a country with buildings dating back centuries, the newness of New Zealand's British-built settlements must have come as a bit of a shock to Harry. His father's church in Linton was over six hundred years old; the town of Lyttelton a mere sixty-two. And with a population of no more than five thousand arrayed on the rocky cliffs it was all a far cry from the crowded cities he would have known in India.

In order to qualify for financial assistance to cover the expense of his 11,000-or-so-mile journey, Harry would have had to have proof that a job awaited him. Only one name comes up in his record of employment in New Zealand and that is E. F. 'Ted' Healy. Healy, a blacksmith-turned-businessman-and-entrepreneur, had made quite a name for himself in and around the town of Blenheim, some 200 miles north of Lyttelton, and would ultimately become an MP and stalwart of New Zealand politics. At the time Harry first met him, he had made enough money from his time as an auctioneer and from the sale of his auctioneering business to local merchants and wool brokers Dalgety & Co. (for whom he continued to work until 1911) that he was able to buy 2,000 acres of virgin farmland. Harry was one of the labourers he had taken on to help him clear the land and get his new farm going.

Another Englishman arrived at the farm a few months later, and he and Harry swiftly struck up a close friendship. George Batters came from a family that had made its fortune in the mines of North Wales, George's grandfather (also named George) having successfully developed the Point of Ayr colliery in Flintshire. George, whose mother died when he was just fourteen, worked for the family enterprise until his father's death in 1911, at which point he packed in the job – which he clearly disliked – and decided, along with his brother Frank, to turn his back on post-Victorian England and seek pleasanter climes elsewhere.

According to his nephew, Malcolm, George sounds to have been a charismatic, extrovert character, artistic and musical, and in the photos of him, always at the centre of any group. It's scarcely surprising that the less than conventional Harry should have become such good friends with him. Or that in the years ahead they should have stuck together through thick and thin.

In 1912 there were two routes out of Lyttelton heading north. One was by train through a one-and-a-half-mile tunnel cut through the walls of an ancient volcano over forty years earlier and opened to passenger trains in December 1867. The other was by a long, winding, far from comfortable road through Evans Pass that emerged into the small seaside township of Sumner and then on through Christchurch. My guess is that Harry travelled by road; perhaps he was given a lift by Ted Healy. Contemporary photos show Healy with a pony and trap, but I wouldn't be surprised if, being a well-to-do businessman, he also had a motor vehicle at his disposal.

However Harry made the journey, once he had left the fjord-like gloom of Lyttelton he would have emerged on the other side of Evans Pass into a very different landscape: a spectacular panorama with high mountains to the north and, soon coming into sight on the western horizon, the long, tall, snow-capped spine of the Southern Alps, running almost the length of the island. For Harry the wide-open spaces would have evoked a distinct sense of terra incognita, as well as a metaphor for limitless opportunities. The rough gravelled road clung to the east coast of the island running parallel to the Pacific

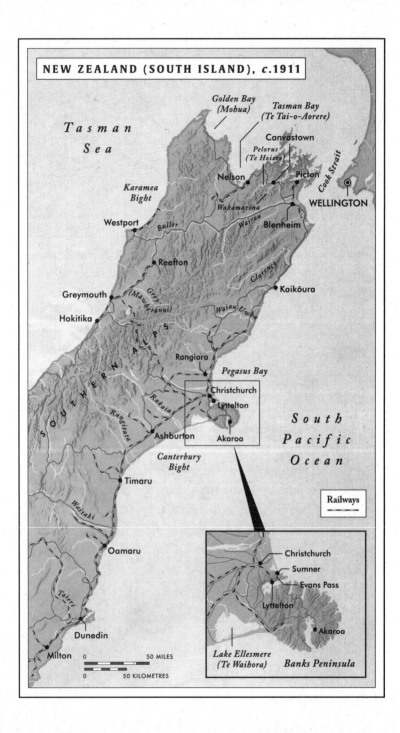

NEW ZEALAND (SOUTH ISLAND), *c.*1911

*Tasman
Sea*

*Golden Bay
(Mohua)*

*Tasman Bay
(Te Tai-o-Aorere)*

Canvastown

*Pelorus
(Te Hoiere)*

Nelson

Picton

Cook Strait

WELLINGTON

*Karamea
Bight*

Wakamarina

Wairau

Westport

Blenheim

Buller

Clarence

Reefton

Kaikōura

Greymouth

*Grey
(Mawheranui)*

Waiau Uwha

Hokitika

Rangiora

Pegasus Bay

Christchurch

Lyttelton

*South
Pacific
Ocean*

Rakaia

Akaroa

Rangitata

Ashburton

*Canterbury
Bight*

Timaru

Railways

Waitaki

Oamaru

Christchurch

Sumner

Evans Pass

Taieri

Lyttelton

Dunedin

Milton

0   50 MILES

0   50 KILOMETRES

Akaroa

*Lake Ellesmere
(Te Waihora)*

Banks Peninsula

SOUTHERN ALPS

Ocean. If he'd been lucky Harry might have seen whales, as I did, when I travelled on this same road in 1996, except that in Harry's time they would still have been hunted, and any whale unlucky enough to be stranded on the shore would have been stripped down to the bone. Nowadays they are protected and the whaling industry town of Kaikōura which Harry would have passed through has been reborn as a whale sanctuary, where locals make money by taking people to watch, but not touch, the whales out at sea. Carrying on up the coast, the road eventually turns inland, towards Blenheim and Canvastown, a small township near the confluence of the Pelorus and Wakamarina Rivers.

The farm Ted Healy was in the throes of purchasing in Canvastown was in an area that a contemporary prospectus boasted as good arable land, with grazing for over 2000 sheep and 150 cattle. Nevertheless, it was unpromisingly known locally as the Wilderness. While the deal was going through, Harry worked at Healy's Auction Mart, staying, according to the Wairau electoral roll, at the nearby Masonic Hotel. Soon, though, he joined Healy, his wife Mary and their six children on the new farm. There was much to do.

Today, Canvastown is close to the heart of the Marlborough wine-growing area. In 1912 it was a small, unglamorous settlement still recovering from the gold rush that had given it its name. Half a century before, a lady called Catherine Pope had found specks of the shiny metal whilst washing clothes in the Wakamarina River. Four years later, as more was discovered, some 6,000 diggers descended on the area, pitching their canvas tents by the river from which they hoped to make their fortunes. In 1864 a total of 24,838 ounces of gold, worth $100,000, were exported from the area. In the following year, however, only 8,000 ounces were found. By the turn of the century little of the legacy of the gold rush remained save for the name of the town. In Harry's time there, Canvastown consisted of a public hall, a school with a Literary and Debating Society in its grounds, and a hotel or two, one of which, the Pelorus, advertised itself as one of the largest and most comfortable hotels in the Marlborough district. The Blenheim–Nelson mail coach passed through every other day.

The farm Healy had bought might have been known as the Wilderness, but the reality was that there was good arable land beneath the thick woodland and forest. Clearance had already begun and trees had been cut down, milled and then shipped out of the nearby port at Havelock. Before Ted Healy could start making more land productive there was a forest of tree trunks to be uprooted. This is where Harry's baptism as a farmhand began, as he laboured at the brutal uprooting work, helped by bullocks and horses that dragged the stumps into piles for burning.

Ted Healy was known and respected as a man who worked hard and got things done. Indeed, in his zeal to have the property cleared, he nearly burned down his own house. But the back-breaking work paid off and, within a year, he had created one of the best cattle- and sheep-fattening properties in the district. Now Harry's labours would have been rewarded with more amenable work, like moving cattle and herding sheep. The wilderness was being tamed. The name, however, lived on – and still does.

The fact that Healy kept Harry on at Wilderness Farm for the next three years shows that the young immigrant was not shy when it came to hard work. But I think there may have been another reason why Harry and his employer were compatible. Ted Healy was Irish. Harry was half Irish. His mother may have suppressed her Irishness, exchanging it for the advancement her English connections brought her, but deep down, in the dark hours, memories of her own parents and their terrible suffering must have constantly edged into her consciousness. And though she had all the benefits of a loving and supportive English family, nothing could erase the awareness that it was Irish genes that had created her and English policy that had orphaned her. I can't help thinking that this unresolved indignation found an outlet in Harry, making him less prepared to accept the status quo than his siblings; more rebellious; more impulsive. He might have inherited some of the formal, buttoned-up traits of his English father, but he had certainly also imbibed the more freewheeling, less conformist characteristics of his Irish ancestry.

And that, I suspect, helped bring him and Ted Healy close together. After many years of bridling at what the British way of life expected of him, Harry had found a place in a country far away that enabled him to be himself, to do the work he wanted and be judged by those he respected. Ted and Mary Healy were his new Irish parents.

And the new parents of George Batters too. George liked a sing-song around the piano, and he had a good baritone voice. His nephew talked of musical evenings with comic songs and favourites from the Christy Minstrels. I should imagine that evenings like this would have been noisily celebrated not just by George and Harry but probably by the Healys as well.

Harry would not have lived in great comfort. He and Batters and doubtless other hired hands would have been put up in what were known as single men's quarters or huts. But then Ted and Mary hardly indulged in a life of luxury either. They lived in an unpretentious bungalow with a shady verandah on which Harry and his fellow workers would surely have taken the odd beer or two. There were no class issues here. And it was a pleasant part of the world to be, with generally mild winters and summers where the thermometer rarely hit much more than a comfortable 68 degrees Fahrenheit (20 degrees C). Blenheim, 20 miles east of Canvastown, and ringed by a bowl of hills, enjoys the reputation of being the sunniest and warmest place in New Zealand.

Ted Healy not only fattened cattle and sheep on the farm but also kept racehorses, chalking up many successes over the years with trotters and gallopers. Harry would almost certainly have learnt, or honed, his riding skills here, and I feel he was the sort of person who, when he wasn't rooting out trees or fence building or helping with the lambing, would have relished the freedom of

a good gallop. Judging by the number of female correspondents who kept up with him after he'd left Canvastown, he also enjoyed an active social life away from
the farm. The Canvastown community was lively and
friendly. There were rifle clubs and tennis clubs and, at
the end of a hard week, Friday-evening dances which ran
well on into Saturday mornings. Big appetites were satis-
fied by legendarily full suppers laid on by the local ladies.
Harry would also have met Māoris, as Canvastown was
the site of one of the marae – traditional Māori meeting
grounds. And he would have experienced something of
the rich Māori culture: an account from the time talks
of a gathering at which 'Mrs Wilson sang "Home Sweet
Home" in Māori'.

Many of those Harry would have drunk and dined
with were immigrants like himself. There was Gavin
Ross, a farmer from Lanarkshire; James Hughes, a farmer
originally from County Monaghan in Ireland; another
from Derbyshire. Would such people have made him feel
more at home, or more nostalgic for places left behind?
Did Harry ever consider following their example and
making a permanent home in New Zealand?

I really don't know. What I do know is that, however
happy he was, when the chance to return to Europe
came, he seized it with both hands.

PART 3

GALLIPOLI

This recently unearthed photograph was taken in one of the training camps in New Zealand. The two figures at the left-hand end of the line-up are almost certainly George Batters and Harry Palin.

Captain Hutton addresses the men of the 12th Nelson Regiment as they prepare to leave Nelson in the autumn of 1914 for combat abroad.

8

OFF TO WAR

———— ◆◈◆ ————

O N 28 JUNE 1914, as Harry was nearing the end
of his second year on the Healy Farm in Canvastown, an obscure event occurred in a far-off
country that was to change the course of his life.

That morning, an Austrian archduke was shot and
killed by a nineteen-year-old Serbian while driving in an
open-top car through the streets of Sarajevo, the capital
of Bosnia-Herzegovina. Harry might well have read the
reports of the assassination that appeared in the New
Zealand press two days later, but if he did so they can
hardly have made much impact on him. He was on the
other side of the earth. It was his third winter in New
Zealand, the calving season had just begun, and there
was plenty of work to do.

Soon, however, it became clear that the shooting in Sarajevo was having repercussions that went far beyond the
frontiers of Bosnia-Herzegovina. International tensions
grew. The great powers of Europe began to mobilise. As

July wore on, the threat of a general conflagration reared its head.

And half a world away in New Zealand, Harry and his friend George Batters, along with a whole host of others, started to pay attention to what was happening in the region of the world that they had only recently been so keen to leave behind.

News that Britain had declared war on Germany arrived in New Zealand just before 1 p.m. on 5 August. Two hours later, Lord Liverpool, the country's governor, made a public announcement on the steps of Parliament in Wellington to an enthusiastic crowd. Within a week 14,000 volunteers had answered the call to travel halfway round the word to defend the Empire. Among the first to respond were Harry Palin and George Batters.

I sense that there was more to the two men's decision than just a surge of patriotism or a simple desire to get back to their families. The fact is that Harry and George were still restless. They knew what they didn't want, but not what they did want. Emigrating to New Zealand had been a delaying tactic, not a solution. Historical journalist Jane Tolerton, who collected the experiences of a number of New Zealand's First World War veterans years later, found that many of them explained their eagerness to sign up in the summer of 1914 in terms of a desire for a new experience. Frank Fougere 'wanted to see it. I wanted to see what was going to happen.' Martin Brooke said he joined up because he 'loved excitement'. For Fred Dill, 'It was adventure, a new adventure, I suppose. Partly that and partly patriotism. We were frightened we wouldn't get there before it finished.' I suspect Harry and George felt much the same way. And anyway, the politicians said it would all be over by Christmas.

Harry and George bade what must have been a poignant goodbye to Ted and Mary Healy and caught the bus west over Pelorus Bridge and along a winding road through the mountains to the town of Nelson on Tasman Bay. There, at the Drill Hall on Harley Street, they enlisted in the 12th Nelson Regiment. George Batters, the 195th man to enlist, was given the regimental number 6/195; Harry, 6/319. The 12th Nelsons were, at the time, a territorial infantry force, not intended for overseas service, but the new local recruits were simultaneously made members of the Canterbury Battalion, which was. The name Nelson was retained to help engender a feeling of local pride, rather like the Pals Battalions back in England – the Leeds Pals, the Grimsby Chums, the Accrington Pals and many more formed to mobilise the spontaneous local expressions of patriotic fervour.

The *Nelson Mail*, alongside advertisements for the latest technological marvels, such as the Edison Phonograph and the Columbia Graphophone, carried reports of crowds cheering the new recruits as they marched behind the band to the strains of 'Lads in Navy Blue', 'True and Faithful' and 'The Regimental Quickstep' on their way to board a ship to Lyttelton.

Only once before – during the Boer War – had soldiers left New Zealand to fight for Sovereign, Empire and Country, and then only a small number of men had been involved. This time was different. A national commitment had been made. National pride was on the line. Marching to war must have seemed the right thing to do at the right time. These were brave men serving a glorious cause. For someone unused to praise, the cheers of the crowds he passed must have buoyed Harry up no end.

Thanks to the military's love of bureaucracy we have a valuable snapshot of Harry's physical condition at the time. On his Description of Enlistment form, with the word 'Infantry' scrawled across the top, are the details of his medical examination. As of 14 August 1914, he was twenty-nine years and eleven months old, stood 5 feet 11 inches and weighed 11 stone 3 lbs. Which was all good. (Or bad, if you look at it another way: had he been under 5 foot 4 or over 12 stone he'd have been automatically disqualified from military service and so possibly gone on to live a long, happy life.) His chest measurements were shown as 32 inches minimum and 36 maximum. His complexion was recorded as 'dark', the colour of his eyes 'brown' and his hair 'black'. Considering he'd been working as a farmhand for two years, it strikes me as a little surprising that he hadn't filled out or muscled up. In fact, he'd lost a few pounds since his Indian medical. He was slim, dark and wiry when he went away to war.

His sight, hearing, heart and lung function were all down as 'Normal'. Ditto to the questions, 'Are his limbs well-formed?' and 'Are the movements of his joints full and perfect?' He was free from 'varicocele, varicose veins, hernia and haemorrhoids'. 'Condition of the teeth' was described only as 'fair', but that was a lot better than was the case with many other applicants. Indeed, some 30 per cent of would-be recruits were rejected because their teeth were rotten and diseased, and even those who made it through the selection procedure often required emergency work. Captain R. D. Elliott, a dentist who sailed out with the 9th Reinforcements at the beginning of 1916, noted that 'the state of the men's mouths generally was more or less deplorable' and that in one month he and a dental assistant had to extract 255 teeth, drill 103 fillings and make 22 dentures.

There is just one observation on Harry's medical report that does stand out. It comes in answer to the innocuous final question, 'Are there any slight defects but not sufficient to cause rejection?' On the dotted line the medical examiner has written 'left testicle atrophied'.

I can't help thinking that a shrunken testicle sounds more than a 'slight defect', and wonder how long Harry had had the condition, and how common or uncommon it was at the time. Online searches suggest sexually transmitted infections and heavy alcohol consumption as potential causes. A doctor I talked to said that the likeliest explanation was mumps contracted during adolescence. The implications, in practical terms, would not have been too serious. One recent study concluded that 'testicular volume does not affect sperm retrieval rates' – in other words, Harry would have been able to father a child. However, he was not to know that and, growing up as he did in an era when things like this would have been thought too personal to talk about at home, and which he was possibly teased about at school, it might have been something that preyed on his mind. Could this be an unexpected insight into understanding Harry? Did he behave differently because he knew he was a bit different?

It clearly didn't matter enough to the authorities to disbar him from service. A total of 88,895 New Zealand men were initially turned down on medical grounds, so for Harry, passing the examination must have given him some reassurance.

He had one more form to deal with before he was officially enlisted, and that was for him to fill in and sign an Attestation. This posed such questions as, 'Are you married?' 'Have you ever been sentenced to imprisonment. If so, where?' 'Are you willing to be vaccinated or revaccinated?' There is nothing remarkable in his responses apart from an interesting answer to question 13, 'Have you ever served in any military or naval force?' Here he has put 'Volunteer India', which suggests that he must have received some military training either while working on the railway or during his time on the tea plantations. A sort of Home Guard of the Raj.

Once he had made his way through the form, he signed it 'HWB Palin' in a strong, confident, rather graceful hand, and then appended his signature again to an Oath of Allegiance.

The transition from farmhand to soldier was complete.

To mark his new status, Harry started to keep a diary. His entries, all in pencil, cover every corner of every page of a slim unlined pocket notebook, measuring 5 by 3 inches (12 x 7.5 cm). It was a quality purchase, with green leather covers, marbled endpapers and a metal clasp. Tucked down in the sleeve is a press cutting from a local paper which mentions that 'Mr H. W. B. Palin, who served four years in India, has joined the Expeditionary Force; also Mr Batters (England). They have been farming in this district lately.' His first entry is for 14 August 1914, the day he left Canvastown for Nelson. 'Passed medical exam and got uniform and became a private in 12th Nelson Regiment'. Or, more accurately, the 12th Nelson Company of the Canterbury Infantry Battalion.

Once at Christchurch, he and his fellow recruits underwent five weeks' training, for which they received 5 shillings a day, with 1 shilling deferred until the termination of service (a small fortune compared to the British Tommies' salary of 1 shilling a day). They were based at the Addington Show Grounds, which had been hastily converted into a mobilisation camp. It was generally thought to be a pretty grim place. A hundred years on it's still a camp, but now provides facilities for tourists and visitors. Judging from recent posts online, it would appear that it still gets criticised. 'Felt old, worn and cramped.' 'Poor showers on a timer.' 'Not a place to relax and feel comfortable.'

Harry's diary entries were usually made on the move and are rarely longer than two or three sentences. Their value is not in their extensiveness but in their spontaneity. Not that he found a lot to write about. For someone itching to go to war he records a frustratingly repetitive diet of route marches and rifle practices, inspections, church parades and the chance to buy official tent photographs, of which half a dozen copies could be purchased for 3 shillings. A potential highlight was a company visit to the Tepid Baths, housed in a grand building on Manchester Street in Christchurch. Built at a time when indoor swimming was becoming increasingly popular, and its health benefits – especially for women – were being extolled, they boasted a sizeable pool warmed by a pioneering destructor plant which turned the city's rubbish into heating. By the time Harry was due to visit they also allowed mixed bathing, previously viewed as morally highly questionable. (As a historian of the baths noted: 'Wet costumes clung to the body and showed more flesh than was deemed proper in mixed company.') Unfortunately, owing to a sore throat and cold, Harry was unable to go.

Two days later, on 19 September, he turned thirty. He describes the day tersely. 'Nothing much on and no leave on my birthday 30th.' But he did note that he had received a letter from Ted and Mary Healy, four letters from his mother, and three from his sister Mary. He also received a cheque for £10 from a friend of the family – a lot for someone who was being paid 5 shillings a day.

Four days after that, the volunteers finally broke camp and marched to Lyttelton on whose dockside Harry had first stepped ashore two years and three months earlier. He would have had high hopes on arrival in New Zealand. He must have had similarly high hopes as he prepared for the adventure that lay ahead, though the kit he would have been issued a couple of weeks before might have warned him that he was not in for an easy time. Along with the jacket, pair of trousers, pair of braces, pair of deck shoes and woollen jerseys, troops

Harry's father, Edward Palin, in his early to mid-twenties.

Edward (*standing eighth from right*) and other Fellows of St John's College, Oxford.

The silver inkstand presented to Edward in 1861, a token of his parishioners' esteem.

The vicarage Edward built at Linton.

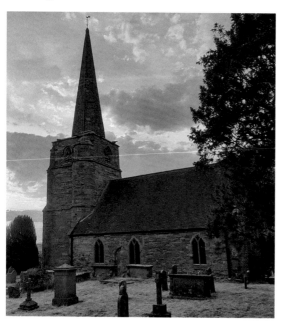

St Mary's Church, Linton, today.

The fountain and connecting water supply erected in 1880 'at the expense of Edward Palin'.

The 'genial' vicar of Linton in later life.

The only surviving photograph of Brita Palin, née Gallagher, c.1901.

Brita's adoptive mother, Caroline Watson.

Harry's brother Richie, who died of typhoid, aged just eighteen.

Harry's bedroom at the vicarage as it is today.

A detail of the stained glass in the vicarage hallway.

St Mary's, Linton: the view that would have met Harry's eyes every Sunday as his father addressed the congregation from his pulpit.

A family occasion: Edith Palin's wedding, 1901. Harry is the awkward teenager on the far right, his brother Eddy the confident doctor on the far left.

A group photograph taken the same day, against the backdrop of Linton vicarage. Harry stands below the ground-floor window, slightly above and to the left of the guest in a top hat.

Harry's first workplace: the grand Victoria station in Bombay.

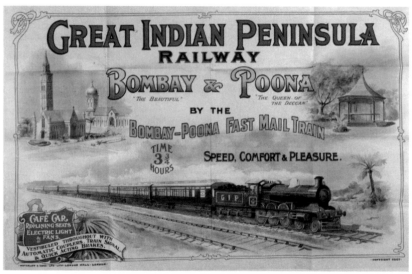

An advertisement for the Great Indian Peninsula Railway, c.1907.

A Victorian-era tea plantation in Assam.

The port at Lyttelton, where Harry first set foot on New Zealand soil.

The Timeball Tower, Lyttelton.

Harry's employers, Ted and Mary Healy, c.1895.

Harry's best friend, George Batters, preparing for war.

The Healys' bungalow at the Wilderness.

Canvastown as it was when Harry first saw it.

The countryside around Canvastown today.

were issued with a cholera belt: a strip of flannel or knitted wool which, wound tightly round the abdomen, was thought to help the wearer avoid the 'chilled stomach' that might lead to cholera and dysentery.

After a regimental photo, with all ranks lined up for inspection by their commanding officer, Sir Alexander Godley, a towering Irishman, the first of the New Zealanders began boarding. It would have been like nothing Christchurch had ever seen before as thousands of officers and men of the Expeditionary Force filed up the gangplanks and into the bellies of the two transport ships, *Tahiti* and *Athenic*, which were to take them to Europe. For security reasons both had been painted grey and renamed: an acknowledgement of the threat posed by the German East Asia Squadron. Harry was aboard *Athenic*, or as she was now, HMNZT 11.

Athenic carried 1,300 men and also 354 horses, stabled in hastily constructed boxes running along the deck. War might have been becoming increasingly mechanised, but the Expeditionary Force nevertheless set sail with some 3,818 horses aboard its various ships. At 5.30 on Wednesday 23 September they weighed anchor. 'Enormous crowd gave us a fine send off,' wrote Harry. And the soldiers, full of enthusiasm, waved back to friends, families and fellow countrymen.

It was the last time most of them would see each other.

In the days that had followed the outbreak of hostilities, the newspapers had whipped the nation into a mood of

gung-ho triumphalism. Such strident headlines as 'Crush-
ing German Defeat', 'Destructive Effect of French Artillery', 'Rapid French Advance' and 'Stories of German
Cruelty and Cowardice' made the war sound both easy
and necessary. In his speech to the departing force, New
Zealand's prime minister, William Massey, seeing 'the
very pick of our male population' sent off to a war being
fought over 11,500 miles away, conjured up a proud, if
convoluted, sense of mission. 'Young New Zealanders,'
he proclaimed, 'will proceed to the other side of the
world to meet Britain's enemies in battle, in countries
where centuries ago the ancestors of New Zealanders
held their own in many a fierce struggle.' Not, of course,
if you were Māori.

The Main Body, as New Zealand's impressive first
contribution to the war effort was known, initially got
only as far as Wellington. Here, partly because of fears
of German warships – the *Scharnhorst* and the *Gneisenau*
were known to be in western Pacific waters – and partly
because of the logistical complexities involved in assem-
bling such a large fleet, they stayed for over a month.
Judging from his diary entry for 7 October, where he
records being 'isolated by Doctor Richie as a chap in my
cabin was taken off to hospital with scarlet fever', Harry
remained quartered on the *Athenic*. But he spent his days
ashore, engaging in target practice and route marches –
one of which, on 27 September, involved an 18-mile trek
in full kit. The monotony was only occasionally inter-
rupted. On 30 September he 'Met Doris Wilberfoss in
evening 7.30, I took her to the pictures, she looked all

right and very chatty.' A few days later he took 'Tea at Wilberfosses and went to church with Doris.' Doris was four years younger than Harry, a society girl from a well-off family, whose activities were mentioned regularly in the papers. How Harry got to know her is a bit of a mystery. Judging from his diary, though, he had quite a talent for being asked to tea with young ladies. The day after tea and church he was not feeling so good. 'Reported sick. Had a temp and sent into hospital.'

On 14 October, exactly two months after he had enlisted, the transports were finally ready to leave. The morning before, Harry had gone up to the Wilberfosses to say goodbye to Doris, and she now came to the wharf to see him off. 'Wrote letters to Jean H, Winnie W, Ethel McR, Fred Jordan, Vera Chapman, Mrs Healy.' That he should have kept in touch with Mary Healy shows how much more cordial his relationship with his New Zealand employers was than it had been with those who ran the tea plantations. Harry never gushed in his diaries, but it's clear he was going to miss the Healys.

As for his women friends, Doris may have been the one who came to wave him off, but she was not the only one to keep in touch with him after he left the shores of New Zealand. Indeed, although Harry is frustratingly sparing with emotional detail, and I have to draw conclusions from the scantiest of evidence, I can't help being struck by the almost obsessive list of correspondents he records in his tightly scribbled diaries as the war proceeds. I find it hard to believe that he would have done so if these people had not meant a lot to him, and I'm struck by how regularly certain names crop up. Doris is one. Another is 'Winnie W', most likely Winifred White. A year younger than Harry, she trained as a teacher, and was registered on the electoral roll in Blenheim in 1914. She was last recorded as living in Wellington in 1938, fifty-three years old and unmarried.

The cheers from the dockside at Wellington had barely died down before instructions came for *Athenic* to drop anchor and wait at the mouth of the harbour. In view of what lay ahead one might think that fortune was reluctant to let them go. The real reason was rather more prosaic: the powers that be were still struggling to assemble a secure escort for these valuable cargoes. Finally, though, the convoy set off, clearing the Heads two days later, escorted out into the Tasman Sea by two New Zealand gunboats, one other from the China Sea fleet and a Japanese battlecruiser, *Ibuki*.

Twenty-four-year-old Private Cecil Malthus from Nelson, handsome, tall, with a thatch of thick black hair, a teacher by trade, was in the same company as Harry and painted a vivid picture of their shared experiences, mainly through letters to his fiancée, Hazel: 'There was a lovely sunset in Cook Strait,' he wrote after the fleet had set sail. 'We passed within sight of Farewell Spit just as they were lighting up the lighthouse, and that was our last glimpse of New Zealand.' The majority of the 8,500 men distributed among the ten war-grey vessels of this convoy were leaving their home country for the first time. Their prevailing mood was captured in another letter from Malthus to his beloved Hazel. 'I don't think half the men realise even yet what they are in for,' he wrote; 'they just treat the whole thing as a picnic.'

Harry would have missed any departure celebrations, as he recorded in his diary that he had come down with a mild attack of pleurisy and had to spend most of the early part of the voyage in the ship's hospital, iodine painted on his side to combat the symptoms. Hospital was perhaps the best place to be as they encountered rough weather on the Tasman Sea. The *Athenian Lyre*, the exotically titled ship's magazine, described in graphic detail the impact of the rough weather on the ship's unfortunate passengers. 'Here, a man sprawled, his head hanging limply, his eyes with a dull, unseeing stare. Another with white face chattered feverishly or hummed a music-hall ditty . . . Presently he would make a sudden dive to the side, and a few moments after would be another recruit to the sprawling, dull-eyed brigade.' So prevalent was seasickness that orders had to be issued reminding those who had false teeth to remove them before vomiting over the side.

Religious observation carried on as best it could, as recorded in the *Lyre*: 'A sadly depleted band, minus a conductor, struggled bravely through the service at church parade.' 'The band will certainly be no small factor in relieving the tedium of the voyage,' it went on. Sport, so often the partner of religion in military life, was encouraged, wrestling and boxing classes both being on offer. Otherwise, the men chatted among themselves or read or lounged around and smoked. Fans of the magazine could consult its pages for brief updates on the course of the war and enjoy the jokey advertisements it ran, such as the one inviting men up to the Boat Deck for dentistry. 'Extract teeth. Absolutely Painless. The Band will attend to drown the shrieks.'

Six days after leaving Wellington, they were in sight of Hobart, Tasmania. The editors of the *Athenian Lyre* waxed lyrical. 'Groups were clustered on the deck eagerly scanning the horizon, with feelings somewhat akin to that which the children of Israel must have felt when gazing on the promised land . . . Memories of mal de mer seemed but a thing of the past and the prospect of feeling firm, solid ground beneath one's feet, instead of a heaving, slithering, sliding deck became more than a possibility of the future.' The rapture continued: 'On all sides one heard learned discussions on fruit culture and the advantages of living in this Garden of Eden, where you have only to sit in the shade, watch your apples ripen in the sun and grow wealthy.' Not an option for the men of the Expeditionary Force, who, after a brief spell ashore, during which they went on a route march through the town, had to leave Hobart just twenty-four hours later. Harry, still recuperating from his attack of pleurisy, and clearly averse to overt celebrations, seems to have had no desire to join his comrades on the march. By the afternoon, though, he had recovered sufficiently to take a walk on deck and scan the shore through a pair of field glasses. 'Big crowd on wharf to see us off,' he noted. 'A lot of v. pretty girls amongst the crowd.'

Lieutenant Hugh Stewart, a Canterbury Battalion officer and author of *The New Zealand Division 1916–1919*, was moved by a different observation. Noting that 200 men had deserted from the Australian troopships that

had joined them at Hobart, he deplored their behaviour
and compared it most unfavourably with that of his own
troops. 'I doubt whether in the whole of the opposing
armies is such a fine body of men, physically and intellec-
tually, as the NZ force.' He might have been less absolute
had he known that four men from the Canterbury Battalion and seven from the Auckland Battalion had also
succumbed to the temptations of the Tasmanian capital
and failed to rejoin their ship.

Soon after leaving Hobart, Harry was given his tobacco
ration and also an inoculation against typhoid. Judging
from the pages of the *Lyre*, the inoculation programme
was not universally welcomed, and quite a large number
of men refused to be vaccinated. The magazine even
went so far as to publish a poem on the subject:

> *Once on a time I was a fairly healthy sort of chap*
> *For all the ills the others got I didn't care a rap*
> *But Doctor Fearless said that to get typhoid I was fated*
> *And that I'd have to visit him and get inoculated . . .*
>
> *The doctor said that what he'd done need cause me no alarm*
> *He'd merely put five hundred million germs into my arm*
> *And in a few days time, he said, he had a treat in store*
> *For he would then put in one thousand million more . . .*
>
> *I may believe in medicine though nasty to the taste –*
> *In patent powders, pills and jubes, and anti-septic paste –*
> *In every kind of strange and evil-smelling preparation*
> *But oh! I never can believe in this inoculation.*

The convoy's next stop was Albany, on the far side of the Great Australian Bight, at the south-western tip of the country. By now Harry was on the mend. The regime of cupping he had been subjected to – blistering his chest to draw the blood out – seemed to have worked, though it left him with quite a lot of pain that persisted for most of the rest of the voyage. He was discharged from the ship's sickbay and able to take a short walk on deck, during which he noted a fleet of Australian troop-ships drawn up in the stream waiting to join them. By the time they left Albany, the vessels and their attendant escorts combined made up the biggest fleet ever to leave Australia. George Wallace Bollinger of the Wellington Infantry Brigade watched the convoy as it headed out: 'I wonder if such a sight as this has ever been witnessed before – thirty-eight ocean liners and five battleships.' The sheer size of the fleet must have fed the aura of invincibility that had been inculcated into the men long before they steamed out into the Indian Ocean.

The heavy seas they had initially experienced soon gave way to calmer waters, but as they moved north-west the temperature became fiercely and unbearably oppressive. On 5 November Harry 'slept on deck. It was A1'. On the 7th it was 'V. hot', and he slept on deck again. 'It is fine, so much healthier than below,' he noted. The *Lyre* put it more poetically: 'Even the sea seemed to be affected by the prevailing spirit and gently heaved under the overpowering sun. The evenings on deck were glorious, it became the custom to take one's bed from below and spend the night in the cool liquid blackness above.'

On 9 November Harry recorded the morale-boosting news of the cornering and forcing aground of the German cruiser *Emden* by HMAS *Sydney*, off the Cocos Islands, in an action in which the *Emden* lost nearly a third of its crew of 376 to the *Sydney's* two killed and thirteen wounded. But while the commander of Harry's company, Captain Brereton, described how immediately 'bands were playing "Sons of the Sea" and crowds of men were singing and dancing', Harry himself seems to have been more taken up with the news that his friend Batters had gone down with measles.

Two days later Harry, on guard that night, heard a rumour that the Australian and New Zealand infantry battalions were to go to India to strengthen the garrison there. Again, rather than considering what implications this might have for the progress of the war, his immediate thoughts were rather closer to home. 'I *may* get a chance to see Ralph [his brother-in-law] and T [his oldest sister, Tissie] again,' he wrote, his spirits clearly rising as he did so.

Nearly a week later, on 15 November, he recorded *Athenic's* arrival in Colombo. A five-funnel Russian cruiser was in port, along with the *Sydney*, which had just arrived, accompanied by an armed merchantman with prisoners from the *Emden* on board. The next day he went ashore with a party of twenty men. 'As I knew Colombo fairly well,' he wrote, 'I was put in front to lead the way.' And, with a clear hint at his familiarity with the Ceylonese (now Sri Lankan) capital, gained during his time in India, he added, 'Had a couple of drinks at the

Bristol and the Lord Nelson Hotels and then went [for] a stroll round fruit market.'

Harry's stay in Colombo seems to have been a low-key one. We know from other accounts, however, that quite a few of his companions were rather less restrained. Mostly farm boys who'd never previously left their home-steads, and who had most recently had to endure being cooped up on a dry ship, they took full advantage of the local hospitality in this exotic Asian capital. Once back on board, eighty-five of them were put on two weeks' hard labour in the stokehold and had black marks in their pay book – effectively, a fine. As one of them, Private Martin Brooke, observed later, 'When troops travel there are always a number who are naughty boys.' Forced to rec-ognise the truth of this, Godley cancelled all shore leave at their next port of call.

Judging from his diary, Harry had some hopes that once the *Athenic* left Colombo it would proceed to India. But that was not to be. When the ship finally set sail on Tuesday 17 November the men were informed that they would not be sailing north to the subcontinent but to 'a destination not yet announced'.

Harry's diary entries can seem frustratingly terse. Lance Corporal William Steven, who was on board the *Tahiti*, describes in his diaries how, in an attempt to cope with the long, hot days on the Indian Ocean, 'two canvas baths, each 20ft by 5ft' were erected on the saloon deck, and orders were given, 'making it compulsory for every man to have a dip first thing in the morning'. He also has a succinct take on the food, making up his own parody of

the dinner menu: ' "Supper Bill of Fare": 1 Cup of doubtful water, 1 piece of doubtful cheese, 1 or 2 Dog or Ship's
biscuits.' Cecil Malthus, disappointed though he was by
the tropics, did at least make the effort to characterise
them to his fiancée, even if in a very negative way: 'They
are so like anywhere else. There are no "skies of molten
brass", all the flying fish we have seen were about the size
of herring, and the dark does <u>not</u> come "at one stride".'
Harry, by contrast, merely repeats in his diary the single
line, day after day, 'Nothing much to note'.

He is not stirred even when things take a more dramatic
turn. Back in early November, as they are on their way to
Colombo, Steven records a storm when 'The decks were
awash all night.' 'Several horses came down . . .' he goes
on to say. 'Many of the fellows on deck ran below and
got their lifebelts. This morning the ship's crew state she
has never rolled like it before. They blame the horses on
the top deck.' We know from different sources that other
ships were even worse hit. The *Wanganui*, for example,
lost sixteen horses and had to pull out of the line to bury
them. Harry, by contrast, sums up the storm in two
words: 'Heavy sea.'

But to my mind, even the brevity of Harry's diary
entries is revealing. They reinforce my impression of my
great-uncle as essentially a man of the moment, a practical man, not much given to romanticising or storytelling
(the unlikely alternative is that he was a martyr to seasickness and wasn't well enough to write). I suspect, too,
that he was unimpressed because he'd seen it all before.
Most of his companions were leaving New Zealand for

the first time. Harry had been back and forth to India, and apparently Ceylon, several times. Most of his fellow soldiers were experiencing conditions they'd never previously had to cope with: Lance Corporal Steven spoke for many when he wrote, 'New Zealanders don't know what heat is.' Heat was nothing new to Harry.

Not that everything was the same. The conditions that Harry would have experienced on board *Athenic* would have been very different from those of his cabin-ticket travels out to India. Sleeping quarters on *Athenic* were down in the bowels of the ship, accessed by a very steep improvised wooden walkway. Bunks were stacked three high, with a yard-wide passageway in between. Washing and toilet facilities were limited, and the fact that beards were not permitted meant a twenty-minute wait to wash and shave each morning. Fearing perhaps the consequences of overcrowding, there were regular inspections by the ship's doctors and dentists. And they were none too gentle. One man, who had had six teeth pulled, complained that 'they gouge them out like a navvy in a shingle pit'.

Privacy was a further casualty of life aboard a warship. Looking back, Ormond Burton, who was serving with the New Zealand Medical Corps, put it well: 'From this time for one, two, three, even four years, a man could not eat by himself or sleep by himself. If he looked at his sweetheart's photograph there was probably an audience, more or less appreciative. If he opened a parcel, there was his own section at least to assist him. If he was miserable he was regarded as a bringer of gloom; if his mate was offensively drunk he could not do more than edge a few inches away from the odorous reality of the exhilarated one.' He did, however, conclude, 'One of the kindly fruits of this enforced proximity was a wonderful growth of tolerance.'

For his part Cecil Malthus wrote of the frustrations of the mess halls where the food was grim, and the mess room was not only crowded, 'it was also dimly lit, hazy, frightfully hot, smelly and sweaty'. Not surprisingly, the men were not always able to bear such conditions with equanimity. Malthus went on to describe how, 'When the orderly officer appeared that day with the traditional "Any complaints?" he was greeted with an almost universal roar of anger, and the next moment was hit fair in the face with an old hunk of cheese.'

The *Athenian Lyre* reported an exchange over tea, the last meal of the day:

ORDERLY OFFICER: 'Any complaints, men?'
PRIVATE: 'Yessir, taste this, Sir.'
OFFICER: 'H'm, rather thin and greasy, otherwise not
   bad soup!'
PRIVATE: 'Yessir, that's what we thought, but the
   Cook says it's tea.'

Despite all this, even the well-read, fastidious Malthus, after initial worries about being quartered so close to the common soldiery, like Burton learnt a lesson in tolerance. 'I find even the lowest of them brave and good natured, and good soldiers too.' Which was just as well, as they were all to spend a lot more time with each other.

Shore leave having been banned because of bad behaviour in Colombo, Aden was passed with little delay, and they steamed up the Red Sea. After the limbo of the long ocean passage Harry was suddenly surrounded by activity as they entered one of the great wonders of the man-made world, the Suez Canal. Less than fifty years old, this feat of engineering had revolutionised travel across the globe, cutting around 4,500 miles off the journey from India to Europe and transforming the relationship between East and West. Not surprisingly there was an extensive military presence along its length, which Harry observed from the deck of the *Athenic*. 'Passed several detachments of Indian troops fortified along the Canal, Sikhs, Goorkhas [*sic*] etc. V. interesting. Cold night.'

They docked at Port Said at 2.30 in the morning on 2 December. 'Very busy all round. 3 French battleships, 1 British Dreadnought – HMS "Swiftsure", 3 torpedo boats and cruisers. Saw a hydroplane on one of the French ships.' After a brief stop for coaling they sailed that afternoon. 'Stood to attention as we left at 2.30 p.m., passing all Australian ships, French men o'war with the band playing. V fine sight.'

That their final destination would be Egypt had remained a secret until the very end of the six-week voyage. Not just from the men, but also, to his intense irritation, from Major General Godley, the commander of the Expeditionary Force. Once it was out, the almost universal reaction was one of disappointment. 'Right up to Suez we were quite positive that we were going to Europe,' a dispirited Malthus wrote.

Harry felt the same way. 'We are bound for <u>Alexandria</u> where we disembark to go to Cairo (?). Not to dear old England for the present. I am rather sorry. In fact very much so, as I may not see Mother and all for a long time, but must hope for the best.'

Two photographs of fellow 12th Nelsons taken by George Batters in Egypt in 1915. His great friend Harry Palin is almost certainly the figure second from left in the top photograph, and may well appear – again, second from left, with his face in partial shadow – in the bottom image.

9

THE CALM BEFORE THE STORM

I HAD WONDERED IF TURNING his back on Britain two or so years earlier had been a definitive burning of the boats for Harry. An irreversible commitment to a new life on the other side of the world. A final break with the family who all shone more brightly than him. I should have known by now that Harry doesn't do irreversible commitments. He goes where the wind blows him. Emigration was not a rejection of a previous life, it was just another symptom of his restlessness. He saw the war as a chance to return to the fold. But as he and his fellow soldiers marched off the *Athenic* for the last time he had to accept that, though it had carried him 10,000 miles closer, home was a long way off yet.

On the dockside at Alexandria the sense of anticlimax persisted, as they were held in marching order for three and a half hours, preyed on, according to Captain Brereton, by local traders who tried to sell them methylated spirit in the guise of whisky. They then boarded a train, but were held for another three and a half hours, before leaving for Cairo. 'Travelling the best part of the night and got no sleep,' Harry wrote. 'Arrived at our destination at 3.30 a.m. V tired and dirty. Had a march of about 2 hours to the camping place.'

The camp was in the district of Zeitoun, 5 miles to the north-east of Cairo, which many years later would become famous for numerous reported sightings of the Virgin Mary. But there was nothing much there when the Expeditionary Force arrived except dust and sand. Even the tents hadn't yet turned up for many of the waiting troops. A Private Thompson summed up their disappointment: 'We certainly did expect to find some grass, but not so this time – simply sand, sand, sand everywhere. We are camped in the Sahara Desert.' On the plus side, they could just see the Pyramids.

The Canterbury Battalion was more fortunate: their tents had already arrived. To the sound of bugles, and the barking of orders from sergeant majors and the adjutant, the men were set to work erecting row after row of them with military precision. Streets were marked with rocks, canteens and messes were opened up. Soon Egyptian entrepreneurs moved in, establishing coffee shops, barbers, bootmakers and bric-a-brac emporiums. The arrival of the Expeditionary Force was a huge boost to the local economy. And so it continued to be. By the end of the war 43,000 New Zealand soldiers had spent time – and money – in Egypt.

So far as the high command was concerned, any interaction between New Zealand troops and the local population spelt potential disaster, and was therefore to be actively avoided. A Special General Order was accordingly issued by Major General Godley advising his men on how to behave 'towards the natives' whilst in Egypt. First it set out its higher purpose: 'Every member of the Force in Egypt is charged with the enormous responsibility of maintaining the prestige of the British race.' Having done that, it proceeded to issue a series of dire warnings. All ranks were 'to avoid conversation with the natives except on matters of business'. In particular there was to be 'no repetition of the regrettable incidents noted in Colombo, of men mixing with the natives, imitating their manner of speech and indulging in badinage'. Troops were to avoid local drinks: 'The native drinks are generally the vilest concoctions possible . . . and cannot be taken with impunity'. That, however, was nothing compared to 'the extreme danger of having any intercourse with native women . . . Syphilis in a most virulent form is rampant in Cairo and men having connection with prostitutes are running the gravest possible risks.'

Despite the dangers the high command saw lurking everywhere, they seem to have been prepared to grant generous leave, and the very next day after their arrival Harry was allowed to ride the 5 miles into Cairo to do some exploring. 'Went with Sammy White and we got two English "Terriers" to show us round,' he wrote. These 'Terriers' were most likely men from the East Lancashires, who were camped adjacent to the New Zealanders, or 'Enzeds', as they called themselves. 'V. much like an Indian city, both in regard to streets, shops,' Harry went on. But it wasn't an altogether successful expedition.

'I shan't go out with White again,' he concluded with barely concealed exasperation. 'He talks such rot and is always looking at his watch.'

The next day, a Sunday, after church parade, Harry went with his old and more trusted friend Batters to the newly built suburb of Heliopolis, a mile outside the camp, where they had beers and went roller-skating. In the days that followed they visited mosques, the Pyramids, and 'some v. nice gardens beyond the Nile Bridge', where they 'lay on the grass smoking etc'.

Rather like Billy Bunter, the penurious cake-eating schoolboy who first appeared in the *Magnet* six years earlier, Harry was always strapped for cash, always relying on a cheque from home to get him out of a scrape. When he went into Cook's in Cairo, the £10 cheque he'd been sent for his birthday was found to be out of date. The next day's plaintive diary entry reads, 'Out on march doing battalion drill etc 8.00 to 2.00 as usual. Absolutely broke.'

Nevertheless he continued his trips into town with Batters – or 'Batty', as he often called him – for haircuts and meals. In the sleeve of his diary I found a tiny menu slip for the John Bulboul Grill Room which offered fish, bread and 'Salade Ham with Cabbagge' for 4 piastres. Alcohol makes a fairly frequent appearance in the diary. 'Had a royal evening; big feed etc and returned home somewhat merry,' Harry writes on one occasion. And on another, 'To Cairo with Batty. B got pretty tight, so I came home alone'. Was there a hint of maturity here? Maybe his greater age and his time in India had taught Harry how to go so far but no further.

To celebrate Christmas Day 1915, they went to the zoo. 'V decent there, must go again. Mooched about town. Wrote some P.c's. Received 14/- pay today.' By the sound of things it disappeared pretty quickly.

Whether or not Harry succumbed to the temptations of the flesh Major General Godley so sternly warned his troops against is unclear. His diaries never specifically mention any sexual encounters. On the other hand, we know that Harry was strongly attracted to women, and we also know that while he was in Egypt he would have visited establishments that were frequented by prostitutes. One such was the Kursaal in Alfi Bey Street, which Harry went to on Christmas evening and which offered – alongside entertainment, live music, dancing and a casino – a large number of ladies for hire. Harry may, of course, have been one of those who simply looked. But he may equally have been tempted. There were, after all, by one estimate, some 60,000 prostitutes in Cairo during the war. In a letter home to his wife Lieutenant Roy Bruce painted a vivid picture of what was on offer in the Wazzir, the brothel quarter. 'Women in open doorways Soudanese, Nubians, displaying their forms and inviting the passers by. Others loaded with jewellery earrings, nose rings, anklets clashing, sitting Sphinx like in their doorways with open beds behind them.' There certainly seemed plenty of opportunities for the twin temptations of drink and sex, or, as one officer put it, the attentions of Bacchus and Venus. And those opportunities would have been taken by many of the soldiers waiting for deployment. In the words of Ormond Burton, 'if

truth be the first casualty of war, then chastity is probably the second'.

While Major General Godley warned against the dangers of illicit sex, he was down-to-earth enough to accept
that when lusty young lads were far from home and in
drink they might well succumb. He therefore arranged for
the men to be given tins of ointment that could be used
before or during intercourse, and ordered each battalion
to have treatment tents dispensing prophylactic solutions
and syringes for post-coital injection. This show of pragmatic tolerance horrified some of his subordinate commanders, one of whom, William Malone, Commander of
the Wellington Battalion, was of the view that instead of
ointments and syringes 'we [should] appeal to the man's
better nature . . . at the same time letting him know of the
awful punishment of certain vice in this country'. Godley's
policy, he maintained, would 'destroy all moral restraint!'

There was another arm to Godley's preventive policy
and that was to keep the men otherwise busy with a full
day's training schedule of drill, fatigues, mock battles,
bayonet fighting, trench digging, route marches and a
series of increasingly ambitious attack practices. Discipline was strict, courts martial common, and when, on 21
December, the *Athenic* returned to New Zealand, those
among the fifty-eight members of the force she took
back with her included, alongside nine invalids and four
with syphilis, thirty-eight who had refused inoculations
and ten 'incorrigibles' guilty of 'misconduct'. The irony
is that these men all survived, while so many of their
better-behaved brethren never saw home again.

The year 1915 was almost a month old when the war for which the New Zealanders had been rehearsing abruptly became a reality. On Monday 25 January, after a day spent writing postcards, Harry recorded his excitement at receiving the news that the 12th Nelsons had been chosen to leave for Ismailia in order to spearhead the defence against a possible enemy build-up: '. . . real active service at last!' he confided to his diary. 'Great excitement of course.' 'No leave in evening,' he continued in telegramese fashion. 'Wrote to Mother and Margie. Only N.Z. sending troops. Busy getting gear in order etc., ready to start tomorrow.' Margie was a name that was to appear in his diaries with increasing frequency over the weeks and months ahead.

Turkey had signed a secret treaty with Germany shortly before the outbreak of general hostilities the previous year, and within months was at war with Russia and, therefore, with Russia's allies Britain and France. In early 1915, aerial reconnaissance had spotted German-led Turkish troops preparing for an assault on the Suez Canal, regarded by the British as of crucial importance, not just because it was vital to Britain's strategic interests in the Eastern Mediterranean but because, as Harry knew well, it offered the quickest route to India. Anticipating the attack, the Nelsons took up position, camping out in thirteen tents on the west bank. Indian troops were already in place. Harry chatted to some of them and was pleased to find that his time out in India had not been entirely wasted: 'Found I could manage fairly well, altho' lots of words forgotten.'

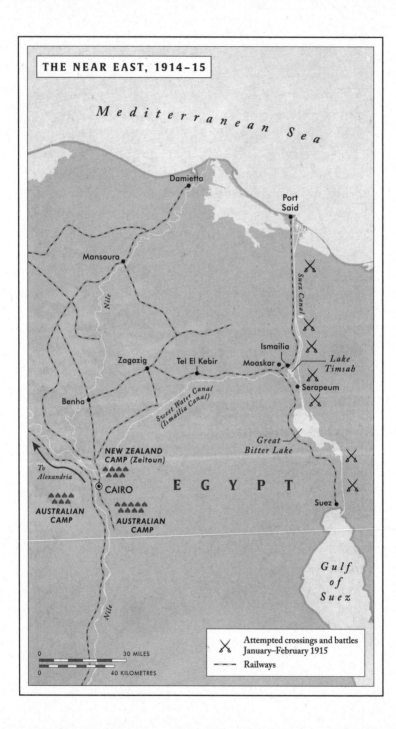

THE NEAR EAST, 1914–15

Mediterranean Sea

Damietta

Port Said

Mansoura

Nile

Suez Canal

Zagazig

Tel El Kebir

Ismailia

Moaskar

Lake Timsah

Serapeum

Benha

Sweet Water Canal (Ismailia Canal)

Great Bitter Lake

NEW ZEALAND CAMP (Zeitoun)

To Alexandria

CAIRO

E G Y P T

AUSTRALIAN CAMP

AUSTRALIAN CAMP

Suez

Nile

Gulf of Suez

0   30 MILES

0   40 KILOMETRES

✕   Attempted crossings and battles January–February 1915

—   Railways

On the 29th a Swiss-German spy was captured, along with two Turkish deserters. Harry was one of those detailed to guard them. On 2 February he was an eyewitness to the first action in the war in which New Zealand troops were engaged. 'Heavy action started after breakfast some way across the Canal and continued some time,' he wrote. 'We could easily see shells bursting in the distance. Some of the N. Z'landers pushed into trenches at midday.' The next day there was more heavy firing at the Turkish lines, largely from a French battleship. 'Prisoners looked v. lame and glad enough to be captured.' But it wasn't all one way. The Nelsons sustained their first casualties of the war. 'Sergt Major Williams wounded in the shoulder and Pvt Ham (10 Platoon) wounded in the neck, seriously.' It turned out that his back was broken.

The Turkish attempt to cross the canal was foiled by superior artillery, seemingly bearing out the popular view that the Turks were nothing more than a 'harmless lot of orange sellers', badly organised and ineffectual in the face of a brutally targeted naval bombardment. The death of Private Ham two days after he received his injury should have served as a warning that the New Zealanders' breezy assumption that the war would be quickly won was misplaced, and that the assumption that the Turks would prove an easy foe to defeat would turn out to be spectacularly wide of the mark.

The diaries of Lance-Corporal Dunton, a fellow 12th Nelson, fill out some of the small details of life for the New Zealanders at that time. Food, as ever, was an obsession and a cause of constant complaint. 'The usual fare,' he wrote, 'is stew, bread, Jam and tea (black) for B/fast and Bread Jam and tea for lunch and what remains of scraps of bread and jam for tea.' It wasn't even good bread and jam, he complained. Fruit could be purchased to supplement the diet, but many were discouraged from doing so when they learnt how the produce had been cleaned in a land where water was in short supply. According to Guy Thornton, a chaplain with the Main Body, strawberries and grapes were reputedly cleaned by their vendors 'by the simple and effective process of placing them in his mouth and licking them vigorously and thoroughly'.

After three weeks in Ismailia, camped beside the canal and gratefully receiving tins of cigarettes and tobacco thrown down from passing ships, Harry and the Infantry Brigade returned to Zeitoun. Corporal Dunton found the ride a lot more agreeable than the bread and jam. 'The railway journey from Ismallia [*sic*] to Cairo is probably the finest I have seen. For four hours the train ran through endless scenes of green pastures, crops and date plantations and on the morning we returned to base it reminded us strongly of a day in September in N.Z.'

Harry's sister Mary had put him in touch with a family called Milton, cousins of some kind, living and working in Cairo. Their generous hospitality must have made life more tolerable for Harry, and on his return from the canal they invited him round for dinner. Predictably, and not unlike his father on a Swiss holiday, Harry noticed the ladies. 'Met a pretty girl there, a Miss Lucas,' he wrote. The next night he was back. 'Had a bath!'

Harry's time in Cairo seems otherwise to have passed without event. While his fellow diarist Lieutenant Hugh Stewart was busy recording the books he read, the philosophy he discussed with fellow officers, the tennis he played, his meals at the Club and the two-day trip he made to Luxor, Harry's diary entries were increasingly reduced to variations on the theme of 'Nothing doing'. Even his visits to the Milton household ended up being curtailed, when Mrs Milton, his hospitable hostess, was obliged to return to England to nurse her sick father.

Having despatched the Turks at Ismailia, everyone was desperate to know where the Enzeds might be going next. There was a rumour that they might be deployed to the Dardanelles, the scene of an ongoing Allied naval attack on Turkish positions. With nothing confirmed, however, and boredom rapidly setting in, such fighting as took place had more to do with frustration than with war. Harry describes how on 10 March the New Zealanders got involved in a brawl with the Australians 'and got well slathered up [probably 'drunk']'. Two days later the Enzeds attacked the East Lancs, whom, Harry wrote with some pride, 'we defeated with great slaughter'.

On 2 April – Good Friday – the unrest escalated into what Harry describes as 'a very serious row in the native quarter'. It began with some disgruntled Australian soldiers getting into an argument with prostitutes in the Wazzir brothel area – either about payment or, according to some accounts, because they claimed the prostitutes had given them VD. By the early evening a fully fledged riot was taking place, with a mob of soldiers smashing windows, grabbing furniture from inside the houses, setting buildings alight and even, at one point, throwing a piano out of a window. Cecil Malthus records the 'shock of seeing a poor Arab boy run over by a car full of mad Australians and instantly killed'. Soon the squaddies were turning on each other, Australians battling New Zealanders. Harry records that the military police – or Red Caps, as they were known – were then called out to restore order 'and several NZ and A were either shot dead or wounded'. The Red Caps, too, were attacked. Two days later, on Easter Sunday, troops, now confined to barracks, burned the camp projector when it broke down.

The breakdown in discipline that Major General Godley had sought to avoid through endless drills and mock battles was now very much on the horizon. There was no knowing how long he could keep the lid on bored, hot, restless, randy young men impatient to join the war.

But things were about to change.

On 9 April Harry noted a sudden burst of activity. 'Packing kits, rolling blankets, receiving Iron Rations, medical inspection etc.' The same day he and the other Canterburys left Zeitoun camp, their home for the last four months, and travelled by overnight train to Alexandria. Here they boarded the *Itonus*, an Australian ship from the Bombay–Queensland run, now commandeered as a troop transport. At 5.00 that afternoon they sailed 'for some unknown destination'.

I don't know how much Harry knew about the progress of the war, and whether he still harboured hopes
of being sent to France. At the time, it must have seemed
the logical destination. It would certainly have been a
regular topic of conversation among those on the troop
transport. Lieutenant Hugh Stewart, aboard another
vessel, the captured German liner *Lützow*, and often busy
playing poker and reading Virgil's *Aeneid*, listened to a
talk by an ex-Irish Guards interpreter about what was
happening elsewhere in Europe and, in particular, on
the Western Front. The interpreter reported that the
British soldiers marched into France chanting, 'Are we
going to win? No! Are we downhearted? Yes!', followed
by roars of laughter, and a rendition of a new version of
'It's a Long Way to Tipperary': 'That's the Wrong Way
to Tickle Mary'.

But any thoughts of France must have started to recede
on the 12th when, rather than continuing to see endless
expanses of open water, Harry noted 'islands showing
up on both sides'. Gradually, the *Itonus*'s destination
became clear: the island of Lemnos, once a part of the
Ottoman Empire, then acquired by Greece after the
first Balkan War in 1912 and now a valuable Allied assem-
bly point. As the ship manoeuvred her way into Mudros
Bay, Harry picked out in the early dawn light an armada
of vessels, dominated by the massively armoured HMS
Queen Elizabeth, complete with eight 15-inch breech-
loading guns, as well as torpedo boats and submarines.
On the shore was arrayed a small city of tents and
marquees.

The next day the *Lützow* pulled into the bay carrying 1,700 men from the Canterbury and Auckland Battalions. Here the men from the *Lützow* and the *Itonus* practised boat landing and disembarkation drills. These had not been part of the training regime in Egypt and must have led Harry to speculate what kind of challenges lay ahead. The weather was nasty, with rain and strong winds. Harry took a day off with a bad cold. He wasn't the only one. Private John Constance, also suffering breathing problems, reported that 'We were all issued with about a dozen packets of cigarettes and matches.' Shocking as this may sound to modern sensibilities, tobacco was at this time considered a health supplement. Good for relaxation, and a cleansing tonic. The great majority of the soldiers who fought at Gallipoli smoked.

Only now were the likes of Privates Constance and Palin to learn what lay ahead. The Australian and New Zealand troops, now officially combined into the Australian and New Zealand Army Corps (ANZAC), were to be part of a two-pronged assault on the Gallipoli peninsula, which lay at the mouth of the 38-mile strait called the Dardanelles. Winston Churchill, First Sea Lord and chief advocate of the offensive, was confident that he who controlled this narrow seaway controlled access to Constantinople (now Istanbul). He who controlled Constantinople controlled Turkey, Germany's ally against our ally Russia. The superior firepower of the British and French navies, aided by amphibious landings to take out the Turkish defences, would, he said, clear the way in a matter of days. He spoke powerfully of the impact a successful invasion of the Dardanelles would have. He saw it as breaking the stalemate into which the war on the Western Front had settled. 'Are there not other alternatives,' Churchill argued, 'than sending our armies to chew barbed wire in Flanders?' More than that, such an offensive had the potential to end the war itself. 'In the Dardanelles,' he urged, 'our armies are separated only by a few miles from a victory such as this war has not yet seen.'

As they wrote their letters home it was clear that this apocalyptic rhetoric found an echo among the young men of the Canterbury Infantry Battalion preparing themselves for the fighting to come. 'Everybody very happy tonight,' Corporal Petrie wrote. Private Tuckwell was inspired by the sight of the huge fleet gathered in Mudros Bay: 'My word, it makes one feel as if he is having a hand in great matters, to be a part of such a great undertaking.' Corporal Mostyn Jones couldn't wait: 'I wish they would hurry up and let us get to work on the Turks.' Sergeant Henry Kitson was ready, too: 'I've got a good red beard to frighten the enemy.'

What they hadn't been told was that this grand, war-winning assault on the Dardanelles was originally to have been a purely naval operation, but that it had not proceeded to plan. The 'orange-selling' Turks had anticipated a possible attack here and had mined the straits, resulting in the destruction of the British warship *Irresistible*, the damaging of another, *Inflexible*, and the sinking of the French battleship *Bouvet*, with much loss of life. The Allied troops were being led to believe that their land assault was to back up the navy. They didn't know that it was now the other way round.

At Mudros Bay, on that last evening before entering the war zone, Harry wrote one letter – to his most regular correspondent, his forty-two-year-old unmarried sister Mary, back in Tonbridge. Did she receive it with dreadful apprehension, with a disbelieving shake of the head? Or did she react with an unusual sense of pride that her feckless younger brother was at last doing something heroic, something that would make the world a safer place?

The Anzacs land in Gallipoli, 25 April 1915. My father believed that Harry Palin was the heroically posed figure on the left.

10

THE STORM

O N SATURDAY 24 APRIL 1915, Harry and his comrades gathered on the decks of *Itonus* and looked across at the SS *Lützow*, on whose bow was chalked the words 'To Constantinople'. Both ships' companies stood to attention to salute the *Queen Elizabeth* as she steamed out of the bay leading a line of six battleships – *London*, *Triumph*, *Queen*, *Prince of Wales*, *Bacchante* and *Majestic* – and seven destroyers, to begin the pre-assault bombardment. The momentousness of what lay ahead affected everybody. Cyprian Brereton, officer commanding the 12th Nelsons, and recently promoted to major, nicely captured the scene in an unpublished memoir. 'Warships were approaching and passing out all day in a general silence and not till they were near could we hear their bands playing very softly their last message. Its simplicity touched us. "The Girl I Left Behind Me" and "The British Grenadiers". And as they slid by, from every throat burst out a great shout in response from our men, followed by dead silence.'

The next day, Sunday the 25th, Harry made his longest diary entry so far: 'Sailed from Lemnos at 7.0 a.m.,' he wrote, underlining the words to emphasise the momentous nature of what was about to happen. 'Just had orders to get ready to land on the Gallipoli Peninsula some time today. Our hard times are about to start! Saw a big battle between our ships and the Turkish batteries, the shells bursting. Magnificent sight.'

It was five in the afternoon when *Itonus* reached its destination. Then things happened quickly. The troops were transferred to a destroyer, HMS *Bulldog*, and from there to small, flat-bottomed wooden boats for the run-up onto the shore. Major Brereton describes how 'Blue-jackets [sailors] received the awkward infantry in their arms and on their toes and swung them aside joking and laughing as though handling ladies at a picnic.' Around them terrified horses and mules dangled from leather harnesses as they too were swung out onto the landing craft. Once the men had crunched onto the beach there was no time to stop and think: 'Scrambled ashore with shrapnell [Harry's regular misspelling of 'shrapnel'] bursting all about us,' Harry noted. Not only did he have to dodge Turkish machine-gun fire, but he had to do so while carrying a pack weighing almost 75 pounds (34 kilos) that contained, among other things, food and water, groundsheets, entrenching tools, firewood, a bayonet and 200 rounds of ammunition. Unsurprisingly, not everyone was able to negotiate this challenge successfully. Harry's fellow 12th Nelson Cecil Malthus, while noting that 'Our casualties were mercifully light – I think only half a dozen in the company – and none were fatal,' recalled how 'We heard for the first time that sickening soft thud of shell fragments or bullets meeting human flesh.'

By an extraordinary chance, an artist was on hand to record the moment Harry landed on Turkish soil. Or, at least, I strongly believe that to be the case. Some years ago I came across a letter written by my father, then fourteen years old and a boarder at Shrewsbury School, to his parents. 'I was looking in an illustrated war paper called "The War of the Nations",' he wrote excitedly, 'when I came to a full page drawing of the force of New Zealanders and Australians gaining the first footing on the Gallipoli Peninsula. There, running up the steep slope, rifle in hand, was Uncle Harry. It is only a drawing . . . but I am certain if you saw the picture you would immediately agree with me, that by some chance, the artist had drawn Uncle Harry.' That my father should have been so sure is evidence enough for me, and now that I've seen the magazine for myself I'm certain that it is Harry, posed heroically, if untruthfully, minus the full, cumbersome kit he would have been carrying. The poster boy of the Gallipoli landings.

In reality the landings were anything but heroic. For Harry, who had been in simulated battles but never in a real one, it was a baptism of fire as the Turks shot relentlessly at them from their vantage point on the clifftops. 'Saw lots of wounded both A and NZ going back to

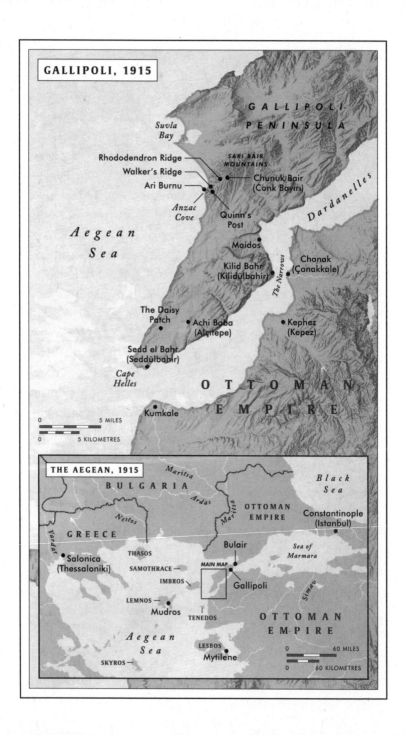

GALLIPOLI, 1915

Suvla Bay

GALLIPOLI PENINSULA

SARI BAIR MOUNTAINS

Rhododendron Ridge
Walker's Ridge
Ari Burnu

Chunuk Bair (Çonk Bayırı)

Anzac Cove

Quinn's Post

Dardanelles

Maidos

Kilid Bahr (Kilidülbahir)

Chanak (Çanakkale)

Aegean Sea

The Narrows

The Daisy Patch

Achi Baba (Alçıtepe)

Kephez (Kepez)

Sedd el Bahr (Seddülbahir)

Cape Helles

OTTOMAN EMPIRE

Kumkale

0   5 MILES
0   5 KILOMETRES

THE AEGEAN, 1915

Maritsa

BULGARIA

Ardas

Maritsa

OTTOMAN EMPIRE

Black Sea

Constantinople (Istanbul)

Nestos

GREECE

Bulair

Sea of Marmara

Vardar

Salonica (Thessaloniki)

THASOS

SAMOTHRACE —

MAIN MAP

Gallipoli

IMBROS —

LEMNOS —

Mudros

TENEDOS —

OTTOMAN EMPIRE

Simav

Aegean Sea

LESBOS —

Mytilene

SKYROS —

0   60 MILES
0   60 KILOMETRES

the ships,' he confided to his diary. 'Saw dead too, poor chaps lying here and there. Left our packs in one place then climbed into a position and dug ourselves in, work going on most of the night. I was on sentry . . . And got no sleep – sniping going on all night.' For his part, Cecil Malthus noted a new sound: 'The continuous rattle of rifle fire with which we were to become so wearily familiar.'

What Harry was not to know was that things had gone wrong from the start. Thanks either to a last-minute change of plan or possibly a simple error, the navy had put the troops ashore in the wrong place. The planned object-ive, code-named Z Beach, had been chosen because it was lightly defended, and offered a wide, flat landing area and comparatively easy access through the foothills. The place where the Anzacs actually went ashore was a small bay, a mile or so north, which was both narrower and steeper; easier to defend, more difficult to attack. The landing area was surrounded by scrubby ridges and gullies through which it was hard to make headway and easy to get lost.

It was to become immortalised as Anzac Cove.

The mistake proved an expensive one. On that first day the New Zealanders sustained numerous casualties, some 146 of them fatal. Among the dead were two of the New Zealanders' most senior officers: Major Grant and Colonel Macbean Stewart, who was mown down as he led his men on, sword in hand. In the confusion, some Anzacs were accidentally shot by their own side.

Harry somehow got himself up to the top of one of the hills, where he and his comrades 'lay about in readiness most of the rest of the day with bayonets fixed. Bullets whizzing about all around us and snipers busy.' For Malthus there was nothing valiant about that first night in Gallipoli: 'A cold misty rain reduced us to cowering misery,' he wrote. They were relieved at 10.00 the next evening and Harry found time to scribble in his diary, 'Came down the hill a bit and got a few hours sleep in the trenches. Pretty tired and sleepy.'

Concerned at the bruising losses already sustained and worried that they might not be able to withstand another Turkish attack, senior ANZAC commanders on the ground suggested possible evacuation. From his base on HMS *Queen Elizabeth*, Sir Ian Hamilton, in command of the Mediterranean Expeditionary Force, refused. 'You have got through the difficult business,' he said. 'Now you have only to dig, dig, dig, until you are safe.'

Before dawn next morning, Harry and his fellow 12th Nelsons busied themselves doing just that, as a fusillade of rifle shots raked their position. The shooting and killing on the steep cliffs began before sunrise. 'Turks fired 1st shot at 5 to 6 a.m.,' Harry's diary reads. 'Our ships started bombardment at 6.30 a.m. and as I write are banging away like anything. Deafening reports but magnificent show. We are fairly safe for today I think – the Queen Elizabeth with her 8 15 in. guns are shaking things up – airplanes all over the place.'

Because of the advantages of terrain the Turks enjoyed, digging in was no guarantee of safety, and already the men were referring to these hastily dug trenches as 'coffin holes'. By mid-morning the fire from the Turkish defences higher up the hillside had become heavier and more pro-longed. Meanwhile, a couple of miles away, at Cape Helles on the southern tip of the peninsula, a combined force of Royal Dublin Fusiliers, Royal Munster Fusiliers and the Hampshires had fought their way ashore, and established a bridgehead, pushing the Turks from some of their for-ward positions. Their losses, however, had been appalling. Two months earlier, Harry had seen how ineffectual the Turks had been in trying to cross the Suez Canal. Defend-ing their homeland, however, they were proving a fierce and implacable enemy, wreaking havoc amid the spurs and gullies of Anzac Cove. 'We shall get Hell tonight I am afraid,' wrote Harry. As ever in war, friendly fire, coming from the opposite direction, could be just as dangerous. In Corporal Leslie Story's diary there's a note that reads: 'Shell dropped short from [HMS] Queen. Buried many of us.'

On the fourth day after the landings Harry was up at four in the morning, using the cover of darkness to carry ammunition up the hastily dug, winding path to their firing position on top of the hill. 'Really ticklish job as snipers busy but got back all right.' In the evening a number of reinforcements were landed. 'Indian, I think,' wrote Harry. A combination of sniper and machine-gun fire kept the Nelsons pinned down over the next few days, but Harry, with what sounds like suicidal cool, managed to get in a swim in the bay, despite the Turks 'land[ing] some shrapnel very close to us'.

So it went on. Days of digging in and securing their positions on the friable cliff sides, as thousands of men

struggled to keep their tenuous hold on sometimes suicidal positions, and were periodically sent on potentially
lethal missions. In Harry's diary there's mention of a friend
he'd made in Cairo, Private Durand of the AIF – the Australian Imperial Force – who was killed whilst carrying
ammunition to the firing line. He was obviously someone
Harry wanted to remember, for I found his name on a
scrap of paper inserted inside the covers of Harry's diary.
'Met this chap on 21st March,' he wrote. 'V. decent'. To
which he added later, 'He was killed 27th April.' Durand
perished fulfilling precisely the same 'ticklish job' as was
given to Harry. Harry was lucky. Durand happened to be
unlucky.

Not surprisingly, it all proved too much for some. At
one point a group of Wellington soldiers were ordered
by machine-gun officer Jesse Wallingford to shoot any
Australians seen fleeing from their positions. It was
tragically ironic that New Zealand troops should
have travelled all those thousands of miles only to be
instructed to direct their first shots fired in anger at
their own side.

The 12th Nelsons successfully moved to a position
defending the coastal hills on the left flank, but found
themselves constantly under fire from Turkish snipers,
one of whom put a bullet through a tin containing the
water reserve. The bullet then travelled through Second
Lieutenant Fred Stane's pocket, breaking a razor before
dropping onto his lap, causing him to leap up with an
indignant cry of 'Hell! The bastard's shot me!' which pro-
voked much tension-breaking laughter.

To me, one of the most surprising things about Harry's diaries at this time is the mix of the murderous and the mundane. On 5 May, for example, he records the 'shrapnell falling around us early', yet follows up that life-threatening observation with the laconic note, 'Two pairs of socks from mother.' Another detail that strikes me is his restraint in describing the horrors around him. On 30 April he sets down the bare fact that a colleague was hit by machine-gun fire. Two days later he writes, in an entirely neutral tone, that 'a chap named Fellowes in 9 platoon' has been shot dead. There's no display of emotion, beyond the observation 'Very unfortunate occurrence'.

Whether or not Harry was as forbearing and phlegmatic when chatting to his mates about the horrors that they were having to endure is a matter for conjecture. Stress-relieving expletives never appear in his diaries, but we know that they were common among the troops, offering an outlet for the anger, frustration, tiredness and fear that dominated their lives. We also know that, even before these men joined up, most would have sworn as a matter of course. As Christopher Pugsley reminds us, 'The language of the trenches was the language of the workplace: the freezing works, the shearing shed, the stockyard, anywhere that men gathered.' Theoretically, bad language had no place in His Majesty's armed forces – a Private Adams, for example, was sentenced to fourteen days' Field Punishment 'for excessive swearing' – but it's hard to believe that such punishments had much effect on men living constantly on a knife's edge. And I find it similarly hard to believe that Harry wouldn't have expressed himself in much the same way as his friends. He may once have been a public school-boy with an Oxford don as his father, but he was perfectly comfortable among the men with whom he served, and he knew how to fit in. Snob he never was.

After the horrors of the first days in the Dardanelles, there was a brief respite. On 6 May Harry and the rest of the Nelsons were taken from Anzac Cove to Cape Helles by the destroyer HMS *Mosquito*. While aboard they were apparently very well looked after, coffee and rum being lavished on them, and once ashore Harry was able to meet up and share experiences with several of his friends, including George Batters, who was in a different platoon.

But this was very much a temporary relief. The Allies had established a southern bridgehead, with the inten-tion of pushing the Turks back and eventually joining up with the forces at Anzac Cove. Two days after Harry disembarked an assault was accordingly made on Turk-ish lines across a stretch of open ground which became known as the Daisy Patch.

It may have had a Beatrix Potter-ish name, but because it offered very little cover it became a scene of slaughter. Private Constance described what it was like to be in the middle of the horrors: 'As we advanced,' he recalled, '. . . the enemy poured a terrific fire into us with machine guns and rifles mowing down our men like rats. What was left of us eventually took up our position after driving the enemy back about three hundred yards. But what an enormous cost it has been to us as dead and wounded are lying all over the ground. Some of them in a frightfully maimed state.' Among the casualties were Major Brereton, who received a head wound, and several of Harry's friends. 'Bell was shot thro' the lungs,' he wrote, 'Bob Hughes [also from Canvastown] killed, I'm afraid . . . Jo Regaldo through the right shoulder by the snipers.'

Harry himself, though, was spared the slaughter, having been given the job of staying back to guard the packs, a task he was kept at for the next three days. He didn't feel he fulfilled the task particularly well, noting gloomily, 'Filthy wet day making trenches awful. Had to stay with packs until a fatigue party came up to take them away. Most of packs missing – I shall probably be blamed for them, but it can't be helped.'

Next day, however, a more satisfying role came his way. 'Capt. Stewart found out that I could speak Hindustani,' he wrote; 'said he wanted me on the permanent fatigue as interpreter.' Not that this made things any safer for him: 'A lot of shells fell at the base whilst we were there,' he went on, 'and gave us a big scare as they were very close to us. A lot of horses killed, one man, and several wounded.' Even so, he clearly relished his new role, recording a few days later on 15 May: 'Things going v well with me, I think. Have fallen on my feet at last. My knowledge of Urdu is very useful.' This whiff of pride is all the more affecting because entries like this come so rarely in his diaries. It also serves as an important reminder that New Zealand and Australia were not the only imperial outposts to contribute large forces to the Gallipoli campaign. It's been estimated that more than 15,000 Indian troops were deployed, and that Indian mule drivers – often working under heavy fire – were crucial to keeping supplies moving.

If an official appreciation of Harry's linguistic skills raised his morale, so, too, did letters from home and abroad – from his mother and sister Mary, from his niece Brita Robertson in Kashmir, 'enclosing a snap of herself on her horse', and from such New Zealand friends as Doris Wilberfoss and Winnie White, who, according to one diary entry, enclosed a pair of socks with her missive. That Harry felt the need to record details of incoming mail so faithfully suggests that they were his means of connecting with a normality beyond the battlefield. A reiteration of all the good things in his life, so far from the ghastliness of Gallipoli.

He himself seems to have been a reliable correspondent – though I suspect not a particularly regular or garrulous one. When he received an assortment of mail and magazines from home that had been wrongly directed to Egypt, for example, he said, 'Sent a Field P.C. to mother, the first since leaving Lemnos.' Field Service postcards were created by the War Office to enable soldiers to make contact with loved ones without risking giving away crucial information. Under the heading 'Nothing is to be written on this side' were a number of pre-printed phrases to be crossed out where not applicable: '*I am quite well*', '*I have been admitted into hospital*', '*I am sick / and am going on well'*, *'I am wounded / and hope to be discharged soon'*, *'I have received your letter dated / telegram / parcel'*, and the heart-rendingly brusque *'I have received no letter from you lately / for a long time'*. Easy to complete, they cost nothing to send, which made them popular. Brita may have felt slightly short-changed to receive such an impersonal missive from her son, but given that in the three weeks since the invasion of Gallipoli, word had trickled out that there had been casualties, even an official postcard bearing his name should at least have been sufficient to reassure her, and the rest of the family, that Harry was still alive.

8 August 1915: the Wellingtons make the ascent towards Chunuk Bair, one of the bloodiest of all the battles fought at Gallipoli.

II

A TIN OF MEAT

———◆◆◆———

B Y 20 MAY THE NEW Zealanders had been ordered
back to Anzac Cove. Harry's voyage on the supply
ship *Eddystone* was uneventful – whatever difficulties the Allies faced on shore, they still controlled
the seas, and were able to transport men and supplies
relatively easily. Moving ashore, however, was a different
matter. Harry's very English penchant for understatement disguises what must have been another frighteningly exposed landing. 'Lots of shrapnell and big shells
falling about the beach making things pretty dangerous.'
Once on the beach the task he was given involved 'loading stores by mules on pack all afternoon' in 'v hot' conditions. Contemporary photographs showing equipment
stacked in a 10-foot wall of crates running the length of
the beach give a sense of the labour involved.

On 24 May, after weeks of close-quarter fighting, he
noted the declaration of a truce between 7.30 and 4.30, to
allow both sides to bury their dead. A whistle was blown

and Turkish and Allied soldiers climbed out of their trenches, swapped cigarettes with each other, and began the grisly work. 'Men who went between the trenches describe it as a fearful sight,' Harry wrote; 'simply thousands of dead Turks who have been there weeks, also some of ours. Major Grant's body was found, also Colonel Stewart's.' Another colonel, Percival Fenwick, recalled the scene more graphically: 'The Turkish dead lay so thick that it was impossible to pass without treading on the bodies . . . Everywhere one looked lay dead, swollen, black, hideous, and over all, a nauseating stink that nearly made one vomit.'

Vic Nicholson was one of those charged with the burials. 'They reckon that no man's land had approximately 500 dead bodies to the acre . . . As soon as you grabbed a corpse by the arm to drag it over to a hole, the arm came off in your hand. So you just ended up scratching a little bit of trench alongside of it, rolling it over into the trench and scraping some stuff back over the top. Nobody handled on that day was buried more than six or eight inches underground.'

At 5 p.m., half an hour after the truce officially ended, a whistle blew and both sides returned to their respective trenches. Within seconds, the fighting had resumed. 'Everybody started firing,' Arthur Bellingham told Jane Tolerton many years later, '. . . you couldn't hear yourself speak.' The contradictions and absurdities of war were not lost on him. 'It's uncanny really to be killing one another one minute and mixing with them the next.' In similar vein, Fred Dill recalled how 'We were always good cobbers with the Turks when we met them privately. We had a great respect for the Turks. They were clean fighters.'

If family and friends back in England and New Zealand reminded Harry of a cosier, safer, more intimate world, they themselves would by now be receiving news that was growing increasingly disturbing. The first reports of the landings on 25 April, which didn't appear in New Zealand's newspapers until 8 May, would no doubt have stirred the nation's pride with their descriptions of the storming of the beaches of Gallipoli at dawn by New Zealand's boys, fighting gallantly alongside the Australians (though in fact, of course, as Harry could attest, they actually landed at 5 o'clock in the afternoon). But a month on from the landing, as the campaign proved to be not a walkover but a ferocious, literally uphill struggle, it became impossible to conceal the fact that many sons and brothers would not be returning. The initial casualty lists published in New Zealand stated that 76 men had lost their lives, and 1,080 had been wounded. The real figure, at Anzac Cove alone, was twice that number.

It was less easy to conceal the truth from those doing the fighting. 'Catastrophe today for navy,' Harry wrote in his diary on 25 May, 'the "Triumph" being sunk by a submarine (Austrian?) about 1.30 p.m. The submarine got away I'm afraid.' They would all have seen it happen. One moment *Triumph* was floating proudly in the bay, confidently blasting Turkish positions on land. The next she burst into flames and within minutes had upended. She was a big ship, one of only two of the 'Swiftsure' class of pre-dreadnought battleships, with a crew of over 800 men, of whom 78 lost their lives that day. Because it was so visible to all, the sinking of a warship had a proportionally greater effect on morale than anything that might have happened ashore, and when the German submarine, U-21, that had sunk her went on to torpedo and sink HMS *Majestic* off Cape Helles two days later, with a loss of forty-nine men, the efficacy of Britain's naval shield must have been called into serious question by those who had previously assumed it would protect them.

June began with no let-up in the heavy fighting. On the 5th, for example, firing continued throughout the night, and while the Canterbury Battalion were successful in overrunning some Turkish trenches, they were soon driven out again. 'A lot of casualties killed, wounded and missing, about 200 in all,' Harry noted. Although he doesn't seem to have been so involved in direct contact with the enemy at this stage in the conflict, he was constantly under fire, as he moved from position to position with supplies and rations. He would see more friends fall victim to carefully aimed bullets over the ensuing days. 'They are terrible pests,' he wrote of the snipers, adding reflectively and mournfully, 'All lives thrown away.'

The New Zealanders were learning fast, though. Soon, thanks to the encouragement of Lieutenant Colonel Malone, the Turkish sharpshooters were being matched by Enzed snipers. Sergeant Harvey Jones, who was one of them, reckoned that, ultimately, 'You got that good you could shoot the left eye out of a fly.'

Other basic problems remained, even if you could find a crevice or a gully out of sight of the snipers or had on hand one of your own to take them out. Food and water supplies were both limited. Fresh water had to be brought over from Lemnos and, because the Turks knew when it was coming, they shelled the ferries carrying it. As for food, the relentlessly basic diet was Fray Bentos tinned bully beef and Huntley & Palmers No. 5 hard biscuits. The main complaint about the biscuits was how dry they were. 'Like chewing a rock,' one veteran, Russell Weir, recalled. For the lucky ones there were army rations made by the Maconochie Company from Aberdeen, which, according to Weir, 'was ordinary stew, but it did have peas and carrots and it was quite good'. Unfortunately, this delicacy was denied the men in the front line: 'The limited supply of Maconochie ration never got past the beach, where the Army Service Corps collared it all.'

Keeping clean was a real challenge. Most of the men's clothing was filthy, and lice were a constant problem. Fred Dill later described how, 'One of our main recreations when we were off duty was to pull our shirts off and crack the eggs and pull the lice off. The whole place was lousy.' 'When the reinforcements came over fresh from New Zealand and from Egypt all nice and clean,' he went on, 'the day after they were there we'd say, "Got any lice on you yet?" And they'd look at us as if they were so disgusted. We'd say, "Look on your shirt." And you'd see the look of disgust on their face when they found a few under the armpits.' As the lice laid their eggs in the seams of the uniforms one way to get rid of them was to pour hot wax from a burning candle down the seams. Effective, but carrying with it the risk of setting the uniform alight.

One way to relieve the constant itching and scratching caused by the lice was to go swimming in the sea – not exactly the safest of activities in any war zone, but particularly risky in the waters off Gallipoli. Hardy, or foolhardy, souls desperate to take a dip were restricted to a few hundred yards between the Ari Burnu headland to the south of the peninsula from which shrapnel shells burst regularly, and the base of Walker's Ridge to the north, from which a constant stream of spent bullets cut up the water, and those fancying swimming away from it all faced a constant shower of bullets restricting any movement further out to sea. 'Every night there was a crowd going in for a swim,' Russell Weir said. 'As soon as we went in the Turks would open with shrapnel. And then there'd be a wild rush to the shore. The next night they'd be out again and in for a swim. You'd lose one or two every night.' Harry was among those prepared to take the chance.

The constant, unremitting presence of dead bodies, with flies swarming over them before lighting on the faces and mouths of the living and on the food they ate and in the tea they drank, inevitably resulted in outbreaks of dysentery. Harry was not spared. On 22 June he confided to his diary, 'I have violent shits again, worst luck.' His condition would have necessitated several visits to what had become known as Latrine Gully, though he also got 'some medicine that did me some good'. Latrine Gully seems to have been a very democratic place. Private Martin Brooke, who was forced to relieve himself there one evening, found that 'on one side was Major McCarroll and on the other Major Schofield'. It struck him as incongruous that he should have been 'Doing my billybobs right in the midst of all the top ranks!' But, as he went on to reflect, this was typical of the relaxed, off-duty ways of the New Zealanders. In this they differed considerably from the hierarchical stiffness of their British colleagues. 'They had special places for officers. Our army was completely different. We often used to call the officers by their Christian names.'

After two months close to the front line, rumours of a rest period started to circulate. But they turned out to be only rumours. At the start of July, with daily temperatures in the thirties and despite 'feeling v. weak from dysentery, which is with me practically daily', Harry and others were moved up to relieve the 1st and 2nd Companies in the trenches at Quinn's Post, a strategically important, frighteningly exposed position perched on the top of a cliff, with the opposing armies, at one point, only 6 feet away from each other. The defence of this strategic pinpoint was to become legendary. 'The story of Gallipoli,' writes Peter Jackson, the New Zealand film director, who has a passionate interest in and comprehensive knowledge about the First World War, 'is the story of a tiny patch of land. Hills and gullies. Every bump, cleft, ridge and gully has a name and they all have stories to tell. The most nightmarish spot was a tiny bit of ground sited at the top of a very steep cliff. This place was called Quinn's Post, a name that still invokes fear and unease in Australia and New Zealand.'

'No-one entered Quinn's without reluctance and fore-boding,' Cecil Malthus wrote. Raising your head care-lessly even a fraction here was to invite a sniper's bullet; and the Turks also regularly lobbed over hand-made bombs. Known to the Anzacs as 'cricket ball' bombs, they were sometimes no more than tins filled with bits of metal, lead, brass and spent cartridge shells. Fortu-nately, the fuses were often accidentally made too long, so that, as Malthus went on to say, 'they lay fizzing for as much as two seconds before exploding, and we gener-ally had time to throw an overcoat over them or dodge round a corner of the trench'. Down below, the beach at Anzac Cove was looking increasingly like a hospital as a constant stream of casualties from the fighting at Quinn's were lined up on the shore, awaiting barges to take them onto ships bound for Lemnos. Passing the wounded as they were taken down were supplies, such as ammunition, water and food, being taken up. Carry-ing them to their destination involved a stiff and dan-gerous climb culminating in several hundred steep steps dug out of the clay. Not surprisingly the combination of fatigues, heavy lifting and the constant close-quarter bomb-slinging meant that no one got much sleep. An hour a night sometimes. And with a sentence of death the penalty for sleeping at your post, it was no wonder, as one man graphically put it, that their nerves were stretched like fiddle strings.

As with soldiers anywhere, the grimmer the conditions, the blacker the humour. A popular poem about the Quinn's Post experience circulated around Malthus's platoon.

> *A man don't need a rifle, he hardly ever shoots,*
> *He only needs a pair of shorts and a hefty pair of boots.*
> *He needs a bloody shovel, to dig a bloody track,*
> *And a bloody box of ammo, to hump it, lump it, hump it,*
> *To hump it on his back.*

The Quinn's posting and the lowering effects of unremitting dysentery may account for Harry's increasingly desperate need to keep in contact with family and friends. Though he's thirty years old and caught up in murderous, seemingly endless fighting, his diary entries make him sound more schoolboy than soldier. On 6 July: '. . . wrote a line to mother asking if she could send me some milk, cocoa etc'. And on 10/11 July: 'Wrote FPC to Mary. Recd letter from mother enclosing note-paper.'

On 9 July Harry received a letter from Mary which must have pulled him up short: 'She said no letter received from me since April 24th. Is it simply so? The delay. I cannot make it out.' The entry for 23 July, the day before he had to return to Quinn's after a brief spell in the reserve trench, is more reassuring: 'Recd 2 Parcels. Mother (50 cigarettes Egyptian), Mary 2 pairs socks and acid drops. 4 letters from Mary.'

Mary was the great constant in his life. Letters from Eddy, the successful country doctor, and sisters Edie and Tissie, appear to have been far fewer and further between. It could be that Mary had more time to write than the others, who were all married and therefore presumably preoccupied with their own families, but I sense that there's more to it than that. Mary, still single, had taken on the task of looking after their mother since their father's death in 1903. Whatever might have been her mother's reservations about her youngest son's fitfulness, now he was fighting for his country, Brita must have appreciated Mary's support as they both lived with the constant fear of a letter of condolence.

By August 1915 the troops had been in Gallipoli for four months. Now the various units of the New Zealand Infantry Brigade were marched to a new position and put on alert for a fresh offensive, a combined operation from land and sea that its commander Major General Godley was confident would give the Allies the great breakthrough they so desperately craved. The role earmarked for the New Zealanders (who were regarded by the high command as more reliable but no less brave than the Australians) was to clear the hills north of an area nicknamed (with heavy irony) Happy Valley, and then to move on to take possession of the strategically important summit of Chunuk Bair, which lay in a commanding position atop the 750-foot-high southern spur of the Sari Bair range.

At about midnight on the 5th Harry and his companions arrived in Happy Valley. Once there, he records, 'Batty fell out' – by which I assume he means that his friend collapsed. Next morning George Batters was taken to hospital with suspected TB. He would play no further part in the war.

Harry was acutely aware that he was about to be pitched into the most brutal fighting he had yet experienced. His diary entry for the 6th cryptically records, 'We move again at midnight, and then mysterious business will start – I will trust in God to help me through.' The same day he sent an FPC to his mother, no doubt aware that this might well be the last time he communicated with her.

Harry describes the action on 7 August at unusual length and with unusual passion:

We were marching up and down the new gully all night dodging bullets. Saw lot of dead Turks about 5. Our first casualty occurred, poor little Tommy Heenan being shot in the throat and died immediately. Sam Penny also killed . . . We continued our career up the hills all hard country to us. Extraordinary sight before us. The Tommys and Gurkhas had landed in the night at the Salt Lake point and there were a crowd of transports, warships etc. all lying about. Things going v well and lots of country taken and any amount of prisoners, some say 5000. The remaining country to be taken consisted in a high ridge and this we were to attempt to take at point of bayonet. The 12th and 13th were detailed for this job and we fell in about 10 a.m. We advanced over a saddle under heavy rifle fire and no casualties. We lay down and then HELL broke loose on us. The Turks brought 75mm guns onto us and they simply poured shrapnel and high explosive onto us with terrible results. There were dozens of casualties, practically everyone getting hit. All officers hit. Poor Priest was hit in both feet terrible wounds. Capt. Houlker (knee) Major Cribb (thigh), Stanier, Duncan, Jervis, all my mates hit. Some killed, amongst them being Meir, Martin Simpson, Sammy White and others. It was an <u>awful</u> business. I got into a bit of a dug out and lay as close as I could and was only slightly hit by shrapnel bullets which did no damage.

Harry's luck had held out, but in the most harrowing of circumstances, and by the very tightest of margins. 'I had a narrow shave – a shrapnel bullet going through my haversack and then into my ration bag through a tin of corned beef and then into the biscuits – I would have had a bad wound in the back, had it not been for the tin of meat.'

In his long description of the battle there is none of his characteristic understatement or grumbles about snipers and flies. What happened on Chunuk Bair clearly shocked him to the core. For someone who clearly flourished in the company of mates and friends, to have lost so many so suddenly must have felt like drowning. And his closest friend Batty is no longer by his side to share jokes about the conditions or awaken memories of their days with the Healys on Wilderness Farm. Harry is losing those he gets on with best. Without them, all that's left is the pain.

For the first time in his diaries Harry admits to fear, and in the concluding lines of this entry there is more than an echo of his father in the pulpit at St Mary's, Linton. 'I have much to be thankful for and must thank God for his goodness to me. I have left a lot of good mates. May God rest their souls.' This time no dissembling, no shrugging of the shoulders can deal with the scale of the annihilation. 'Nelson Co. only musters about 50 men now [out of a full strength of 225]. It's awful, awful.'

And it was not yet over. On 8 August, a Sunday, when Harry would normally have been on church parade, he and the rest of the Canterbury Battalion, relieved from the front line, had to stand to all night digging a fire trench on Rhododendron Ridge, deep enough to create a safe position for directing fire on the enemy. It was his third night without sleep. Though away from the fiercest fighting, he was witness to an unending procession of casualties being brought down from Chunuk Bair by the stretcher bearers. There was talk of some of the mortally wounded being finished off by their fellow countrymen.

'A lot of dead all round near the trenches and the stench dreadful,' Harry wrote on the 9th. He could, however, take heart at the news that the New Zealanders had fought their way to the top of Chunuk Bair and taken the summit. And there was some other good news circulating. 'Capt. Stewart reported this morning that Achi Baba had fallen, so hope it's true at last. Heavy firing still going on and Turks being driven further back and back.'

Like so many rumours of war, it wasn't true. Achi Baba hadn't fallen. And the possession of Chunuk Bair, the highest point and the furthest inland reached by the Allies, hobbled by a mixture of confused aims and uncoordinated orders being given to very tired men, proved to be short-lived. (Christopher Pugsley gives us a snapshot of exhausted infantry preparing to attack while 'sucking pebbles to moisten dry mouths'.) It subsequently became clear that although the Wellington Battalion had heroically captured the summit and the Auckland Mounted Rifles then fought their way through to back them up, no other reinforcements, apart from some of the Otago Battalion, arrived to help secure the gains made. The New Zealanders went on to hold the position for two days. When they were eventually relieved by British forces, of the 760 men of the Wellington Battalion who had taken the summit, only around 70 emerged unscathed. Such gains as had been made were then swiftly swept away, with the British forced to retreat in the face of a Turkish counter-offensive under the highly effective leadership of Mustafa Kemal, later known as Kemal Atatürk, the founder of modern Turkey. The Turks proceeded to consolidate their hold on the peak the New Zealanders had fought so hard to take.

Years later, Colonel Temperley, who took part in the battle, expressed his frustration at the lack of support for the men who tried to hold the summit. 'The New Zealand Infantry Brigade,' he wrote, 'was for 48 hours . . . at the throat of the Turkish Empire and had certain events turned out differently, the Turkish army would have been beaten, Constantinople would have fallen and the war might have been shortened by two years.'

As it was, 852 New Zealanders perished during the fight for Chunuk Bair. Among them was Frank Gilderoy Batters, George's younger brother. He was nineteen.

The fight for control of the Gallipoli Peninsula now returned to a destructive period of attrition. The Turkish troops, much encouraged by the re-taking of Chunuk Bair, dug in and could not be dislodged. At sea, German submarines struck another blow, sinking the troopship *Royal Edward* on her way from Alexandria to Lemnos. It was the worst troopship disaster of the war. Eight hundred and sixty-one men perished. 'A terrible thing,' Harry wrote in the diary.

But he was not one to brood. Not for him the whys and the wherefores. He had survived many months of battle in Gallipoli, enduring appalling conditions and witnessing horrific carnage, without apparently suffering any physical or mental scarring. Like many of his fellow soldiers he had become inured to the horrors that he'd witnessed, dealing with them by getting back to some kind of normality as quickly as possible and focusing on what mattered most: the friendships he had made, the comrades who had survived. He was scarcely unique in this. In a recent documentary about the Falklands War of 1982, I was struck by the observation made by one of the British soldiers involved that, 'In war it's not country or Empire or King or Queen you're fighting for. It's for the man to the right of you and the man to the left of you.' I'm sure 'twas ever so. Soldiers on the battlefield have to do dreadful things but they do them together and the bond thus created enables them to deal with the pain collectively rather than personally.

Maybe his ability to keep a daily account of his war experiences with a stub of indelible pencil in a 5 by 3-inch diary was a small part of his resilience. In it, he doesn't see himself as a hero, or a participant in a great moment of history. He doesn't use words like destiny or mission. He is simply there, doing a job, unsaddled, it seems, with ideas of seniority or expectations of responsibility. Which I'm sure was not usual for the son of such a well-off, well-educated middle-class family, but which may have been the key to his survival. And like his fellow soldiers he wouldn't have talked much about his battlefield experiences to those who hadn't been there. He would have kept quiet and kept on.

On 20 August Harry was called to do interpreting duty with the Indian troops, and the day after that he recorded 'a magnificent swim and washed my clothes'. This was followed by a morale-boosting parcel delivery. 'Brother sent 100 cigts. and Agnes [his sister-in-law] sent tobacco (2 tins), matches box, soap, boracic powder [a disinfectant] and 4 papers. V. acceptable and must acknowledge as soon as possible.' Evidence that even in the jaws of hell, Private Palin found time to write his thank-you letters.

After more than four months on the peninsula, during which time he had been largely accepting of the snipers and the smells and the mortar shells, a bout of ill health made him think seriously in terms of trying to get out. On 27 August, after a twenty-four-hour spell on guard duty, he reported, 'Not feeling too good, headache, dizziness etc. Must try for a trip to Lemnos.'

However, even though his stomach problems worsened ('Very crook in the stomach again awful pains,' he wrote), the trip to Lemnos didn't materialise. There were so many ahead of him, waiting on barges to be ferried across to Mudros Bay. A total of 1,435 had been wounded in action but even more, nearly 1,700, were sick with dysentery and enteric fever. Harry was deemed fit enough to be put on stretcher duty, helping carry those even worse off than himself.

It was turning colder now and only the letters and papers sent by Mary and his mother kept up his morale. That and a church parade on 12 September: 'Listened to the Maoris, they sing awfully well together in their own language.'

Then, almost abruptly, he found himself back on the beach at Anzac Cove where he had first made landfall twenty weeks earlier. Not to fight, however. 'At midnight went aboard SS Osmanieh which sailed for Lemnos at 2 a.m.,' he wrote. 'I had a bit of a sleep on deck, but pretty chilly and wet.' But at least, for the first time in four months, he was out of harm's way.

Harry and the rest of the Canterbury Battalion, reduced from a total of over 1,000 to 9 officers and

230 men, disembarked at Mudros at midday on 15 September. They were part of a general and long overdue withdrawal of all the ANZAC forces. The official New Zealand First World War History quotes blunt statistics. 'At full strength they would have numbered 18,000; just 4,000 stumbled into the "rest camps".'

As they sailed into Mudros Bay, Harry's spirits were lifted by the sight of 'a magnificent looking boat', the four-funnelled Cunard liner *Aquitania* riding at anchor, towering over the assortment of cruisers, paddle steamers, hospital ships, fishing smacks, submarines and supply barges that filled the harbour. 'I'm glad I've seen her at last,' he noted. But once ashore, all glamour faded. Conditions for the men were deplorable. Despite the fact that they had been ground down by weeks and months of war, there was no transport laid on. They were expected to walk the 3 miles to the camp at Sarpi, carrying full equipment. The fittest made it in two hours. Some took as many as twelve. And once they arrived they found that the camp was nothing more than a bare, stony, treeless site, with a few candlelit marquees. They had to spend the first night of their 'rest' in the open. To add insult to injury, the next morning 'A very heavy thunderstorm broke over us and it came down in buckets and the ground got simply swamped.'

And Harry was not well. He might have got away from the Turks, but not from the enemy within. On 17 September he recorded, 'Visiting the latrines a good deal today.' Two days later, his condition was deemed serious enough for him to spend his thirty-first birthday in hospital.

Fortunately, this turned out not to be as bad as it sounds: 'after a lot of delay landed in the 1st Canadian Base hospital. Had v. good night in a <u>real</u> bed with spring mattress.'

He was not the only one to be suffering from the legacy of Gallipoli. Sergeant Bollinger of the Wellington Battalion estimated that 'Over 25 per cent of the men are parading sick, most suffering from terrific pain in the stomach. They seem to have broken up completely.'

Another eyewitness, one of the reinforcements freshly arrived from Egypt, noted how muted and subdued the men seemed to be. An old friend was, shockingly, almost unrecognisable, 'his hollow face matching in colour his sun-faded tunic and forage cap'.

Meanwhile, good news from the Western Front was fed through to them, which Harry noted in his diary. 'French advanced 30 miles?' he wrote questioningly, scarcely believing what he had heard. 'And English took 29,000 prisoners – V[ery] G[ood].' After the failure at Gallipoli, he wanted to believe more than ever that he was still on the winning side. But bitter experience had taught him that his side didn't always tell the truth.

On 1 October, Harry found himself marked down 'to go to England'. Many others with wounds or medical problems had already been evacuated there – indeed in September 1915 there were more New Zealanders convalescing in England (2,927) than there were serving in Gallipoli (2,840). One can only begin to imagine what joy the prospect must have brought him. But jubilation was short-lived as it turned out to be a clerical error. He was going to Convalescent Camp instead. The enteric infection had not disappeared – it was noted down on his Casualty Form as diarrhoea – and for the next two weeks Harry found little time or enthusiasm to make any diary entries. How ill he was is hard to know, but considering he had managed to scribble in his diary whilst the bullets flew on Gallipoli, this long silence suggests something serious. Another name for enteric fever was typhoid, and he had watched that take his brother's life.

By the end of the month he was pronounced fit again. On 1 November he reported for drill, and after a long lay-off the daily diary resumes. Nothing about the war, but plenty of news – and a few treats – from home. 'Found a food parcel from mother sent by Barker's London full of lovely groceries for me.' Brita, his mother, now in her early seventies, still seems to have had plenty of energy left. Determined to help the war effort, she had just joined her local Quarry Hill branch of the Voluntary Aid Detachments – mainly middle-class or upper-class British women who volunteered to help with the lowliest jobs in the hospitals. The New Zealanders who experienced their help after being evacuated from Gallipoli were highly approving of the VADs. Various Assorted Darlings, they called them.

Harry's nearest and dearest continued to rally round. He received 'a parcel from Edie containing chocolate, soup and a tin of cocoa', and on the day he reported for duty again, a 'parcel from Margie containing paper and envelopes, cotton reel, buttons and a cake of soap. Also a v. nice snapshot of the dear girl herself. She's much fitter looking nowadays.'

Margie, who Harry first mentioned in his diaries while stationed in Egypt, was Margaret Sale, the twenty-nine-year-old daughter of a New Zealand-born farmer-turned-university-professor and his wife, also Margaret. The family lived in London. Margie was one of three women whose names and addresses Harry listed in the back pages of his diary, along with Miss Batters, sister of his close friend George, who lived in Enfield, and a Miss G. Tickell who lived in New Zealand at 105 Riccarton Road, Christchurch, and who was George's fiancée.

Judging from the number of times she wrote to him and from the observations of her improved fitness, Margie Sale seems to have meant more to him than the others. How close they had become is unclear, but that they were still writing to each other over three years after he had left England suggests that something was making the heart grow fonder. And that his emigration to New Zealand was never intended to be permanent.

The diaries end at Lemnos in November and don't resume for three months. With winter coming on, the campaign was winding down and there wasn't so much to write about.

The expedition had been a failure. And an expensive one. An estimated 300,000 Ottoman Turks died defending their country. On the attacking side, the British and French had taken some 250,000 casualties, the Australians 28,000. Out of a total of around 17,000 New Zealanders who fought at Gallipoli, there were 7,473 casualties: 2,515 killed in action, 206 killed by accident and disease, and 4,752 wounded. By the end of October 1915, over 2,000 of those New Zealanders who'd fallen over themselves to join the fight for King and Country had been sent back home, unfit for future service. Batters included. The whole affair had been badly planned and badly executed. Many contemporary critics thought it was misconceived in the first place, placing troops in a region where even military success might have had only a limited impact, and diverting them from the Western Front where the war would ultimately be won or lost.

Sometime in December Harry departed from Lemnos for the last time. As he left to board ship he would have passed a large enclosure which had not been there when he arrived. It was the East Mudros military cemetery, where lay the remains of those soldiers who arrived but never made it back. Heading south he would have made out the outline of Asia Minor on the eastern horizon, where Troy once stood; to the north-west the island of Samothrace. His father, steeped in classical history, would have given anything to visit these ancient sites. His son couldn't wait to get away from them.

Harry had been very fortunate to emerge from such a ferocious conflict with barely a scratch. He also came through without a promotion: there is no mention of any recognition of his services over the four and a half months he spent in the thick of it.

When he opened a new diary on 25 March 1916, he was still Private Palin 6/319. And he was back in Egypt.

PART 4

FRANCE

EGYPT. - Landscape with the Pyramids of Giza.

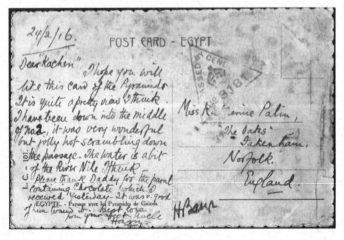

24/2/16.

POST CARD - EGYPT

Dear "Kachen" I hope you will
like this card of the Pyramids
It is quite a pretty view I think
I have been down into the middle
of No 2, it was very wonderful
but jolly hot scrambling down
the passage. The water is a bit
of the River Nile I think —
Please thank Daddy for the parcel
containing Chocolate which I
received yesterday- It was v. good
I hope I round it. Best love
from your affect uncle
Harry

Miss Katherine Palin,
"The Oaks"
Fakenham.
Norfolk.
England.

EGYPTE - Paysage avec les Pyramides de Guizeh.

A postcard written by Harry while in Egypt to his niece, 'Kachen'.

12

TO THE WESTERN FRONT

———————

B Y THE TIME THAT HARRY was safely back in
Egypt, the evacuation of ANZAC troops from
the Dardanelles was well under way. All the Australians and New Zealanders were withdrawn by Christmas. The last of the British forces left in the first weeks
of 1916.

It was an elaborately and craftily executed operation.
Malthus described how 'We were kept busily on the
move up and down the saps and trenches, so that the
amount of movement would be as usual.' Performances
by regimental bands further confirmed the impression that nothing untoward was occurring. Rifles were
mounted with triggers wired to tins into which water
dropped until the pressure caused the triggers to be
pulled, helping create the semblance of random fire long
after the last man had left.

The invasion had been a total disaster. The retreat
was, ironically, a spectacular success.

Harry soon settled into his new quarters near Ismailia, at the Moaskar (or Moascar) Isolation Camp. It was, as the name suggests, a bleak place, surrounded by desert – the only points of interest visible being the tall masts of the barges on the Sweet Water Canal (now the Ismailia Canal), which feeds into the Suez Canal, and which lies to the west and south. As Alexander Aitken, one of Harry's fellow evacuees wrote, the survivors presented a sorry sight. 'All clothing was frayed, torn, sun-faded. Parade-ground drill had degenerated, men sloped and ordered arms by the principle of least action in a single circular movement, avoided saluting, kept step but little else.' Their appearance contrasted strongly with that of the fresh and enthusiastic reinforcements recently arrived from New Zealand, who, Aitken said, 'looked like young Apollos, physically fit, sun-browned, spick and span, executing their movements before us with all that click and swank of simultaneity so dear to the military eye and ear'. 'They looked with critical sadness on our rough state,' he added; 'they were disappointed at having missed Gallipoli, as though it had been the Hesperides.'

No doubt Harry would have been plied with endless questions by the eager new arrivals. What had it been like to land at Anzac Cove? Was it true that he'd been involved in the attack on Chunuk Bair? They would have regarded such exploits as exciting and heroic. But Harry, like most veterans of fierce fighting, would probably have said little in reply. How could he possibly have got them to comprehend the terror and the tragedy involved, the friends wounded and the friends lost? It was easier to say nothing. His diary entries reflect the mental journey on which so many soldiers must have gone. In New Zealand he had eagerly recorded the daily regimen of route marches, the rifle training, the sham attacks. Now, after four months of brutal warfare, he was back doing the same training but exhibiting none of the interest and enthusiasm that had been apparent the previous year.

As I turn the pages of his new diary, which he begins in mid-February 1916, I hope to gain more of an insight into my often inscrutable great-uncle. Sometimes I wish he could be more poetic, as Alexander Aitken is when he describes the mirages he sees at Moaskar: 'Cavalry on the skyline would seem to be splashing in a silver lagoon. Once, glancing back from the marching column I saw the whole of Ismailia reflected in a lake of shimmering air.' But then I have to remind myself that Aitken wrote his memoir after the event; Harry's brusque, unembellished diary entries capture the moment, with no time for analysis or the benefits of hindsight. And while he remains emotionally elusive, I have seen moments when the passivity cracks and he lets loose, whether it's about the death of a friend, or the sudden ferocity of battle, or the disappointment of not going home. The one thing the diaries have taught me is that he doesn't want to be let go, to be unremembered. If he had, he wouldn't have gone to the effort of recording his experiences in the thick of battle.

Nor do others want to let him go. Myself included.

The essence of Harry is often to be found in those carefully noted lists of mail received and sent. It's easy to mock someone who religiously records every pair of socks and every jar of Bovril, but it's their way of reminding themselves that someone out there still cares about them. Such humble items become the valuable parameters of their lives. More important to Harry than the records of casualties and battlefield strategies, they're reminders of the friends and friendships to be enjoyed when the war is over.

I have a postcard, complete with family nickname, written by Harry while he was in Egypt to his niece Katherine, Eddy's daughter and my aunt. The tone is not that of someone who is happy to be away from family but of someone who wants to come home.

Dear 'Kachen'

I hope you will like this card of the Pyramids. It is quite a pretty view I think. I have been down into the middle of no. 2, it was very wonderful, but jolly hot scrambling down the passage. The water is a bit of the River Nile, I think. Please thank Daddy for the parcel containing chocolate which I received yesterday – it was v. good of him to send it.

Best love from your affect. uncle, Harry.

On 18 February 1916, his first entry in his new diary records that he was in Cairo, staying, happily, with the Miltons.

Three days later and 3,000 miles away, the Germans began a massive offensive on the French lines at Verdun, using storm troops and flamethrowers. Fought out over ten months, it would prove be the longest battle in modern history. It would also turn out to be one of the bloodiest. By the time it ground to a halt, some 377,000 Frenchmen and 330,000 Germans had become casualties.

The diary entries for Harry's brief stay in Cairo show him out and about, meeting new people, as well as catching up with old friends. His eye for the ladies remains undiminished. ('Saw the tennis girl again looking v smart and pretty,' he writes.) His desire to keep in touch with those who matter to him is similarly apparent. A day's leave on Sunday 26 March, for example, is partly spent writing postcards. One each goes to Jean Hutcheson and Fred Jordan, both friends from his New Zealand days. The final postcard he lists as having written is altogether more poignant: it's to his old friend and fellow farmhand George Batters, who after three months at a clearing hospital in Eastleigh in Hampshire, following his physical collapse in Gallipoli, had now arrived back home in New Zealand. Harry would never see Batty again. The *Press* newspaper in Christchurch reported of him that 'in the severe weather in Gallipoli, in the cold, wet trenches, he contracted lung trouble and after being treated for some considerable time at home, was invalided to New Zealand and is now an inmate of the Cashmere Hills Sanatorium and is making splendid progress to recovery'. George Batters died there, from tuberculosis, in March 1920. He was twenty-nine years old.

At the beginning of April Harry's life takes a new direction. He's now attached to the newly formed New

Zealand Division, consisting of twelve infantry battalions formed into three brigades, and is undergoing medical checks and training with new weapons in anticipation of imminent deployment. His immediate concerns, how-ever, are more mundane. His entry for 5 April 1916 would win no literary prizes, but it puts you immediately in his shoes, or in this case, in his bed. He's at Port Said, and this is his last night in Egypt. 'Didn't sleep too well owing to mosquitoes and BUGS! in the bed!' He uses capitals very sparingly, so they must have been serious bugs.

The next morning, as part of the 1st Battalion, the Canterbury Regiment, of the New Zealand Division, he boarded the Cunard liner RMS *Franconia*, which sailed for France at 10.30. Accompanied across the Mediterranean by two destroyers – deployed to combat the increasing threat of torpedo attacks from German submarines – she sounds to have been the troopship of dreams. Harry and his comrades, instead of being squeezed into bunks in a crowded hold, were allotted cabins of their own. For Cecil Malthus, *Franconia* was 'By far the most com-fortable ship we had ever been on . . . The weather was perfect, we had virtually no parades, and in general we really had the feeling that we were tourists travelling at His Majesty's expense.' Albert Gridley, from Blenheim, with whom he shared a cabin, was similarly impressed. 'Grid was a man of few words,' Malthus recalled, 'but I can certainly remember his beautiful slow smile of satis-faction at all these luxuries.' Alexander Aitken was 'quite bewildered by corridors glowing in these early hours with electric light, uniformed and attentive stewards standing there, cabins with white sheets and pillows'. Harry, ever the pleasure-seeker, found such luxury after years of simple living very hard to take, recording, two nights after boarding, 'I had a much better sleep owing to removing the mattress.'

What Cecil Malthus called 'our pleasure cruise' lasted a week. A week of cloudless skies and a halcyon sea. Time out of war.

They saw no land until they were past Sardinia, where their destroyer escort left them. 'Apparently it is safe in these waters,' Harry noted. Turning into the Gulf of Lyon, they ran head first into a mistral which whipped up the sea, forcing them to drop anchor in the roads at Marseilles. They rode out the storm next to the P&O liner SS *Moldavia*, which was playing a similar waiting game until it was safe to disembark. 'Rumours that a submarine got a French steamer about 2 hours before we came along last night,' wrote Harry; 'if so, lucky for us!' The rumour mill was, on this occasion, accurate. The ship that went down was the *Vega*, a cargo vessel, sunk 80 miles east of Barcelona. Her crew of thirty-three were all rescued.

Six months later it was the *Franconia*'s turn. The ship on which Harry and his comrades enjoyed an almost magical interlude was torpedoed and sunk by the German submarine U47, 195 miles east of Malta. She was not carrying troops at the time, but twelve of her crew perished, as 'the most comfortable ship we had ever been on' went to the bottom.

Once on French soil, the Canterburys marched through the streets of Marseilles to board a train to take

them northwards to the battlefields. Malthus, a Franco-
phile, enthused, 'We got an amazing welcome. I dare say
the people had some queer ideas as to where we'd come
from, but anyway it was from the ends of the earth and
we had come to save *La France* so they milled around in
the wildest excitement and made our progress difficult.
Our Captain Gray was heartily kissed by a fat businessman, to the joy of the troops, and a number of the said
troops broke ranks to do some kissing and hugging on
their own behalf.'

Harry was in a similarly chirpy mood as they set out.
'The Colonel told us we'd be 60 hours on the journey,
so we shall see plenty of France!' he wrote. 'Got a fine
carriage.'

The train was a mix of carriages and wagons (some
of which had 'Hommes [Men] 40, Chevaux [Horses] 8'
stamped on their sides). The carriages had compart-
ments complete with maps and railway guides, but the
wagons offered more room to stretch out and beds of
straw to sleep on. Harry, however, doesn't seem to have
taken advantage of these facilities and consequently
'Had a rotten night as no room to sleep'. Travelling at
little more than 12 miles an hour the train reached Lyons
at 5 a.m., Macon at 8.00 and passed Dijon, 197 miles
from Paris, at 1.15. After months in the desert, the sight
of green fields, orchards and medieval villages initially
made the slow journey a treat, but as the weather
worsened the further north they went the sense of pleasure diminished. 'Going towards Amiens,' wrote Harry.
'V. cold, wet, sleet and hail etc.' Aitken caught the sense

of anticlimax as they neared the battlegrounds: 'Landscapes winter-bitten, drear bleak and northern. Branch-railways of military purpose, a multitude of French troop trains, thickets of barbed wire everywhere, and a general pervasive miasma showed at this point we could not be far behind the front line.'

What must have been a poignant moment for Harry came as the train reached the northern end of France. Running through Étaples and Boulogne, it slowly passed along the coast, tantalising him with a view, through the hail and the sleet, of the grey-green waters of the Channel. 'Only 22 miles from England,' he wrote. Jubilantly? Despairingly? Bearing in mind Kierkegaard's dictum that life can only be understood backwards, but must be lived forwards, one must assume that from his side of time, seeing England on the horizon must have been a glimpse of good things to come.

The next night's entry came after they had U-turned from the coast and run inland to disembark near the Belgian border at Hazebrouck. The journey from Marseilles had taken them fifty-five hours. By this stage Harry's spirits had been quite lifted. 'Had a fine sleep. It's hard to believe that I am only about 80 miles from home now! I must look after some leave when we settle down.' There was no note of apprehension at being close to another bloody battlefield. Right now, being in France meant, in some ways, being closer to normality.

The next day, with Harry and his comrades camped in rows of bell tents in damp fields near the ancient village of Morbecque, any mood of optimism they might

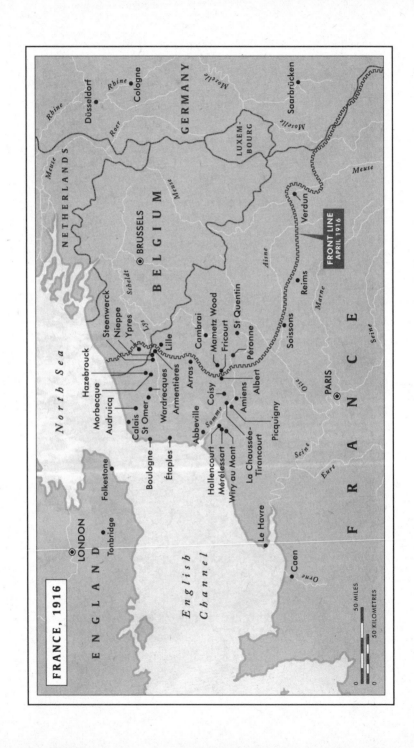

have felt must have been severely punctured. To start with there was a three-hour route march in full kit. Then the troops received their first instruction in dealing with some of the many challenges that fighting in northern France presented. No doubt the Anzacs would have been relieved to learn that they would no longer have to cope with the extreme summer heat and the mountainous terrain that had helped make the Gallipoli campaign so treacherous. But the Western Front offered plenty of dangers and challenges of its own. Poison gas, for example, unknown in the Dardanelles, had been deployed here since 1915, and Harry had to undergo respirator practice accordingly. Alexander Aitken later recalled how even route marches in France differed from those undertaken in preparation for Gallipoli: they uncomfortably demonstrated, he said, 'the difference between Egyptian sand and Flemish cobbles'.

Then there were the new weapons and fighting techniques that had to be mastered. The improvised 'cricket ball' bombs that both sides lobbed towards each other at Quinn's Post had been superseded by the Mills bomb, an altogether more sophisticated hand grenade with deep grooves carved vertically and horizontally on the case to maximise the shrapnel damage on detonation. Standard bayonet training was now supplemented by 'New Bayonet Fighting' that involved learning precisely how and where to plant the weapon for maximum effect. Neck preferred. Anywhere on the chest risked embedding the blade in the breastbone and so making it difficult to extract. Stabbing it into the groin rarely caused death but did result in such agony that the victim would instinctively grab the bayonet and try to pull it out. Some of the training demanded specialised one-week courses at various schools of instruction for officers and selected other ranks – grenade schools, gas schools, schools of camp sanitation among them.

For Harry, there was a more immediate, pragmatic concern. 'No money.' Because of some procedural problem, most of the battalion had received nothing since they left Moaskar camp. Harry was down to his last few pennies. And to compound his dour mood there was 'No hope of any leave.'

Tuesday 18 April was another wet, cold day. 'This camp is a brute,' wrote Harry, following this observation with the better news that after more respirator practice in the afternoon, they were to be moved out of the tents into billets. Harry and the rest of his platoon were duly allocated a barn, 'fairly warm and plenty of straw'. Next day, in better mood, he and his friends strolled into Morbecque to acquaint themselves with one of the local estaminets. These were smaller equivalents of the British pub – basically cafés where you could buy drinks, have a cheap meal, and often gather round a piano for a sing-song. Harry had a beer for a penny and noted, 'Rather a fine girl in the pub bar.' Cecil Malthus was equally impressed. 'I have a great admiration for the girls who run these places,' he wrote. 'There are no men, of course, but the girls need no protection but their own good sense and tact.' To raise Harry's spirits further a rumour was circulating that those who had fought longest at Gallipoli without taking leave – men such as Harry – were to be given priority for the next home visits.

The opening of Harry's entry for 25 April reads rather like a newspaper headline: '1st Anniversary of the Landing at "Anzac" by the Australians and New Zealanders.' It's an occasion that, over a hundred years later, remains the most important national day of remembrance on both sides of the Tasman Sea: Anzac Day. Yet Harry's objective phrasing here almost makes it sound as though he hadn't been involved. Perhaps he was uncomfortable at the recollection – or at the thought of the recognition of personal achievement that goes with such occasions.

What did give him cause for celebration, though, was the news that he was to be granted leave after all: '8 days from Boulogne,' he wrote, 'so that's decent.' And, as the weather took a turn for the better, that welcome news was followed a few days later by the arrival, finally, of some long-delayed pay: 'Francs 30 = £1-1-6.' There was no question of paying it into a savings account. Instead he stuffed it in his pocket and went that afternoon to Hazebrouck 'for a chance to spend some cash and have a feed'.

Hazebrouck, which Alexander Aitken described as 'not an attractive town', was a 4-mile walk from the camp. Its population had been swelled by refugees from those French and Belgian border towns overrun by the Germans at the start of the war. 'Some were lace-makers. One might watch, in a certain corner window, the graceful finger-juggling of three Belgian ladies, evidently sisters, the tiny bobbins flying up, crossing and recrossing in an intriguing figure,' wrote Aitken. Harry, I'm afraid, showed no interest in such picturesque details of French provincial life. The bald entry that appears in his diary that night is, 'Late to bed as a big number fairly stewed with wine etc.'

As Harry prepared for home leave he was suddenly informed that the place he had been promised had now been allocated to one of his fellow Nelsons, Cecil Malthus. The two men's experiences in Gallipoli had been much alike, but while Harry had remained a private, Malthus had subsequently been promoted to sergeant, and that seniority guaranteed him preferential treatment. Harry was not one to brood over ranks or promotions in his diary, but when they affected home leave he was understandably irritated: 'I should have gone 1st had not Malthus got [his sergeant's] stripes,' he complained. 'Wrote to Mother to tell her I'll be home next week.'

The days must have passed slowly: endless dull army routine, with only the occasional break for recuperation and relaxation. It's perhaps not surprising therefore that even the tiniest departure from the mindless norm merited a mention in Harry's diary. A 'hot shower bath down in Morbecque' is given the same attention as a route march and a disappointing score in the rapid firing course. The issuing of a new helmet – the rounded 'Brodie' pattern model – is deemed worthy of a short entry and the assessment 'Pretty heavy.'

Such a judgement of the new Brodie was scarcely surprising, as in Gallipoli Harry would have been used to wearing the far more comfortable New Zealander's soft-top campaign hat, known affectionately – because of its very distinctive shape – as the 'Lemon Squeezer'. The brainchild of Lieutenant Colonel Malone, inspirational commander of the Wellington Battalion who perished at Chunuk Bair, it had furrows running vertically from a point on top, rather than the single horizontal furrow to be found on the wide-brimmed bush hat of the Australians, thus ensuring that rainwater poured off it rather than gathered in it, and simultaneously providing the New Zealanders with something that marked them out from the rest. The war created many opportunities for the Johnny Enzeds to forge a national identity stronger than anything that had existed before. The 'Lemon Squeezer' was one very visible element.

Harry wasn't the only Enzed to regret the replacement of soft-tops with Brodies. Cecil Malthus seemed to speak for all his mates when he wrote home, 'They are said to be a grand Idea, but they are uncomfortable, and we regret our old slouch hats, which have been "called in".' The weight of the helmet and the heat it generated clearly took some getting used to.

So, too, did the anti-gas respirators: grey-flannel hoods covering the head and shoulders that had circular eye-pieces and a rubber mouthpiece cut into them that gave their wearers a chilling, ghost-like appearance. A new model had been introduced a few months before – the 'PH Hood', impregnated with Phenate Hexamine, a newly discovered coating offering improved protection against chlorine and phosgene poisons. On 1 May, after the usual rifle bayonet fighting practice, Harry and his comrades were taken to a field near Morbecque to observe a practical demonstration of the new respirator. Once the British officer in charge had told them how to recognise the smell of gas, and how to adjust the helmet and operate the exhale valve, he led them along a 30-yard trench, which a hissing cylinder was supposedly filling with chlorine gas. Some scepticism was expressed by the assembled troops when it was revealed that one of them had carried a frog through alive.

However tedious and onerous the day's regime in camp, Harry and his mates were free to make up for it later. 'To village in evening for drink etc.' Despite the distant rumbling from the east and the occasional flare of a rocket soaring into the night sky, the reason for their being in France seemed a long way away. Meanwhile the proprietors of the wine shops and cafés along the cobbled streets of Morbecque asked no questions, but puffed on their pipes and served up watery beer and made money while they could. In a sense, everyone was holding their breath.

On 2 May, reported Harry, it was 'cooler and some rain fell', but the big news was of 'an "alarm" parade last night at 10.30 p.m.' 'Practically half of the chaps were drunk,' he wrote, 'but fell in somehow.' Not that the experience of a surprise parade provided any kind of cautionary lesson. That evening they went back to the village: 'same as last night', Harry tersely recorded.

The next day, another route march, followed by more bayonet fighting lessons, followed by 'my usual stroll to the village' in the evening and, with it, the risk of another alarm parade. But Harry, phlegmatic as ever, was prepared to chance his arm. 'Rumours of a "Brigade Alarm" some time tonight,' he wrote, 'which might be a dinkum move [Australian slang for a genuine prospect], but somehow I don't think so.' As it turned out he was right. There was no alarm, 'altho' everyone was ready and slept with clothes on'.

The following day Harry's home leave was at last confirmed. 'We (Ted Cousens and I) are going to England tomorrow morning, Sergt Gridley in charge. I am going to Tonbridge direct. Got orders to report at 7-0 p.m. in full marching order (minus cartridges) at Orderly Room. To Hazebrouck and put up at Hotel du Nord for the night.'

Sergeant Albert Gridley, 'Grid', had been Cecil Malthus's cabin mate on the *Franconia*, and while stationed at Armentières, often shared a dugout with him. ('But I lost touch with him on the Somme and have never seen nor heard of him since.') Judging from the affectionate way Malthus talked of him, Harry was in good hands. Gridley saw Harry and Ted Cousens safely onto the Folkestone ferry on Friday 5 May, after a 'terribly slow' six-hour train journey to Boulogne. By half-past two that afternoon, almost exactly four years since he had left for Wellington on the SS *Rotorua*, Harry was back in the land of his birth.

His sisters Mary and Edith met him from the train at Tonbridge station. They were both in their early forties by now. Frustratingly, Harry gives little away about this long-delayed reunion other than to note, 'Both looked v. fit.' At St Helen's he was welcomed by Eleanor and her children Pauline, Sylvia and Paul, and his mother Brita, now in her seventies. 'Mother looks very well too,' he noted.

It might be tempting to assume that the rest of the afternoon would have been filled with the joy of seeing each other again and catching up with all that had happened in the intervening four years. But other things were on Harry's mind. 'To the town and got a shave and haircut. Bought a shirt 6/11. Left watch to be repaired.' I understand that. The first thing I want to do when I come home after a long time away is the ordinary stuff. I want to go out and buy my favourite coffee, or the new pair of shoes I've been promising myself for months. The social catching up can wait. For Harry, who, after all, had been living a pretty basic life on the farm in New Zealand and one of spartan extremes in the army, the opportunity to indulge in a few creature comforts must have been overwhelming.

Diary entries over the next few days give the lie to any notion I might ever have entertained of Harry being anti-social, awkward or uncomfortable in company. On the contrary, he seems energised: busy chasing up family and friends, one day in London, another in Norfolk, another back in Kent. In this one week in May, Harry, free from the oppressive world of orders and duties and enemies and killing skills, comes alive. I learn more about the people he knew and the things he liked to do than at any other time of his life.

On the Saturday morning he's shopping in Tonbridge with his mother and the girls. Mary takes him to see a Mrs Gordon, cousin of the Miltons who had looked after him so well in Cairo: 'v. nice and pretty.' He takes a walk with Mary and Eleanor ('Nellie') in the castle grounds. 'Afterwards tea and then went to the tennis courts and also called at the Furleys.' Family numbers swell in the evening as Edith and her husband Geoffrey (now in the navy, and, according to Harry, looking 'v. fit in his uniform') come round for supper.

And then there's the rekindling of his friendship with Margie Sale, who seems to have been the nearest to a sweetheart that he ever had and with whom he'd been corresponding regularly during his time in Gallipoli. He wired her on that first full day at home. She then wired him a number to call her on when he came up to London.

The next few days proved similarly busy. On Sunday he went to church with his mother and two sisters. While I can't be sure how much religion meant to him, I suspect that, as the son of a vicar, he would have regarded churchgoing as part and parcel of the weekly routine. He didn't stop at a morning service, either. That evening they went to another one in Tonbridge School Chapel. 'V. nice chapel and service.' As ever, Harry wasn't giving much away.

On Monday Harry took the 8.50 train to Charing Cross. From there he proceeded 'to the NZ offices No 13 Vic. St', the headquarters of the New Zealand Expeditionary Force in England and the first port of call for any Kiwi soldier on leave. ('You can't walk down the Strand without meeting a New Zealander,' wrote Cecil Malthus, who had been there just a couple of weeks earlier.) Number 13 Victoria Street was at the heart of a network of facilities for New Zealanders that included four hospitals across the south of England – including one, at Weymouth, specifically for those who had suffered wounds or contracted diseases at Gallipoli – and a number of dedicated convalescent homes. It also oversaw reserve depots and a training area, Sling Camp on Salisbury Plain, where a huge kiwi, known as the Bulford Kiwi, would later be carved into the chalk of Beacon Hill. It's still there, an indelible reminder of New Zealanders in England in the First World War. The New Zealand Rifle Brigade trained at Brocton in Staffordshire, the Machine Gun Corps at Grantham and the engineers, tunnellers and Māori reinforcements trained, appropriately perhaps, at Christchurch in Hampshire.

At the office Harry met 'a Miss Wood' who, he noted, knew the Dampier-Crossley family in New Zealand. Christopher Dampier-Crossley was the cousin of Edward Palin who may conceivably have encouraged Harry to emigrate those few years earlier.

Once he had left 13 Victoria Street, Harry 'Rang up Margie No: 1019 Putney' and then went to her work address, which he recorded at the back of his diary as being 'Lord Roberts Memorial Workshops, Fulham'. He found her 'in due course and looking I thought, fairly fit tho' thin'. They spent some time together. 'She showed me round the toy works, most awfully interesting. All disabled soldiers working and their daughters etc.' Then it was 'Back to Piccadilly to lunch.'

After buying a ticket for an upcoming trip to Norwich he went 'back west and called on Mrs W who was very glad to see me'. This, I assume, was the Mrs Wright who sent him such regular food parcels; on this occasion she gave him a pound. He then collected Margie from her place of work and took her to Piccadilly. 'We first of all had an excellent dinner in Soho at "Le Chantecleer" and a very enjoyable little tête à tête,' he confided in his diary. 'Afterwards to the "Lyric" (Upper Circle) and saw the play "Romance". Lovely thing, tho v. sad. The main actor is Owen Nares, and the leading lady, lovely actress and in beautiful clothes, Doris Keane.' What he didn't mention is that the play, by the American dramatist Edward Sheldon, centres on an opera singer's intense affair with a young clergyman – not quite the story of his mother and father in reverse, but near enough.

Afterwards Harry took Margie home in a taxi to her parents' house in West London. 'She was v. sweet to me then, allowed me to kiss her, the darling old girl. I am still dreadfully fond of her and she of me, I think. Had a little chat, smoke and W & S [whisky and soda] at Denham cottage.' He then returned to his lodgings at Peel House on Regency Street at 12.40 a.m. He was tired and probably a little over-wrought. It had been a full and frantic day.

The following morning, he took an early train from Liverpool Street to Norwich to see his elder brother Edward, then working at the Norfolk and Norwich hospital, which offered special provision for the treatment of wounded servicemen. Eddy was now forty-seven. His two children – Edward Moreton, my father, and Katherine, or Kachen, as Harry called his much-loved niece – were fifteen and seven respectively. 'He looked v. fit and well' was Harry's characteristically minimal description of my grandfather. Or anyone he met who was not actually at death's door. They lunched at the hospital, after which Eddy's wife, Agnes, along with Kachen, came to see him. It was a lightning visit, but he had been 'V. glad to have seen them.'

His descriptions of these family reunions are frustratingly abrupt. To some they might even come across as cold. But that's another trick of hindsight. We expect more because we know that Harry won't see them again. For Harry, not a natural writer, it's enough just to record whatever he can in a whirlwind visit. There'd be more time on his next visit. And when the war was over, all the time in the world.

Harry went shopping in town the next morning with Mary and Nellie and 'got Margie a pretty little brooch'. They met up with the rest of the family for lunch at a Lyons Corner House, then went on to see *Joyland*, the long-running revue at the Hippodrome on Leicester Square.

At 5.30 the party broke up and his two sisters walked through Trafalgar Square to Charing Cross Station to catch the train to Tonbridge. For Harry, with only two days of leave remaining, it was clear where his priorities lay. At seven o'clock, having met Margie for an early supper at the Chantecleer, he took her to the Wyndham's Theatre in Charing Cross Road to see *A Kiss for Cinderella*, a 'sweet little play'. ('We had lovely seats,' he also noted.) Written by the author of *Peter Pan*, J. M. Barrie, it's a contemporary take on the Cinderella story that touches on various wartime themes, such as food rationing, Zeppelin raids, blackouts and the plight of children whose fathers are fighting and dying in the trenches. Malthus, who also saw it while on leave, quite enjoyed its 'naïve sentimentality'.

Unfortunately for Harry, his evening did not end as happily as did the play:

> Afterwards drove back to Bedford Park by taxi. M. v. sweet to me, the dear. Put the question to her on parting, but I fear it's no good. Poor darling, she was awfully cut up about it I'm afraid. God bless her. I love her and I think she loves me, but not enough to marry me.

Harry doesn't dwell on her decision, so it's difficult to tell how hard it hit him. On the one hand, he was now in his early thirties and, after the years of roaming the world in order to find himself, had at last decided that whatever the future held for him he wanted Margie to be part of it. On the other hand, over those meals at the Chantecleer and the long taxi rides out to Chiswick, he and Margie would surely have endlessly rehearsed the wisdom of making a binding commitment to each other in the middle of a war. Margie's family remember her as quite a driven, ambitious woman; she certainly looks strong and composed in a photograph taken of her around that time. So perhaps it was just a question of Harry's dream colliding with Margie's reality. They nevertheless remained in touch, and Harry must have hoped that when the war was finally over, there would be another opportunity to pop the question.

But he never saw her again.

The next day he 'wrote to M'. I assume this must have been Margie, though I can't be sure, and Harry has left no hint as to the contents of his letter or his state of mind. It seems telling to me, though, that without Margie as his focus, his day appears to have been rather aimless: 'To the City by bus and walked about there a bit. Saw a young girl with a club foot. Saw Westminster Abbey and St Paul's. Bought a pipe. Had a good lunch, oysters etc.'

'Last day!' Harry's diary begins on Friday 12 May. The exclamation mark is the only hint of there being anything special on his last day in England. 'Did some shopping in morning. Had my photo taken. In afternoon finished shopping. Went in to say good bye to Mrs Gordon after tea. She looked awfully pretty and gave me a v. kind welcome and met a Miss Marjery Hewson.'

Was Harry's attraction to women as one-dimensional as it appears? Were they either pretty or not pretty? Was he as superficial in his appreciation as he sounds? I might have said yes, had I not read his expressions of love for Margie on this week back home. There was something deeper there, I think. Something beyond the fit and the pretty. He just wasn't good at expressing it.

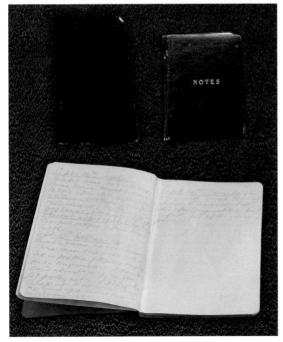

Harry's Gallipoli diary, open at July 1915. Note the tiny pencil stub.

Various of Harry's war diaries. The diary at the bottom is open at the last entries he made.

The *Tahiti* and the *Athenic* (which carried Harry to war) at the dockside, Lyttelton.

Cairo, 1915: a postcard sent from Zeitoun camp by one of the Enzeds to his family at home in New Zealand.

The New Zealanders' camp at Zeitoun. A cricket match is in progress.

Major General Alexander Godley, commander of the New Zealand forces. Born in England, Irish father.

Lieutenant Colonel Malone, commander of the Wellington Battalion. Brave, much loved, he died leading the assault on Chunuk Bair.

A German postcard celebrates the attack by Turkish forces on the Suez Canal, 2 February 1915.

The Anzacs land at Anzac Cove, Gallipoli, 25 April 1915.

The 1st Anzac Corps headquarters.

May 1915: a Turkish envoy mounts his horse, after arranging a brief armistice.

Enzed troops and dugouts at the foot of Walker's Ridge.

Peter Jackson and I think this is a 'probable sighting' of Harry, half-standing in a shell-hole at Cape Helles.

Another probable sighting of Harry, holding a Lee-Enfield rifle (which had recently replaced the Boer War-era Lee-Metford). The photograph was taken with a portable Kodak on Rhododendron Ridge in early August 1915. Note the camera case in the foreground.

(*Above*) The lemon squeezer. (*Left*) The cap badge of the 12th Nelsons.

A New Zealand corporal in full marching kit.

The love of Harry's life, Margie Sale.

Wyndham's Theatre, where Harry took Margie before he proposed to her in May 1916.

Soldiers of the Wellington Regiment form a trench on the Somme by joining up shell craters, 15 September 1916.

On the move: New Zealanders on the road between Amiens and Albert, September 1916.

The attack on the village of Morval, 25 September 1916.

The name on the wall: Caterpillar Valley Cemetery, March 2023.

On Saturday 13 May Harry left his mother's house at 6.00 a.m. and was at Folkestone by 9.00, only to be told that the boat would not leave until 7.30 p.m. 'So got a train back to Tonbridge and got home in time for lunch giving everyone a big surprise.' I'll bet.

After a second lot of goodbyes he went into town, had some tea, caught the train to Folkestone and was back in France by eleven o'clock that evening.

A lieutenant with the 4th Battalion, New Zealand Rifle Brigade, rests in his dugout in the Close Support Trench near Chard's Farm, Armentières.

13

WAITING

———◈———

THE NEXT DAY HE REJOINED the battalion back at Hazebrouck. Here they changed onto a train that headed due north to Steenwerck, in French Flanders, almost on the Belgian border, before disembarking for three hours' sleep, and then continuing by bus to Armentières. It took them thirty-six hours to travel some hundred miles.

They were now in one of the quieter sectors of the Western Front. L'Epinette Salient, located between Ypres and the Somme, was so quiet indeed that it had acquired as its nickname 'the Nursery'. It was all a far cry from the Dardanelles. Newly promoted Sergeant Cecil Malthus, having boasted to his fiancée Hazel that 'I am quite a good soldier now and take things just as they come without feeling much nervousness or strain from the presence of danger,' went on to reassure her, 'But then the danger, in the state of quiet prevailing on this front at present is nothing compared with Gallipoli.'

For his part, Lieutenant Lawrence Blyth, one of the veterans who told his story to Jane Tolerton, described how 'The Huns and the British forces had sort of come to an arrangement not to hurt one another. We took over from an English division, and the English lads said, "If you leave the Germans alone, he'll [*sic*] leave you alone."' 'Which,' he mused, 'was a pretty sound theory.' 'But,' he concluded, 'we hadn't travelled 12,000 miles to sit on our backside and wait for the Germans.'

Armentières turned out to be somewhat like Hazebrouck, 'a dour, unpleasing little manufacturing town' in Malthus's opinion, with a pre-war population of nearly 30,000 now reduced to some 6,000. The Germans had briefly occupied the town after the outbreak of hostilities, before being pushed back by Allied forces, and stories of the appalling atrocities they had supposedly committed against Belgian civilians had swiftly circulated. The women and children left behind after the able-bodied men had been called away to fight, however, appeared to harbour no particular hatred of the Germans, leading some to speculate that the stories had merely been part of the propaganda war. Now those of the townspeople who still remained were busy servicing the British Army, and most of the key buildings such as schools, convents and small factories had been commandeered for military use. Harry himself was billeted in an old factory in the town centre.

Mornings for the New Zealand troops were enlivened by a visit from a local shopkeeper and her daughter, Zoë Duriez, who brought round hot black coffee in pails. Zoë also waitressed at one of the local estaminets. She was hugely popular with the Kiwis. Cecil Malthus summed up her qualities. 'Always friendly, always smiling, always obliging, she had a quick tongue and a sturdy right arm, and well deserved the respect, affection and gratitude of all hands. She must have received an impossible number of proposals, but her answer to all and sundry was a firm and cheery *"Après la guerre."'*

Harry's return to active duty was a gentle one: a day on fatigue loading firewood, followed by a stroll around town in the evening. Margie was still very much on his mind. He had written to her a few days before and now received a reply which he recorded, briefly, in his diary: 'Such a sweet little note, also a lovely knife from her.'

On 20 May his company moved from Armentières to the trenches some 4 miles east of the town. As elsewhere on the Western Front these were arranged in three parallel lines. The first, immediately facing the enemy, was the firing line. At Armentières it ballooned out in a semi-circle, which became known as 'the Mushroom' and which was described by the 12th Nelsons' commanding officer, Major Brereton, as 'a maze of rotting trenches and weeds'. So close did it come to the German front line – at some points within 60 yards of it – that the two sides were able to indulge in early-morning banter. This would generally begin as an exchange of salutations, and degenerate swiftly into a barrage of insults: the hope was that someone would be so outraged by something the other side said, he would pop his head above the parapet and so be picked off. Not all communication was spoken. Henry Sissons of the Auckland Infantry Battalion remembered a sign held up in one of the German trenches. It read, 'Welcome, New Zealand'.

Constant caution was required. A brief moment of carelessness, a casual glance over the parapet, could all too often prove fatal. Snipers were on constant alert. One New Zealand sniper, Jack White, reckoned, 'I was a pretty good shot, and you'd know you wouldn't miss. That was the rotten part of being a sniper.' One story he told reveals both the fragility of life in the trenches and the humanity that still survived there, despite everything. One morning, he recalled, a stretch of the enemy's protective parapet had come down, revealing a German having a wash over a basin. 'I thought, I can't shoot him like that. Every sniper had an observer, so I said to mine, "I'll give this bloke a fright." So I fired at the basin. The chap bolted for his life.' 'That was the only time,' he concluded, 'I deliberately missed.'

About 150 yards (137 metres) behind the front trenches were the support line trenches, which were the most strongly fortified, and a further 500 yards behind them, were the subsidiary lines, which is where Harry and the 12th Nelsons were initially deployed. The various lines were interconnected, and they also contained occasional zigzags, both to ensure that any enemy soldier who managed to penetrate the lines would not be able to fire straight down them and to give the defending soldiers views to the side as well as straight ahead. Because the Flanders plain was so low-lying and prone to waterlogging, the defences had to be built from the ground upwards to avoid flooding, and the pathways had to be lined with duckboards.

In many ways, the trenches were like small towns, containing everything needed for communal life – hospital posts, kitchens, latrines, observation bays, operations dugouts for meetings. But life in them was unremittingly tough. Not only was there the constant threat of an enemy bomb or bullet ending your life, you were also living at the bottom of a 12-foot-deep (3.6 metres) V-shaped ditch in which rainwater never drained away in winter and flies filled the air in summer. When it was cold and damp, you ran the risk of developing trench foot, a condition that caused your feet to swell and often resulted in serious infection. When it was hot and dry, you had to contend with the stench of excrement and dead bodies. Trench fever (a louse-borne disease), dysentery, pneumonia and scabies lurked constantly. And then there were the 'large, well-conditioned rats' that Alexander Aitken recalled only too vividly 'scampering along parapets or gnawing at haversacks in the dug-outs'.

The daily routine was nothing to write home about, either. Unless he had already been on night duty, Harry would have been at stand-to, in full kit, from 5.00 in the morning. At 5.30 the daily rum ration was issued. If no attack was expected, he would then be stood down for breakfast: oatmeal and bacon if he was lucky, although by this stage of the war meat had been rationed to 6 ounces (170 grams) per man per day. After that, Harry might spend the rest of the morning cleaning his rifle, checking the remainder of his equipment and doing the constant repair and maintenance work required to keep the trenches as strong and safe as possible – fixing barbed wire, shoring up collapsed walls, laying duckboards, replacing sandbags strafed by enemy machine-gunners. The afternoon was time for sleeping, reading or writing letters.

There was no privacy. Men slept sitting up, crammed together at the bottom of the trench or else in dugouts. Washing was an occasional luxury. Even shaving could be tricky. A member of the Rifle Brigade, recalling how insistent senior officers were that a smooth jaw was essential to good morale, described the improvised technique that had to be developed: 'We used to shave in our hot tea in the morning. We always had our shaving gear because we had a little haversack with our razor and soap and brush, and dipped it into the tea and lathered it.'

Harry's diaries contain no complaints about trench life. Like so many of his companions, he seems to have adopted a stoical, even fatalistic, view. Discomfort and danger were things not so much to be dreaded as to be endured. A typical late May entry simply reads, 'Decent dugout. Turned in.' There was little action. Some shelling but few casualties. He'd also been serving for long enough to know that it was best to be sceptical when heart-warming stories of great military success came his way. On one occasion he noted, 'The Australians made a bit of a raid on a German trench – took a lot of prisoners and trench mortars,' but then immediately followed this with 'Do not know if the story is true.' The entry for the following morning reads, 'No truth in the story,' after which he moved on to more important things: 'Recd an old letter from mother dated 12th April, which had been travelling all over the place after me.'

On 28 May the First Battalion was relieved at 10.15 in the evening and marched back to Armentières, arriving just before midnight. 'Back to our old billets and very glad to be between the blankets again,' wrote Harry.

If Harry was right to be wary about the rumours and claims that constantly swirled round the trenches, there was one gaining attention by mid-June that was very much rooted in reality: 'This big advance the papers talk about,' as Cecil Malthus referred to it in a letter home. ('May it come soon and end this rotten war,' he added.) First discussed by the British and French top brass the previous December, 'this big advance' had originally been conceived as a massive offensive along the upper reaches of the Somme River that would inflict a decisive blow against the Germans. Now that French troops had to be diverted to resist the German onslaught at Verdun, a more limited attack was agreed that would relieve pressure on the French while wearing the Germans down. It was nevertheless destined to be one of the biggest battles of the war. The front in Gallipoli had never been longer than 2 or 3 miles. The Somme front would stretch for 25 miles. Here, artillery would engage in creeping barrages, incrementally landing missiles further and further back into enemy positions. Massed infantry battalions would then move forward under cover of these barrages, bombs and mortars blasting the way ahead of them. Tanks would be employed for the first time. To feed the insatiable need for more men, conscription had been introduced in January 1916. The man in command of British forces, Douglas Haig, saw the conflict to come as a battle of attrition, in which the enemy would be worn down by the relentless application of superior force.

Harry must have realised by the end of his time there that Gallipoli had been a waste of lives. Now, less than 200 miles from the cafés, clubs and dancing girls of the West End, he and his fellow soldiers in the New Zealand Division were being prepared to risk their lives yet again. In the fields of France the opposing armies were building a potential for destruction that would be greater than in any other war in history. And Harry would soon be in the thick of it.

In immediate terms, though, all that mattered to Private Palin 6/319 was a comfortable billet and a letter from Margie. His diary entry for 29 May even manages to make it sound as though he were on holiday. 'Did not get up until 8 a.m. Nothing on in the morning. For a stroll in town and got some paper etc. Stood "beers" to the section. No parades in afternoon.' The following day's entry records 'a splendid bath' and 'change of clothes' in the morning at an old garment factory whose dyeing vats had been filled with hot water for the purpose; if you were lucky, once you had bathed yourself and washed your clothes you could hand them over to some local women who would dry and iron them for you. But reminders of the war were never far away. The same day, Harry noted that the Germans had bombarded the town and that a number of people had been either injured or killed.

Harry's diary entry for 31 May shows perhaps more than any other the gulf between the lived experience of the individual soldier and the vastness of the events that swirled around him and in which he played his part. For Harry, this particular Wednesday was yet another day of route marches, bayonet practice and an hour and a half of drill. More importantly, it was a day when he received letters from his mother (with a 5-shilling postal order) and 'a <u>sweet</u> one from Margie', acknowledging that 'She has received the "Anzac Book" all right' (this was a collection of stories, cartoons, poems and other diversions compiled by the soldiers themselves; it was a big hit in the summer of 1916). Elsewhere, though, big things were happening. The high command were meeting to confirm the nature of the summer offensive to come. And in the North Sea, the one great naval engagement of the First World War was being fought – the Battle of Jutland.

With this entry for the last day of May Harry had filled every inch of his slim black diary. He concluded it with two pages full of addresses, lists of photographs to be sent, and an inventory headed 'To Carry in the Pack':

1 Balaclava
1 Holdall (bootlaces, shaving gear, toothbrush)
1 Greatcoat
1 Housewife [sewing kit]
Mess tin in cover to be carried upright in strips of pack
    outside

1 Singlet
1 Cardigan
1 Shirt or singlet
1 pr trousers or shorts
1 pr drawers
2 Blankets in oil sheet round pack
Knife, fork and spoon in haversack

The most brutal summer of a brutal war was about to begin, but for now Harry waited comfortably enough in Armentières, with his mates around him and the constant stream of letters from home reminding him of what he had to look forward to when it was all over.

It occurs to me to wonder where Harry's loyalties lay at this time. He had, for the last three years, lived and worked and fought amongst New Zealanders. Did he see himself as one of them? Did he ever intend to become a New Zealand citizen? Had he developed a New Zealand accent? It's impossible to know for sure. Part of me feels he had so espoused his family during his week's leave that by now he would perhaps have been happier living back in the land of his birth. After all, his girl was English and his mother and sister were living comfortably in Kent. And yet here he was surrounded by New Zealanders, taking orders from New Zealand officers. Had he considered where he might go when it was all over? The 100 or so miles back to England? Or the 11,000 miles and more back to Canvastown?

One thing was for sure. The world in which he had grown up, the ordered, unchanging, comfortable world of a country vicarage, was no longer there to go back to. The patriarch had died nearly thirteen years ago and the family had dispersed. Perhaps that lack of an anchor served Harry and played to his strengths. He had become a citizen of the world, unencumbered by expectation and with little emotional baggage. Whatever might come out of the current global upheaval, there was a fair chance Harry would be riding it out as he rode out the months in Gallipoli, ready to fall in with whatever lay ahead. Lack of self-analysis could be one of the secrets of his survival thus far. He strikes me as very much a man of the here and now.

Harry, I suspect, would go where the wind blew him.

With his previous diary now filled, he started a new one in a 4 by 2½ inch (10 x 6 cm) notebook, bound in soft purple leather with the single capitalised word 'NOTES' embossed tastefully on the front in gold leaf. It would almost have fitted in the palm of his hand. Given the amount of gear he had to carry with him, it was sensible to take something he could slip easily and accessibly into a shirt pocket. Unlike the functional khaki-covered wallet in which he carried the photos of his brother Eddy and Agnes his wife, this was not an army-issue notebook, and looks more like something one of his womenfolk might have bought for him at some smart London stationer. Perhaps it was a gift from Margie.

Harry's account of his life in France continues, with a bit of drama, on Thursday 1 June 1916.

'The Huns bombarded an Observation balloon in evening and the two observers had to jump out and get to Terra Firma by parachute. It was a thrilling sight. They landed on French soil, but the balloon drifted away over the German lines.' Harry would have first seen observation balloons during his months of service in the Dardanelles. He would also have seen a few examples of that other wonder of modern aerial warfare: the aeroplane. In France he was destined to see many more, although they were not remotely as ubiquitous as they were to be in the Second World War. Like the observation balloon Harry saw being bombarded, they were used for reconnaissance, and then increasingly became involved in dogfights with enemy planes. At this stage in their development they were pretty crude affairs. The cockpits in the early fighter aircraft like the Sopwith Pup, and its later more famous successor, the Sopwith Camel, were open to the elements and the pilot's hands often got so cold that it became almost impossible to fly the plane and press the machine-gun buttons at the same time.

Two other dramas that Harry recorded in early June were rather less close to home, if no less keenly felt. The first was the Battle of Jutland, which Harry finally learnt about on 4 June, some five days after it had begun and three days after it ended. 'News in today's paper of a sea fight in North Sea,' he wrote. '12 British vessels destroyed. No record of German losses however. It must be regarded as a reverse I'm afraid.' In fact, it was less of a reversal than a stalemate. The British sustained greater losses – fourteen ships and 6,094 men to the Germans' eleven ships and 2,551 men – leading the Kaiser to make the claim that 'The spell of Trafalgar has been broken.' On the other hand, the British could claim a strategic victory, since the deadlock meant that they remained in control of the Atlantic.

Four days after reading of the Battle of Jutland, Harry registered more visceral shock at the news that Lord Kitchener and all his staff, who were on their way to Russia to bolster support for the war, had been drowned when HMS *Hampshire* hit a mine laid by German submarine U-75 just 2 miles north-west of the Orkney Islands. Only a dozen men survived out of the 749 on board. The historian James W. Irvine has likened the public reaction to that which followed the death of President Kennedy or Princess Diana. 'Everyone who was alive then would remember the moment they heard about Kitchener's death.' Harry's reaction was unequivocal. 'Very sad and terrible thing, for our fine Chief to be killed that way.' The very fact that Harry referred to him simply as 'Chief' shows in what esteem the ageing Kitchener was held. He had transcended rank and position to become the embodiment of the British bulldog spirit. He had seen off the rebellious Boers and his recruiting call in 1914 – 'Your Country Needs You!' – had been answered by millions of young men.

For Harry these early days of June passed uneventfully. In fact he seems to have spent as much time as possible away from the front and wandering into town. He was there on the 2nd when a spontaneous Alarm Parade was called, out of the blue, at 7.15 in the evening. 'I managed to fall in all right tho' still in town at 7.00 p.m.' He must have raced back. A few days later he 'went for a stroll in town in evening and read the papers at Union Jack Club' – presumably a French offshoot of the original Union Jack Club founded in London in 1907 to give non-commissioned soldiers somewhere to go when off duty. For Private Harry Palin this was the only club he could call his own. By contrast my maternal grandfather, who was also in France at the time, and who was a lieuten-ant colonel and a DSO, would have had plenty of clubs to choose from. He survived the war and became High Sheriff of Oxfordshire.

That Harry should have had such a relatively easy time was down to the fact that his sector remained rela-tively quiet, despite efforts by Major General Godley and Lieutenant General Birdwood, the GOC of the Austra-lians, to keep reminding the men stationed in the Nur-sery what they were being paid for (at least they *were* now being paid). To this end the two officers ordered eleven raids against the German lines in three months. The New Zealand Division suffered 2,500 casualties.

My great-uncle was spared these raids, but even so he wasn't altogether free from danger. The tone of his entry for Friday 9 June is classic Harry: a mix of the mundane and the terrifying in the life of a man with no particular game plan, a man who is just keeping his life together on a day-by-day basis. Reading it made me understand why the First World War gave birth to surrealism. 'Posted letters to Doris W, Nellie, Baba, Helen B, Margie, Mother, Mrs Wright. We go back to the trenches tonight.

"Minenwerfers" especially objectionable.' Minenwerfers, also known as 'minnies' or 'German sausages', were missiles weighing over 200 pounds (97 kilos), which were fired high into the air from trench mortars. They could clearly be seen twisting and tumbling down towards defensive emplacements. They weren't terribly accurate, and Harry makes them sound like troublesome flies. But they could blow people apart. Equally lethal were the high-velocity, high-explosive shells fired from smaller-calibre field guns that were known colloquially as 'whizz bangs'. They couldn't be seen coming over, but they could certainly be heard: it was the whizz of the incoming shells, followed by their explosion on impact, that gave them their nickname.

The next day it was 'fairly quiet until about 4.45 p.m. when the Huns started to "straffe" [Harry's regular misspelling of 'strafe'] with H.E. [high explosive] and aerial torpedoes [missiles packed with black powder explosive and dropped from the sky]'. Harry, in his typically understated way, describes this as a 'V. unpleasant experience', but then gives an indication just how terrifying – and lethal – such attacks must have been. 'We chased out to the end of No 6 post while the danger was on. I shall know in future where to get to another time and waste no time about it.'

On Sunday the 11th, 'No aerials came over today, only a few shrap [shrapnel shells, designed to explode in the air and shower hundreds of small round pieces of lead over the trenches]. Beastly wet day.' On the 12th, 'The Huns put over some big "minnies" and other bombs. V. wet and miserable all afternoon and night.' The attacks carried on into the next day. One of his mates, Bob Brownlee, was a casualty, 'wounded in shoulder and jaw today by a surprise whiz-bang shell. Not v. bad I think.' The following morning, 'poor old Bob Brownlee had passed out at the Field Ambulance station. He must have been badly hit inwardly.'

Over the next few days things took a turn for the better. His platoon was relieved from their front-line position back to one which Harry described as ' "a home" compared with our last on the firing line'. 'Very cheering news from Ypres,' he went on to record. 'The Canadians have retaken all the lost trenches. The Huns had got mixed up with their own men and had been cut up by their own guns.' The next day he jubilantly wrote, 'Russians got 6000 more Austrians and are now only 30 miles from Poland. Also a Baltic Sea fleet smashed up a German convoy of merchantmen and destroyers.'

For once, his ability to see through the propaganda failed him. It was, of course, all wild, unsubstantiated rumour, fed out to give Harry and all those flea-bitten foot soldiers being bombarded in their muddy trenches the sense that what they were going through was matched by others' efforts elsewhere, and to remind them that they were still on the winning side.

On the 17th and 18th there were gas alarms, but fortunately the wind was blowing away from the Allied lines and danger was averted. As the New Zealanders waited for the air to clear, a morale boost for Harry arrived in the shape of a parcel from Mrs Wright, enclosing 'potted meat 4 tins, OXO 2 tins, Spanish plums 1 tin, toffee 1 tin, marmalade 1 tin'. In between 'a lively artillery duel' and some minnies dropping around him, Harry coolly answered Mrs W's letter and thanked her for the parcel and its contents.

On 20 June Harry and the 12th Nelsons were re-deployed to the reserve trenches. Even here there was plenty of work to do, much of it unglamorous. 'On night fatigue as per usual,' he wrote on the 23rd. 'V. wet night and the trollies v. hard to work.' The trollies had to be run down to the depot, filled up with anything from sandbags, sheets of corrugated iron, barbed wire and timber to food and petrol cans filled with chlorinated water, then pushed up to the lines. They were moved mostly at night and in total darkness.

Three days later they were back in Armentières. The artillery exchanges continued around him, but were far enough away not to threaten the town. He was able to go to the YMCA and hear a band called the Drinkeroos, and the next day to take 'a fine hot dip and a change' at the baths. On the last day of June he went to the pictures.

Compared to the days in Gallipoli, often racked with dysentery, eating a crude, unchanging diet and sleeping in ratholes, Harry had had a relatively easy time in France. Cecil Malthus nicely captured how many of the New Zealanders must have felt during their early months on the Somme. 'In some respects our existence was more satisfying than civilian life, because it was corporate not competitive, and characterised by a sharing and acceptance that banished all worries and cares.' 'Of course,' he added as a rather major caveat, 'it must be said mortal danger was just around the corner, and our contentment was largely due to a sense of respite and a longing for the luck to last.'

At the start of July the luck began to run out. On Saturday the 1st the Germans bombed the town during the day, scoring a direct hit on the church of Notre Dame. 'Knocked down the church steeple and made a fearful mess,' Harry noted. Church spires were regular targets as they could be used for surveillance, and this was the last one standing in Armentières. Cecil Malthus recorded the 'great indignation at this outrage among the pious townspeople'.

On that same morning, 50 miles to the south, things were worse – much worse. After a seven-day rolling bombardment during which 1.5 million shells were fired at German positions to soften up the enemy, the ruinous battle of the Somme, designed to end the stalemate of over eighteen months of trench warfare, had begun. It was to be by far the biggest test yet of Britain's largely volunteer army.

Gunners of the New Zealand Field Artillery load ammunition near Albert, September 1916.

14

THE ROAD TO THE SOMME

———◆———

A T 7.30 A.M. ON 1 July 1916, on General Douglas
Haig's orders, 100,000 British and Allied soldiers
of Sir Henry Rawlinson's Fourth Army poured
out of their trenches and headed for the German lines.
They assumed that the previous week's merciless bombardment would have destroyed German defences and
German morale. They were wrong. The Germans had
hunkered down in their trenches. The barbed wire that
protected them had survived. Instead of the expected
walkover, the advancing British soldiers were scythed
down in their thousands by raking swirls of machine-gun
fire. The British army gained 3 square miles of ground but
sustained its highest-ever casualty toll for a single day's
fighting. An astounding 57,470 casualties were recorded,
among whom were 19,240 dead. In one morning almost
as many lives were lost as in the entire Boer War.

It was much quieter on the Armentières salient, and
on 2 July Harry had time to write to Margie before

heading back to the trenches. Even so, it was clear that things were beginning to hot up. Harry recorded relentless strafing by the Germans as he and his comrades headed for their 'old supports', as well as 'A great deal of bombing going on, also H.E. [high explosive] etc.' He also noted that there had been significant Allied casualties: 'The 16th Waikatos [a regiment within the Auckland Battalion] got a terrible dump last night, being bombed and buried in their bivys [bivouacs], a lot of casualties. I fear about 110.'

As July wore on the intensity of the fighting increased. Understandably, Harry clutched at any sign of normality – he even underlined the news of a postcard from '<u>dear Margie "to wish me well"</u>'. But he also noted increasingly heavy firing from the German lines. On 7 July there were 'Luckily no casualties, tho' the trenches got torn up badly.' Saturday 8 July was altogether tougher. As hard a day as any Harry had experienced since Gallipoli. 'The Huns started to give us a lot of shrapnel from 10.00 a.m. and so on to dinner time,' he wrote. 'We returned the compliment with H.E. after they had sent H.E. first.'

Much worse was to come:

The Huns straffed us by surprise starting at 9.15pm when we had just 'stood to'. It was absolute HELL for nearly 2 hrs. I came through all right, but am a fearful wreck. Joe Rankin seriously wounded in neck, old Mac pretty badly hit. Kelly, Hickey, Tyrell, Jack McLeod, Jim Smart, Sergt Smith and Wyllie, all more or less badly wounded. Patchett and 1 other in No 12 killed I think.

Capt Grey and Lieut Morrison both wounded and Sergt Major Thomson and Sergt Carrington both killed, burned by a 'Minnie' in their body. Altogether 27 casualties in 12th Nelson Coy. During the straffe the Huns raided 'The Mushroom' and practically wiped out the entire garrison, all buried by bombs etc. Standing at their post, a fearful mess I believe. Lieuts Connolly and Harman killed and 3 other officers wounded. We expected the Huns to come over anywhere after raiding the mushroom and were well prepared with bombs etc, but our guns threw over a magnificent curtain of fire into 'no man's land' and nothing more happened. A big lot of German dead outside our parapets in mushroom I hear, so they did not come off Scot-free. It was a terrifying experience and shook most of us up badly.

Such bodies as could be recovered were eventually buried at the Bonjean Military Cemetery at Armentières; 452 men who served with the New Zealand Expeditionary force lie there, with a further 47 whose bodies were never identified listed on a separate memorial. It's the largest national cemetery outside New Zealand.

The next day, a Sunday, Harry's diary entry comprises two sentences which, yet again, seem to sum up the madness of war. 'Received a letter from Mother and a box containing peppermint creams from Mary . . . Poor little Joe Rankin died of his wound, on 10th July RIP.'

The Germans kept up the pressure, with a gas attack (fortunately, thwarted by the wind) and another sustained artillery bombardment that began at 11.30 on the night of the 10th. 'It was a most awful experience while it lasted, as the Huns simply poured down H.E.'s on to us.' For once, Harry's usually phlegmatic outlook gave way to furious indignation as he went on to record what he felt to be the utter inadequacy of the Allied response. The weapons deployed responded 'feebly' in his view and were 'only a few 18 pounders at that!' 'It was pure and simple murder, as for every one 18 pounder fired the Hun sent back ½ doz H.E. and "minniewerfin". 11 Platoon's casualties were very severe. 3 killed (Gibson, Freddy Meares and Jack Gossiff). The 2 latter buried in their bivy during the 2nd straffe. Poor little chaps, game to the end!'

There was no sleep for anyone that night. 'The early hours were very trying as we did not know if the Huns would come over or not . . . I am nothing but a bundle of nerves and feel awful. Am on a day post now as well as night on a/c of there being no men scarcely to carry on.' In the midst of this appalling tension Alexander Aitken heard a flute playing in the German trenches, with 'unfamiliar airs, German folk-songs'. 'This was melting while it lasted,' he remembered, 'but with true German gallows-humour the unseen flautist, knowing that we must be listening, modulated into a travesty of the Dead March in Saul, bizarre and truly macabre. To me it seemed to say "For you tomorrow night, *Kameraden*!"'

On the 13th Harry was seeing the doctor at the dressing station for a debilitating cold when the New Zealanders mounted an attack, 'the 2nd Otago going over under cover of dark.' The terrible mauling they received caused

Harry to vent his sense of anger and frustration at the Allied high command for the second time in just three days. 'Heard that the row was another failure. Most of the men getting smacked up by shrapnel and machine gun fire before they could get into the Hun trenches.' '<u>When</u>,' he asked, 'will the Authorities take a hint that these raids are no use and only breaking the men's hearts!'

Alexander Aitken expressed his own indignant anger a touch more elegantly:

> . . . that so-called Christian Europe . . . should be offering up its young men to the Moloch [god] of war, while pacifist non-Christians of other continents – Hindus, Chinese, Muslims – must surely be looking on, perplexed at this urge to suicide. Did Christianity, not of saintly individuals but of nations and sects and denominations, contain an impulse to aggression?

As ever, though, standing beside Harry the soldier was Harry the romantic. '<u>Received a lovely long letter from Winnie White,</u>' he wrote. 'She has agreed to call me by my Christian name, was charmed with the little things I sent her from Egypt and thought me not at all a forward person!' Given Harry's clear love for Margie, this might appear to be a case of epistolary two-timing, were it not for the fact that all Winnie White had agreed to was to stop calling him Mr Palin. Their relationship was clearly an innocent one. In fact, it seems typical of Harry's encounters with women. He appreciated good looks and 'fitness', but in an almost abstract way. As with his father on his summer holidays, there seems to have been much looking but no touching. I can't help sensing that something held Harry back, perhaps his Victorian upbringing, perhaps a lack of sexual confidence (the atrophic testicle?), perhaps a tendency to idealise. Whatever the facts of the matter, I feel I should not question his motives as he faced another summer in the trenches – just be glad that Winnie White's letter meant so much to him. In any case, he decided the same day to write to Margie again (as well as to his sister Mary and Mrs White), and 'gave all three letters, hers, Mary's and Mrs W's, to Capt. Taylor to censor.' Harry and his comrades may not have been privy to what the Allied commanders were planning, but that didn't prevent their letters from being read by their officers, just in case they let slip some crucial military detail.

Next day, Harry expressed further fury at his superiors. 'Rumours that we are not being relieved from the trenches for another fortnight . . . It's a shame if it is true, as men are all more or less worn out with the continual straffing.' One can almost feel the stress and strain of shell shock pushing his anger up an octave. 'Curse Gen. Godley, he is only thinking of <u>himself</u> and <u>his</u> honours! <u>He</u> does not know what it is to sit through a bombardment on the firestep in the front line!!' The fire step was, of course, the most exposed position in a trench, which soldiers mounted in preparation for, or to repel, an attack. Harry would have known it only too well.

He went into Armentières next morning with the intention of finally seeing off his cold with a hot bath, 'but on arriving there found that there was nothing doing as it was a Sunday!' 'Had 1½ hours leave,' he went on, 'but had no money so could only go to the Y.M.C.A. and look at papers. A letter from Mary, with '2 others enclosed', proved a useful distraction. 'All Linton and Aston news,' he noted. Aston Crews is close to Linton and somewhere Harry would have known well from his childhood. Who could forget a village whose main thoroughfare is called Cut Throat Lane? In what appears to be a non sequitur he goes on to record that 'The Kohnstanns [*sic*] have lost their son Jack "killed in action". V. sorry.' The Kohnstamms were a prominent Jewish family living in Hampstead. Jacob, 'Jack', their eighteen-year-old son, served with the North Staffordshire Regiment. Jack's older brother, Norman, had seen action in Gallipoli and was to die in 1918. How Harry knew this tragic, talented family is something of a mystery.

On the 17th, alongside a letter from his mother, he received a box of chocolates from Margie but noted, underlining the words, that there was '<u>no letter</u>' to go with them. As so often, I'm left to tease out the possible significance of this. Was Margie backing off? Was her turning down of his proposal of marriage more final than I initially thought? The entries in his diary certainly seem to suggest that while he continued to send letters and cards to her, fewer came back the other way. I'm left to conclude that as the days passed in Armentières, Harry might have been thinking more of Margie than she of him. But I simply don't know.

He wasn't one to brood, though, filling his time with a visit to the baths first thing next morning, and then an expedition in search of his cousin, Harry Dampier-Crossley, in Nieppe, a village a couple of miles outside Armentières on the other side of the Lys River. There were baths here too, housed in a disused brewery and improvised from eight huge beer vats, each of which could hold twenty men at a time. Dampier-Crossley was with one of the DACs – the Divisional Ammunition Columns – whose job it was to haul heavy artillery equipment up to the front lines. They had dinner together: Harry, Harry and Dampier-Crossley's friend Hughie Kyle.

Next day my great-uncle was on fatigues at the Mushroom, where so much blood had been shed ten days earlier. 'Quiet up there,' he wrote, noting, almost as an afterthought, that a man on truck-pushing fatigue, doing exactly the same job as him, had been killed the night before. The tasks allotted to Harry proved heavy work: 'Had to carry an iron girder to no 1 location [where he lived and slept]'; 'Dug our possies [positions] under the fire steps in case of "straffes".' He wasn't the only one digging. On 24 July he described how 'In one of the bivys here you can easily hear someone (probably Fritz!) mining underneath, the noise of the pick is quite easily heard.' Mining had become an increasingly important element of warfare on the Western Front. Two huge mines named Lochnagar and Hawthorn were detonated at the start of the Battle of the Somme. These would be dwarfed a year later by the coordinated explosion of nineteen mines, releasing a force of 1 million pounds of ammonal explosive, at the Battle of Messines: it was the world's biggest man-made explosion before the atomic age.

Back in Armentières, some quieter nights followed, capped by one of Mrs Wright's specials, this one consisting of '2 tins salmon, 5 tins potted meat, some cigarettes (Egyptian) and some more almond toffee. She is being very kind to me.'

On the 29th he recorded, 'Rumours that we have got to stay on in trenches over Sunday, then going to the Somme to reinforce the Australians.' As usual with Harry, there is no editorialising here, no hint of apprehension. He would have had some inkling from the papers and from gossip passed up the line just what a transfer to the Somme would mean, but either the full extent of the disaster was still being successfully concealed, or he was exhibiting extraordinary sangfroid. I suspect it was more the former than the latter: further evidence that those fighting a war are the last to know exactly what or why. Perhaps if they did, they might start questioning whether they should be fighting at all.

As it was, he followed the news of a possible Somme posting with a positive entry: 'Glorious summer's day. Too good for the trenches.'

On the last day of July, after he had spent the morning firing 85 rounds and keeping the Huns 'busy replying', Harry at last received a promotion: 'Capt. Down informed me that I had got one stripe given me.' He was entirely unimpressed. 'I said I didn't particularly want it, but he said I must take it. So I suppose I must.' And that was that. Harry Palin was now a lance corporal. 'Very hot all day. Got leave to take our tunics off. On guard 2/30 to 4/30 pm.'

As I look through his notebook I wonder whether it was that night that Harry carefully crossed out 'Private' on the flyleaf and inserted 'L/Cpl'? Or did he remember to do so days later? I can detect no hint of celebration, just the amendment, in its most minimal form:

L/Cpl HWB Palin 6/319,
12th Nelson Coy.

What seemed to exercise him more that day was what he recorded as 'Official War News'. 'Rumania has joined the Allies. Lemberg has been taken by the Russians and 76000 prisoners. We put up a poster with the above news to show to the Huns in the "Mushroom".'

On 2 August came the wearily predictable retraction: 'The War news of yesterday was <u>not</u> correct after all. Something fishy about the thing.'

By 3 August the positives of promotion seemed to be sinking in. Having noted that he was 'looking after a fatigue party working up in no. 2 location', he reflected, 'It seems v. funny to me to be <u>looking after</u> and not actually <u>doing</u> the fatigue. Some advantages seem to be attached to a stripe.' Not a swelling of pride exactly, but an acknowledgement that he was certainly no worse off as a lance-jack.

Another apparent perk swiftly came his way. On Saturday the 5th he was told he'd been selected, along with ten others from the 1st Canterbury Infantry Battalion, to attend a course at grenade school. 'It will be a nice holiday from what I can hear,' he wrote. 'Short hours.' He duly reported to regimental headquarters the next morning where his spirits were further raised when he was issued 'a new rigout i.e. tunic trousers, putties and a hat'. 'Quite a swell now!' he mused proudly. Unfortunately, the course, at Pont de Nieppe, proved to be harder work than he had anticipated. No bathing in the beer vats; instead five days of intensive theoretical and practical training, during which he was expected to master not only the principle and nature of grenades, but the differences between the ones used by the Allies, and those deployed by the Germans: '3 hours in the morning and 3 in the afternoon. Had lessons in wiring, bombing squads and their various duties, bomb throwing etc.' Practical tests included bowling at marks in the open and from the trench. 'Interesting work,' noted Harry, 'but . . . we're not allowed to sit down at all so it's pretty tiring as we are all soft after 5 wks in the trenches.'

The idea of life in the trenches being 'soft' may seem odd at first, but, of course, what Harry means is that he and his fellow soldiers had been physically quite inactive over the previous weeks. They'd had fatigue duties to carry out, of course, but otherwise had been keeping their heads down and waiting, while the shrill and thump of whizz bangs and 'minnies' constantly jarred their nerves.

Ever the optimist, Harry wrote on Friday the 11th, 'Last day, tomorrow being tests in which I shall all pass – <u>I don't think</u>.' Possibly to his surprise, he was proved wrong, and was able to record with some pride the next day, 'I got through my tests all right, our examining Sergt a v. decent chap, gave plenty of time to a fellow.' As ever, army life was accompanied by a flurry of private correspondence. He wrote to his mother and Margie, and noted his intention to get in touch with the rest of his family. On the evening of his exam success, which he celebrated with a visit to the pictures, he documented the receipt of a clutch of letters from his female correspondents: '3 from N.Z. i.e. Winnie W, Ethel McRae and Kate D-C [Dampier-Crossley]'. He also received one from Margie, revealing that 'She's going for a fortnight's holiday to the North.' 'Dear girl,' he added. 'I hope she will have a good time and come back quite fit and well.'

Harry spent Sunday 13 August cleaning up and packing his gear for another move. The tone is resigned. 'Rumour hath it that in a day or so we go to Steenwerck marching, then take train to Dieppe or some coastal port (en route for ? perhaps Salonika or Egypt).' 'It will do me,' he concluded, 'anywhere.'

If there is such a thing as negative eloquence it comes across here. As ever with Harry it's the more powerful for being understated. There is no talk of home or of the war possibly being nearly over. Harry, like so many others who are being led into these bloody battles, is too tired to protest. The war still had two more years to run: for me, Harry's words of quiet resignation, rather than of patriotic fervour, explain how that could have been possible. 'It will do me, anywhere.'

Two days later, most of the support facilities had closed down but Harry and his companions had still not moved: 'We have to do all our own cooking today as we are shifting out tonight . . . Huns shelled the town and there were a good many casualties.'

Sergeant Malthus paints a picture of a very tired outfit that eventually left Armentières on the morning of 16 August for the 6-mile route march to the nearest station at Steenwerck. It seems to have been chaotic: 'After the long period of immobility in the trenches, with little sleep and under great strain, they were in extraordinarily poor form physically, and that morning's short march was their worst performance ever. Before it was even half over some were dropping out exhausted and could not be induced to continue. Luckily there was plenty of time for them to rejoin us before the train left.'

The train carried them 19 miles to Ebblinghem, just west of their old stamping ground at Hazebrouck. Then yet another route march, 5 miles this time, to Wardrecques in the Pas-de-Calais. Harry noted, undramatically, 'Quiet little village. V. tired and footsore on arrival.'

The days at Wardrecques offered a change of heart and a change of mood. 'Had a magnificent sleep last night,' Harry wrote on Thursday the 17th. 'Fine straw beds. Feet much better.' Infantry battalions took the state of the men's feet seriously, with trained chiropodists on hand to make sure that the troops were able to sustain these long route marches. It comes as no surprise, therefore, that Harry noted that alongside the usual rifle inspection, there was also a foot inspection. Events later that day do make me wonder, though, whether senior officers were at all sympathetic to the men's plight, as Harry recorded 'Standing for 2¼ hours in the afternoon for the Colonel to make an inspection then route marched for about 1½ miles before getting back to billet.'

The Nelsons clearly enjoyed their brief break from the war, billeted as they were in farm buildings in a peaceful country village. Malthus enthused that 'The countryside was a perfect picture, very closely settled with plenty of villages.' At the time, he recalled, 'harvest work was in full swing', although in the absence of any able-bodied men it had to be undertaken by the local women who struggled to bring in the crops before they rotted in the fields. 'Our assistance with the harvest was sorely needed, and would have been gladly given, but our command had other ideas.' Alexander Aitken was similarly taken with the country around Wardrecques. For him it had 'the undertones of history, for the quiet, tree-shaded roads and wooded parkland where our route marches took us had known the camps and campaigns of English soldiers in those French wars of four or five hundred years before'.

Route marches weren't the only reminder of wars past and present. The Nelsons also had to undergo bayonet practice and company and platoon drill ahead of an inspection by General Plumer (later Field Marshal Herbert Charles Onslow Plumer, 1st Viscount Plumer and Commander of the Second Army), one of the few First

World War generals to emerge from the conflict with his reputation enhanced. Harry, with his well-known aversion to pomp and circumstance, sounds as though he wasn't able to do the occasion justice: 'I am v. rough in drill,' he admitted ruefully, before perking up with the thought, 'but then everyone else is as bad.'

They finally left Wardrecques on Sunday 20 August and spent the day travelling by train to Calais, passing on the way a small town called Audruicq where Aitken noted 'portentous piles of duckboards, fifteen or twenty feet high, which, by their augury of a winter campaign, extinguished any hopes that the war would end in 1916'. From Calais, and a snatched glimpse of the Straits of Dover, the train continued along the coast to Boulogne and Abbeville near the mouth of the Somme. A mere hundred miles as the crow flies from the house in Tonbridge where his mother and sisters awaited his latest news.

'At Abbeyville [sic] where we got out,' Harry wrote, 'we found that the march was going to be 12 miles to billets! That was a great bit of news . . . We set sail at 10.30 p.m. It was a brute of a march and after about 5 miles my feet gave out and from then onwards was pure misery but I hung on. Scores fell out and camped on the road.'

They marched on into the night, hungry (they hadn't eaten since midday) and kept ignorant of where they were heading. 'The officers . . . kept on telling us it was "only a mile",' Malthus recalled, 'until the men received this announcement with ironical cheers and cat calls; then everyone sank into moody silence.' They finally arrived at their destination, a tiny village called Mérélessart, at four in the morning. And woe betide anyone who wanted to collapse at the end of it all. 'The Col gave <u>Hell</u> to everyone who fell out. Rather too much, I think,' was Harry's judgement. On arrival, he was made Acting Corporal of the Battalion Guard, 'Escorting prisoners etc.' His view was that it was a 'V fine place where HQR's [headquarters] are billeted at Chateau with a Countess and all.' Major Brereton's crisp depiction of Mérélessart was less complimentary. 'Their men were all away in the trenches and the women, children and cripples made a living weaving scrim on homemade looms.'

I have walked into Mérélessart myself. Not at four in the morning and not with a thousand exhausted soldiers for company. I strolled towards it through flat fields on a long, straight road. It is a small, plain village of red-brick houses with few facilities. The chateau is grand, but a bit run-down. I stood at its gates, just as Harry did when he was Acting Corporal of the Guard. He wasn't allowed into the house itself. And neither was I.

As there was little chance of his getting leave for a while, the family rallied round to make sure he was comfortable in his new quarters. Among other things, his brother Eddy sent him a letter with £2.00 enclosed, with which he was to buy a watch. Harry duly went into nearby Hallencourt, 'quite a nice town of fair shops', where he bought a watch for 30 francs (about £1 3s). He also changed two postal orders, buying socks with some of the proceeds. The day's events are captured in his diary in a brief display of stream of consciousness. 'Bought socks (1 pr), butter, bread, saw some rather pretty French girls . . . The watch did not go well at first, but will probably improve.'

Harry's optimism proved misplaced, and watch problems become something of a recurrent theme over the next few days. On Thursday the 24th, 'To Hallencourt in evening. Had to exchange watch as it would not go, and got one at frs 22, the balance being refunded.' The following day, 'My watch has gone amok on me again. Shall go and get my old one again tomorrow.' And finally, 'To Hallencourt in evening and got my old watch back, the damage was frs 3/50.'

When he wasn't struggling with poor-quality French time-keepers, he was busy rehearsing for the combat to come: 'Platoon drill in morning and route march in afternoon' (23rd). 'Drill and attacked a wood in morning. A route march in afternoon . . . My feet rather sore' (24th). 'Drill, gas helmet wearing, bayonet drill, bombing etc. in morning' (25th).

And when he was neither taking his watch back nor doing army drill he was writing to or thinking about women. On the 24th he 'Saw all the same pretty girls I saw last night.' On the 26th he 'Wrote letter to <u>Ethel McRae and Kate D-C</u>.' On Sunday the 27th he received a 'Weekly Mirror' and a letter from Nellie and walked into Wiry au Mont for a stroll where he 'Saw a young girl with a lame leg and one a good deal shorter than the other.' The next day he wrote to Margie in London and Winnie White back in Blenheim, and having walked again to Wiry, 'Had a yarn with the girl with the gammy leg. Rather a good sort.' On Tuesday his spirits rose on the receipt of 'a very nice letter from Margie now away on her holiday having a good time'. He was to write to her again, but that seems to have been the last time he heard from her. She was later to marry, to have a family, and to pursue a very full and active life. Margie Sale died in 1974 at the age of eighty-nine.

Over the next four days, they practised 'wood fighting' – that is, learning how to fight in the wooded terrain of the Somme. ('It was a difficult problem and most company commanders had only vague ideas of tackling it,' according to Major Brereton.) They were taught about creeping barrages, which were becoming such a feature of the Somme offensive. And they were also treated to a lecture with the exotic title of 'The Spirit of the Bayonet'. 'A mixture of realistic good sense and grim humour,' according to Malthus, it was delivered with theatrical panache by a huge red-headed major of the Gordon Highlanders who had apparently been awarded the DSO just for giving the talk.

It closed with a bloodthirsty imprecation: 'You will bayonet all you meet, dead or alive, wounded or shamming, and take no prisoners.' The Gordon Highlander did not say this purely for effect; he meant every word. As Major Brereton noted, 'At that time this teaching was general in France, as it was fully realised that our only hope of ending the war lay in killing Germans without scruple. The Somme battle was planned to that end, attacking always behind overwhelming artillery barrages, not so much to gain ground as to destroy men and so break down the spirit of their army.'

From Brereton's point of view, the stay in Mérélessart served two purposes. The first was to prepare the men as fully as possible for the practicalities, challenges and tactics of the slaughter to come. The second was to restore their physical condition with games (which Harry never refers to) and regular food and rest. He observed that the men 'called this process "fattening up for the killing"', though, he went on, 'they were not the least depressed by the idea'.

On 1 September Harry saw the 'young lame girl' one last time. 'She gave me "bon soir".' The next day they left Mérélessart, 'The inhabitants extremely sorrowful at our departure.' They marched east towards Amiens, arriving at their next billet at the village of La Chaussée-Tirancourt. It was near enough to the town of Picquigny for Harry and Charlie Downes, one of his platoon, to stroll there in the evening.

It was while they were at La Chaussée-Tirancourt that Harry learnt that 'Major Brereton has put me up for a commission.' When I read this, I felt a surge of pride for my great-uncle. At last, I thought, his abilities were being recognised. But that brief mention is all we have. Typically, Harry has nothing more to say on the subject beyond the statement, 'I had to give him particulars of my education etc.' There are no further references in his diary to the proposed accolade and all that it meant and would have entailed. Life carried on as usual with its drill and attack practices and pleasantries exchanged with local French girls.

On the evening of 6 September, having gone out 'to see the French girls, and spent a pleasant time', he learnt that 'We are leaving tomorrow worst luck.' The following day, after a 'v. sad parting with the girls', during which 'the little one gave me a charming kiss', Harry and his fellow Enzeds set off on a four-hour march to Coisy, a few miles north of Amiens. It proved to be a 'God-forsaken place' with 'awful billets', at least according to Harry. And that perhaps wasn't surprising. At the time, there was such pressure on the main roads to and from the Somme battlefield that troops were often deliberately sent round the houses to avoid them, and so ended up in villages like Coisy that were wholly unprepared to receive them, certainly in such large numbers.

In her book on the Battle of the Somme, Lyn Macdonald vividly describes the logistical challenges involved: 'The Pioneer troops,' she writes, 'were slaving night and day to keep the battered roads from disintegrating altogether under the strain of the constant trundling of wheels, the incessant tramping of feet, the pounding of shells that the enemy sent over in unremitting, nerve-racking salvoes.' She then goes on to give an indication of the sheer numbers of men and vehicles involved:

During the twenty-four hours when the Anzacs were moving into the line, census takers managed to count two thousand four hundred and twenty-three motor vehicles . . . Five thousand four hundred and four mounted officers and one thousand and forty-three men riding bicycles who stumbled or dodged as best they could through the long column of transport . . . The Control Post unfortunately did not manage to make a complete count of the infantry moving to and from the line. The nearest approximate figure . . . was twenty-six thousand five hundred and thirty-six.

Even in the midst of all the mayhem, Alexander Aitken, who had himself just received a commission, managed to find a moment of peace in the company of an aged Frenchman, the only man who seemed to be left in Coisy village. Standing beside each other in an apple orchard, 'We listened together to a sound like distant breakers on a coast, a steady and even rolling, except where here and there a larger explosion would surge up and seem to command a momentary silence.' The old man recalled the Franco-Prussian War of 1870–71. 'So it had been then, and now it had come again, but worse.'

Next day the Enzeds left Coisy at 9.30 in the morning for an encampment about a mile and a half from the town of Albert. It was another long march – six hours in all. And it took its toll on Harry. 'Had to get my feet dressed by medical Coy,' he recorded at the end of it all. By now they were very close to the front line where the fiercest fighting of the Somme campaign was taking place. Sergeant Malthus experienced a sudden, oppressive fear of what lay ahead. 'I found myself face to face with the fact I had been dodging for days: I was horribly, abjectly, afraid of the coming push . . . What I felt was by no means the certainty of death, but the fear of overwhelming, intolerable, long-continued pain.'

What did Harry feel? Knowing him, as I don't, I'd say he reckoned he was on the right side of the statistics.

He could take heart from being one of that tiny number who had survived Gallipoli without a scratch. Here in France, he would know that for every chance of being killed in the fighting, there were two of getting through unharmed, and that even if wounded, the chances were that the injury would not prove life-threatening. Many soldiers talked longingly about their hopes of 'getting a blighty' – in other words, of being injured sufficiently seriously to be repatriated to 'Blighty' (Indian army slang for England or Britain).

Meanwhile, he marched on, as did Malthus and all those thousands of others drawn inexorably into the stream of traffic that flowed towards the battle. The highway from Amiens to Albert, according to Malthus's graphic account, resounded to the 'thunder of wheels and of horses' hooves, the shouting and cursing of the drivers . . . against the background of the ominous sound of the endless bombardment.' This, he said, in an echo of Aitken's poetic imagery, 'swelled a little at times, like the rolling roar of a great sea'. Or as Harry described it all, 'Guns sounding v. loud. Saw a lot of Hun prisoners along the road. Pretty tired but feet no worse. Had a good bathe in a river nearby.'

On 8 September they were moved again, this time to a camp near Fricourt, where they were to spend three days. From their position they looked down on the remains of Fricourt village and beyond it the woods that were being so fiercely fought over – Mametz, High Wood and Delville Wood, rechristened Devil's Wood by those who fought there. Harry was born and brought up in the countryside. He knew every inch of the woods around Linton and would have thought of them as special places of peace, quiet and boyhood adventure. The tall trees swinging and creaking, protecting him with their splayed boughs and thick, indestructible trunks. Magical places. The woods of the Somme which lay ahead were hellish, brutalised places, stripped bare and devastated by men intent on killing each other. A metaphor for the horrendous arc of Harry's life, from protection to pulverisation.

When I walked the Somme battlefield in the steps of the New Zealanders I paused for a while on one side of a shallow decline, and looked across at Mametz Wood, nearly a hundred and seven years after Harry and his fellow infantrymen made camp nearby. It looks innocent enough. A gentle green slope climbs innocuously up towards it. Trees rise, tall, bushy, calm in the unmoving air. Birds fly in and out. It's an oasis of perfect peace. But even today it's impossible not to be reminded of what happened here over a century ago: on a hill just behind, a fierce red dragon rears up from a plinth commemorating the men of the 38th Welsh Division who took this wood after a ferocious battle in which 4,000 men were killed or injured. When the poet Siegfried Sassoon approached Mametz in 1916 he saw it 'looming on the opposite slope, a dense wood of old trees and undergrowth, a menacing wall of doom'. When Harry slept there two months later, the limes, oaks and hornbeams had been reduced to a carpet of shattered stumps. The smell of death clung to what was left of the undergrowth. And as he lay down for the night he would have known full well that although the Germans might have been forced out of Mametz Wood, they were camped out in deep trenches, in other woods nearby, waiting to fight back.

Harry would have known this to be the case, but not brooded about it. Indeed, I suspect he would have looked at me pityingly if he'd read what his great-nephew had just written. On Saturday 9 September, while in the heart of the wood, Harry found room for one last entry in his densely packed, hand-sized purple-covered notebook: 'Had to sleep out in the open and was rather cold as there was a heavy dew and mist in morning.' Typical Harry. Matter-of-fact, practical, with neither judgement nor speculation. Just another day. 'Some parades in morning and afternoon inspections and such like.'

The 'afternoon inspections' would have involved checking that each man's kit was in a state of readiness for action. Harry would have moved up into battle with rifle and bayonet, waterproof sheet, mess tin, bundle of sandbags, pick or shovel, iron ration, shirt and socks, soap, water-bottle (well filled), gas mask, field dressing, shaving gear, 200 rounds of ammunition and two Mills bombs (more if he wanted). He had to leave his completed diary behind, but he had invested in a new one for when the battle was over. It was an altogether stouter affair than the one he'd squeezed his experiences into before. Strong blue cardboard covers, inside one of which he listed the names of the members of 11 Platoon 9 Section: 'L/Cpl Palin, Pvts Woodham, Simpson A., Clough, Roberts H, L/Cpl McIsaacs S., Pvts Proudlock,

Downes and Pacey.' Against the names of Downes and
Pacey he wrote 'sick'.

The page opposite is neatly inscribed:

Lance Corporal HWB Palin
6/319 12th Nelson Coy.
1st Cant. Infty. Batt
New Zealand E.F.
France
Sept 10th 1916

Home address:

'St. Helen's'
Tonbridge, Kent
England

Almost every other page is blank.

*A barrier across a sunken road at Morval on the day of its capture,
25 September 1916.*

15

THE LAST MAN

———◦———

ON MONDAY 11 SEPTEMBER, Harry Dampier-Crossley, with eight horse teams from the Divisional Ammunition Column, was delivering gun emplacement materials ahead of the upcoming offensive. Like Harry, he kept a diary and in it he noted that he looked out for his cousin among the troops moving up into the front line. 'Couldn't see Harry Palin,' he wrote; 'he was away on fatigue in the trenches.' He spoke to some others he knew – Garry Upton and J. Tonkin, with whom he had 'a long yarn'. They showed him their proposed line of attack. 'They knew what they were up against and would be lucky if they came out.'

Harry Dampier-Crossley's information about his cousin was accurate. Lance-Corporal Palin's morning was taken up with 'Physical, bayonet fighting, gas helmet, platoon drill', followed in the afternoon by 'section drill, short lecture and platoon drill' ('Awful rot,' he wrote, presumably in reference to the lecture). He was, however, able to take some time off to inspect some of the German trenches taken on 1 July. 'Marvellous sight,' he wrote, 'and huge dugouts some 50 feet deep or more.'

On the 12th Harry Dampier-Crossley was 'Out with teams all day. Carting to batteries in Death Valley.' This was one of a trinity of valleys that branched off from Mametz Wood, the others being known as Happy Valley and Caterpillar Valley. The New Zealanders would have passed through all three of them on their way to their front-line trenches. 'In the evening Harry Palin came down to our camp to see me. Looking very fit and well. Gave him a pair of sox as he was short.' (Harry, feet squeezed painfully by weeks of route marches, could never have enough socks.) For his part, Lance-Corporal Palin made no mention in his diary of meeting his cousin, noting merely: 'Parade same as yesterday, same times. Managed to miss fatigue after all – Received 3 letters.'

Next day Dampier-Crossley was busy all day 'carting ammunition for the big push'. After tea, with his friend Hugh, he 'walked up the hill to see and say goodbye to our boys who go into the trenches. Saw Harry Palin, Garry Upton and Jack Tonkin.'

All of them for the last time.

Harry, who may possibly have mentioned to his cousin his sighting that day of his first tanks ('Extraordinary machines'), now moved, with the rest of the 1st Battalion, nearer to the German lines, from Fricourt and Mametz Wood up towards High Wood and Longueval. The Germans had begun a heavy bombardment, and, as Harry Dampier-Crossley put it, 'Things were very lively.'

'We were quite close to a wagon when an 8 inch landed almost on it,' he went on. 'Men, horses and wagon went flying. There wasn't much left of any of them.'

The following day – Thursday 14 September – my great-uncle made his final diary entry. It was, as ever, matter of fact: 'Very cold wind blowing almost wintry. Pretty cold after being wet thro' last night. Got off the morning parade.'

Harry Palin and the rest of the 1st Battalion were in reserve when, at 6.20 on the morning of 15 September, the 2nd New Zealand Infantry Battalion 'hopped the bags' and headed for the German lines, just over 400 yards away. Accompanied, for the first time in war, by tanks. It was, by the standards of earlier Somme offensives, a success, with ground gained and many German prisoners taken. 'Reported 5000 captured the first day,' wrote Harry Dampier-Crossley. 'Poor chaps ripped and torn in all directions.' But it was at the expense of many New Zealand lives. 'Our casualties are big. 50% or more.' Official figures put Allied losses at 1,200 wounded and 670 dead or dying.

The arena in which Harry found himself is so tranquil now that as I passed along quiet roads, over gentle hills and through sparsely populated villages, it took a real effort of the imagination to conjure up the inferno that it had once witnessed. I recalled the description by Corporal Cecil Howden, a Gallipoli veteran, of the vast encampment that then stretched over the countryside.

It reminded him, he wrote, of Lemnos days, but was on a much greater scale. 'Here there are tens of thousands of horses and mules, also thousands of great motor-wagons, and all working at top speed. Railways and trolley lines go everywhere too. Balloons are up – something like a score at present, and aeroplanes are dodging in and out among the clouds by the dozen . . . flashes from guns and shells are constant too, and star-shells are always rising and falling up at the line.'

It was now time for Harry and the rest of the 1st Canterbury Battalion to move into the front line. They were ordered forward to Grove Alley, from which they would mount an assault on the German-held Goose Alley. Malthus later described what Harry and the others experienced: 'The enemy had been fully alerted, and the moment we appeared over the ridge every gun was on us . . . 9 and 11 Platoons [11 was Harry's] sprinted for it and got through tolerably well, though their losses were heavy enough. But 10 and 12 met the full weight of a terrible bombardment, plus a sizzling stream of machine-gun fire.' Orders were then given to call off the attack and return to Grove Alley. For the next few days the men were kept in line in muddy trenches with little protection against the freezing cold. 'We became unspeakably weary, dreary and sick of it all,' wrote Malthus.

Cecil Malthus and Harry had come a long way together since signing up in the Drill Hall in Nelson two years earlier. Now there was a parting of the ways as Sergeant Malthus, busy digging and sandbagging in one of the trenches, hit a half-buried bomb that blew off part

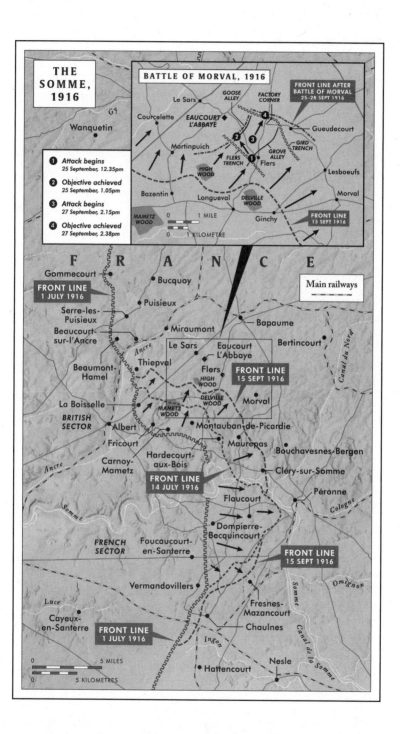

THE SOMME, 1916

BATTLE OF MORVAL, 1916

FRONT LINE AFTER BATTLE OF MORVAL 25-28 SEPT 1916

1 *Attack begins* 25 September, 12.35pm

2 *Objective achieved* 25 September, 1.05pm

3 *Attack begins* 27 September, 2.15pm

4 *Objective achieved* 27 September, 2.38pm

Le Sars
GOOSE ALLEY
FACTORY CORNER
Courcelette
EAUCOURT L'ABBAYE
Gueudecourt
Martinpuich
GIRD TRENCH
FLERS TRENCH
GROVE ALLEY
2 **3**
1
Flers
HIGH WOOD
Lesboeufs
Bazentin
Longueval
DELVILLE WOOD
Morval
MAMETZ WOOD
0   1 MILE
0   1 KILOMETRE
Ginchy
FRONT LINE 15 SEPT 1916

F R A N C E

Gommecourt
FRONT LINE 1 JULY 1916
Bucquoy

Puisieux

Serre-les-Puisieux
Miraumont
Bapaume
Beaucourt-sur-l'Ancre
Ancre
Le Sars
Bertincourt
Eaucourt L'Abbaye
Canal du Nord
Main railways

Beaumont-Hamel
Thiepval
Flers
HIGH WOOD
FRONT LINE 15 SEPT 1916

La Boissolle
MAMETZ WOOD
DELVILLE WOOD
Morval

BRITISH SECTOR
Albert
Montauban-de-Picardie

Fricourt
Maurepas
Bouchavesnes-Bergen

Carnoy-Mametz
Hardecourt-aux-Bois
Cléry-sur-Somme

Ancre
FRONT LINE 14 JULY 1916
Péronne

Somme
Flaucourt
Cologne

FRENCH SECTOR
Foucaucourt-en-Santerre
Dompierre-Becquincourt
FRONT LINE 15 SEPT 1916

Luce
Vermandovillers
Somme
Omignon

Cayeux-en-Santerre
Fresnes-Mazancourt
FRONT LINE 1 JULY 1916
Chaulnes
Canal de la Somme

0   5 MILES
0   5 KILOMETRES
Ingon
Hattencourt
Nesle

of his right foot. The stretcher bearers moved quickly to get him back behind the lines. He had sustained an injury that wasn't life threatening but that was definitely 'a blighty'. He took no further part in the war.

The following morning Harry and the rest of the Nelsons prepared for the next push, intended to advance on – and, hopefully, capture – the strongly held German line known as Gird Trench. In the official history this action, which took place between 25 and 28 September, is called the Battle of Morval. The New Zealand Division was tasked with securing the right flank and opening up a line from Goose Alley to Factory Corner. While they waited a cricket match was organised by the New Zealand troops in reserve. Alexander Aitken later recalled that the night before the attack one of the officers suggested they have a sing-song. 'We sang, a little self-consciously at first; songs already beginning to be rather out of fashion, from the *Scottish Students' Songbook* . . . "Riding Down to Bangor", "In a Cavern, in a Canyon" and others like these, and for a close "Vive l'amour, vive la compagnie".' 'We saw no irony then in these words,' he went on; 'we might have, could we have foreseen that at the same hour three nights later almost all the singers would be lying dead or wounded in no-man's-land.'

The attack was launched at 12.35 p.m. on Monday 25 September, with the troops moving forward behind a creeping barrage of covering fire. The massed lines of infantry easily overran the enemy positions and pushed the Germans out of Goose Alley within twenty-three minutes. By 1.05, according to the history of the

Canterbury Regiment, 'the battalion had captured all its objectives, with only slight casualties'. This first day of the battle was regarded as a great success. Two of the three objectives, Lesboeufs and Morval, were taken, leaving only Guedecourt to be captured. It fell the next day to dismounted cavalry.

That night Alexander Aitken was on duty after midnight. 'The sky had cleared and was now of great beauty.' Somewhere in the middle of all this Lance Corporal Palin must have felt that he had ridden his luck once again.

The following two days were spent consolidating the new front line. On the evening of the 26th word came from headquarters that a new objective had been identified, to be captured during the afternoon of the 27th. It was Gird Trench itself. Strongly fortified, the German defences consisted of two parallel trenches, Gird Trench and the connecting Gird Support Trench. They lay on the other side of a crossroads, known – because of the beet factory that stood there – as Factory Corner. Andrew Macdonald, in his book *On My Way to the Somme*, described the ground leading up to the trench as 'a carefully constructed killing zone, one laced with barbed-wire entanglements and bristling with cleverly-sited machine-gun posts'. The Gird trenches were defended by freshly deployed soldiers of the Bavarian Reserve Regiments who had relieved other units of their formation during the night.

On the morning of Wednesday 27 September the attacking troops – 1st Canterburys on the right, 1st Aucklanders in the centre and 1st Otago on the left – were moved into position before daylight, in order to avoid detection, though zero hour was not set until 2.15 in the afternoon. It must have been agonising to be battle-ready, but to be held for so long. Private Howard Kippen-berger looked along the line of men of which Harry was one. 'They were a wretched looking lot,' he thought, worn down by days on the offensive, 'mostly too tired and sleepy to talk.'

At three minutes past zero hour watches were syn-chronised. The creeping barrage burst over no man's land and the start of the assault was signalled. The bat-talion moved forward with Harry and the 12th Nelsons in the first wave. Eight minutes had been allowed for them to cross the 1,000 yards to the German trenches. Alex-ander Aitken, running like hell, describes what this felt like. 'In an attack such as this, under deadly fire, one is as powerless as a man gripping strongly charged electrodes, powerless to do anything but go mechanically on . . . all normal emotion is numbed utterly.'

The official history again: 'The attacking company was held up for a short while by bombers and machine guns, but the latter were silenced by our Lewis Gunners, and all the objectives of the battalion were captured by 2.38 p.m., with slight casualties.' Among the 'slight casualties' was Alexander Aitken who was hit twice only a few yards after crossing the road. He remembered looking to one side and seeing thirty of the men in his platoon crumple and fall, only two going on. He took shelter in a shell-hole, blood oozing from his ankle, as bullets whizzed above him. He eventually managed to crawl back to his lines, under cover of nightfall. That was the end of Aitken's war.

Another of the 'slight casualties' was Great-Uncle Harry.

When I revisited the Somme to retrace his footsteps, the one place I wanted to see more than any other was the 1,000-yard stretch of French farmland across which he raced towards Gird Trench that September afternoon. I found it, quite easily. There is a useful landmark: an isolated house at the junction where the beet factory used to stand. On one side, a facade of cream walls and green shutters, with a row of dormer windows, faces onto the road. The other side of the house, looking out onto the slope up which Harry would have charged, is almost concealed behind thick, dark ivy. As I passed I noticed cars in the yard. To my surprise they had British number plates, but I could see no one about. Behind me, the road from Longueval to Bapaume was quiet as I started to walk up towards the top of the rise, in the direction of Gird Trench. To follow the assault line accurately I had to step across a shallow ditch and into a field green with the shoots of winter wheat. Aware that I was treading on sprouting crops I looked guiltily around me, but there was no one watching. After a few more steps I suddenly felt the full weight of where I was and what I was doing. Somewhere in this anonymous field, beneath my increasingly muddy boots, was the shell-hole in which Great-Uncle Harry took cover and from which he never emerged. The sun had come out, a breeze had got up and skylarks were wheeling above. I'd reached the end of his story and the end of my search.

I still vividly recall the moment I first saw the official form that now resides in the New Zealand Military

Archive. Serial no 3a, titled History-Sheet, it logs the precise moment of death of 'L/Cpl Palin, Farmhand'. Under the heading 'Message and Remarks' is written in red ink and a spidery hand, the testimony of the 'man of few words' and 'a beautiful slow smile' who had shared a cabin with Cecil Malthus and who accompanied Harry on his last visit home in May 1916.

6/242 Sgt Gridley states on 27th Sept L/cpl Palin & myself were in the same shell-hole just before the taking of Gird Trench. Palin was just getting up to fire when he was shot through the head. I was next to him and I'm sure he was killed outright.

I like to think of Sergeant Gridley and Lance Corporal Palin side by side in that last afternoon of Harry's life, maybe sharing family news as they waited for the final attack. And I take some comfort from the thought that Harry died in the arms of someone who knew the names of his mother and brother and sisters and girlfriends.

The report concludes:

Finding: Killed by a bullet on 27th September 1916.

I'm aware that the official record may conceal an even more distressing truth. If on that September afternoon near Factory Corner Harry had indeed died of a single bullet through the head, at the end of a successful assault when there were only 'slight casualties', one might assume that his body would have remained intact and accessible and that Sgt Gridley would have had time to lay him down, note where he'd fallen and pass the information on to the medical orderlies so that the corpse could be retrieved for proper burial. And yet, no identifiable trace of Harry has ever been found.

The Bavarians who were defending Gird Trench were not, by all accounts, trained snipers. They were fighting back with machine guns, bombs and grenades. They weren't seeking to eliminate individual soldiers with surgical precision. They were looking to wipe out swathes of them with heavy weapons. The question I'm left pondering, therefore, is whether Harry's death was as surgically clean as Albert Gridley claimed.

I have read that when bodies had been blown apart it was customary to spare the feelings of the family by describing their deaths in palatable euphemisms: 'Died in action.' 'Killed instantly.' The single-bullet account made Harry's death seem uncomplicated, instantaneous and heroic. The supreme sacrifice. But what Sergeant Gridley described so precisely was never backed up by any corroborating evidence. It took forty-eight hours for the battlefield to be cleared. And Harry was described as 'Missing in Action' for almost a month.

The only conclusion I can draw is that either Harry Palin died from a single bullet wound and was buried where he fell, or that he was obliterated.

A mile or so from where Harry was killed, near the village of Longueval, is the Caterpillar Valley Cemetery.

Neat rows of identically proportioned headstones stretch away in perfect formation, white as snowdrops against the trimmed green lawns around them. On each head-stone is either the name of the soldier buried there or, if the body could not be identified, a plain stone with the inscription devised by Rudyard Kipling, 'A Soldier of the Great War, Known unto God'.

If there was no body to recover, if the remains of the loved one had disappeared into the mud, his name would be inscribed on a Wall of Remembrance as being among those 'Whose Graves Are Known Only to God'. In the Somme offensive, 1,272 men, 60 per cent of all New Zea-landers killed, are memorialised in this way. Fathers, Uncles, Brothers, Lovers. Lost without trace.

And there, on the Wall of Remembrance at Caterpil-lar Valley Cemetery, between 'Morrison J.' and 'Scrim-shaw R.A.' is 'Palin H.W.B.'

At the time of Harry's death, Harry Dampier-Crossley's diary paints a portrait of a beaten and demor-alised enemy. 'The German machine gunners have been found chained to their guns. Their front trenches practic-ally empty when our men went over. Our casualties are very light as far as we know yet.' Even the weather had turned fine and warm after weeks of rain.

But a much less rosy picture was painted by Rifleman Sidney Gully, who described some of his fellow soldiers returning from the Battle of Morval as 'half demented during the last couple of days. Unshaven, unwashed, covered in mud and lastly but not least almost devoid of energy and only half-fed.'

What's pretty sure is that when Harry's luck finally ran out, it was all over instantly. No time to prepare, no time to settle scores or hold a hand. No time for anyone to mourn, and no body to mourn over. That was it. Time's up.

He was no longer around to enjoy any more of Mrs Wright's jam, or read Mary's chatty letters or try on the umpteenth pair of socks his mother had sent him. Nor was he there to see the message from his commander-in-chief to the government back home: 'The New Zealand Division has fought with greatest gallantry in the Somme Battle for twenty-three consecutive days, carrying out with complete success every task set, and always doing more than was asked of it. The Division has won universal confidence and admiration. No praise can be too high for these troops.'

Almost a week later, on Tuesday 3 October, Harry Dampier-Crossley was shifting unused ammunition back to the dump at Montauban. The first news of recent casualties was coming in as the men of the 1st Canterbury Battalion made their way back from the front lines. 'Heard that poor old Garry Upton was killed in the first advance, also Lieutenant Tonkin,' he wrote. Of the fourth member of that group that had gone for tea and a walk before the battle began there was no sign. On 6 October he reported, 'Carting 18 pounder shrapnel. 3 loads to Montauban Dump.' 'Could find out nothing about Harry Palin at all,' he went on.

It was nearly two months before his cousin finally found out what had happened.

Wednesday 15 November: 'Fine, cold wind, frost. Heard yesterday that Harry Palin was killed on the Somme. The last man to be killed, just as the company was coming out. Then was told again that he was missing, which is much the same as being reported as killed.' Nobody seemed to be sure. After all, Lance Corporal Palin was a very small fry in a very big war.

A week or so after Harry was killed the New Zealand Division were pulled out of the Battle of the Somme.

When his family first heard of Harry's death, and what they were told about it, is not recorded.

Photos, diaries, a medal and a few personal posses-sions were sent to his mother in Tonbridge. She was still grieving for her son when news came through that her daughter Edith's husband, Geoffrey Ashmore, had been drowned when HMT *Transylvania* was sunk by German torpedoes on 4 May 1917.

Nor did the death and destruction cease when the guns fell silent. Scarcely had the war ended in November 1918 than the first of four waves of a deadly influenza pandemic began. Spanish flu, as it was called, ran ram-pant, infecting a third of the world's population and kill-ing many millions of people.

The hopes and promises with which Edward and Brita had embarked on life together and which were personi-fied in the loving family they had created around them at Linton lay shattered. Their world had gone for ever.

On Wednesday 30 July 1919, those in Linton scan-ning their *Hereford Times* would have read an account of another family death – of Brita Palin, née Gallagher, at her home in Tonbridge, at the age of seventy-five. The report concluded, 'It is believed that the sad bereavements her family suffered during the terrible war may have hastened her end.' Brita's body was brought to Linton for interment and was buried in the churchyard following a service led by her son-in-law Paul Jerome Kirkby, rector of Saham Toney in Norfolk and Eleanor's husband. On her gravestone Harry is remembered with this inscription:

Henry William Bourne Palin
Killed in action on the Somme 27 Sept 1916 aged 31
years *Pro Patria*

It seems to say everything about Harry that they got his age wrong. He had been thirty-two for nine days when he was killed.

After the war, the mess and the mud, the miserable circumstances of Harry's death were tidied into fine words. A heavy bronze memorial plaque was sent to his brother Eddy from the New Zealand Government 'in respect of the above named deceased soldier . . . I sincerely trust that this will be of some little consolation to you in the sad loss which you have sustained.' It was dated 10 January 1924. Just under seven and a half years after Harry vanished.

For its part, the British government included his name on a scroll of remembrance, even though they couldn't actually remember him. It came with the stirring words:

He whom this scroll commemorates was numbered among those who, at the call of King and Country, left all that was dear to them, endured hardness, faced danger, and finally passed out of the sight of men by the path of duty and self-sacrifice, giving up their own lives that others might live in freedom. Let those who come after see to it that his name may be not forgotten.

This could be a fitting epitaph to Henry William Bourne Palin, 6/319, but not to Harry Palin, a far more complex mix of faults and flaws and talents and virtues. He would, I'm pretty sure, have had no time for the patriotic cliché. He wouldn't want to have been summed up. Harry was a work in progress, still searching for lasting happiness when he died.

He was a drifter; a free, if not always totally happy, spirit, living from moment to moment, refusing to be typecast. He didn't care for fame or fortune. He was permanently short of money. On his death his estate was valued at £78 7s and 6d.

Great-Uncle Harry became one of the many thousands known as the 'Missing of the Somme'. Yes, I would like him to have been a war hero, to have won a VC and stayed alive to march past the Cenotaph in his fifties honouring his fallen comrades. At the very least I would like him to lie in a grave with his name on the headstone.

And I would like him to have been as admired as his father and his brother.

But he was just another human being at a time when men far more distinguished than himself decided that there were things worth killing each other for.

His life seems a distant era away, and yet if Harry had survived his last battle, he would have been fifty-eight when I was born. If he'd lived to the age I am now he could have been at my twenty-first birthday party.

He and I are not that far apart.

The official record of the death of Harry Palin, killed in action on 27 September 1916.

THE HUNT FOR HARRY

My primary materials for this book came, most suitably, from Harry Palin's niece, Joyce Ashmore. She was the eldest child of Edith Palin, and it is at her mother's wedding to Geoffrey Ashmore in 1901 that we see Harry in a photograph for the first time.

Without Joyce's appreciation, collection and protection of the family records, and her decision to pass them down to my father and myself, this story might never have been told.

I have to credit my own curiosity for the next move. I had seen the potential for a film based on Edward and Brita's love story and teamed up with Tristram Powell (who had directed my seaside holiday film *East of Ipswich*) to make *American Friends*, which was released in 1991, with me playing Edward, Trini Alvarado as Brita and Connie Booth as Caroline Watson. The film prompted a response from the then vicar of St Mary's, Linton, the Revd Allan Ricketts, in the form of two very well-researched booklets about the family, which he called *The Palin Assignment*. A wealth of further local detail was gathered by the very active members of the Linton and District History Society. Roger Davies was my linkman here and I owe him an enormous debt for so thoroughly scouring parish records, censuses, birth and death records and local papers to create a framework of the Palin family's lives.

In 2015, the History Society organised a comprehensive exhibition at St Mary's to mark the 150th anniversary of Edward Palin's induction as vicar. I went down to Linton and gave a talk about my family, clutching the pulpit on which my great-grandfather's arms had so often rested. Later, as research for the book gathered pace, I was lucky enough to spend two wonderful days at the vicarage that Edward and Brita built, and which is now occupied, and scrupulously looked after, by the Hodgson family. Enquiries at Edward's college at Oxford, St John's, also produced some gold dust: the earliest photograph I have of Edward Palin, unearthed by the college archivist Michael Riordan.

My early research efforts had very much focused on Edward and Brita's story. But in 2008, while preparing a film for the BBC's *Timewatch* documentary series called *The Last Day of World War One*, I was shown the name of H. W. B. Palin on a memorial wall at Longueval, one of the great battlefields of the Somme, and the fascination with Harry I first felt when Joyce showed me the photograph of him in uniform was reawakened. Appreciating my interest, the battlefield historian Paul Reed, who accompanied me while we were filming, later took me on my first visit to Factory Corner and to the spot nearby where Great-Uncle Harry was killed.

I became ever more determined to track down the least conventional, and least documented, of all Edward and Brita's children. Fortunately, there were sufficient clues in Joyce Ashmore's material to allow me to make progress on various fronts. For example, a mention of Harry spending some time in India working on the railway and for a tea plantation led me, via genealogist Emma Jolly, to the Glasgow-based owners of the Finlay's tea plantations, and to their archive in which were held reports on their employees going back over a hundred years – one of whom was H. W. B. Palin. These reports not only fleshed out the character of my great-uncle but gave a rare insight into how he was seen by others. Not always flatteringly.

The other great treasure that Joyce Ashmore passed on was the clutch of slim notebooks, written in densely packed pencil, that contain a day-by-day account of Harry's war experiences. From these I learnt that during the conflict he had fought at Gallipoli and the Somme, not with the British, but with the New Zealand Army. That inevitably invited the question as to what he was doing in New Zealand in the first place, and whether he went alone. Fortunately, there was a clue, in the form of the regular mention in the notebooks of his best friend at the time, George Batters. Paul Bird of my company Mayday followed up on this, and was able not only to confirm that Batters and Harry worked at the same farm, but to track down George's nephew, who shared family stories and some priceless photos of Harry and his friend, off duty and letting their hair down in Egypt. Meanwhile a friend in New Zealand, Rosie Belton, discovered names, addresses and photos that provided me with a visual and verbal portrait of the Wilderness Farm where Harry and George worked, and of Ted Healy who owned it.

When it came to Harry's war service I was helped both by his notebooks and by the military's endless love of bureaucracy. We may find form-filling an irritant, but to those interested in the past it is invaluable. It was from Harry's army records that I gathered priceless nuggets of information that ranged from what he looked like to how he died.

A stroke of further good fortune followed on from a chance connection with an eminent New Zealander obsessed with improving our understanding of the First World War. I had first met Sir Peter Jackson in Wellington back in the late 1990s when he had asked whether I'd like a part in a film he was planning. I was too busy travelling at the time, which is why you won't see me in *The Lord of the Rings*, but years later I was bowled over by the technical skills he used to transform our perception of life on the Western Front in his film *They Shall Not Grow Old*. I decided to get back in touch with him to tell him of my interest in Harry Palin's career with the New Zealand Army.

The floodgates opened. Peter sent me stacks of information, a massive tranche of books, and an invitation to tour Gallipoli together. Most excitingly of all he had a huge selection of First World War photographs. A new portable Kodak camera had come out in 1915. It was affordable and easy to use and, though not permitted on the battlefield, allowed the men to take informal photos of each other, so breaking the stranglehold of official war photographers. Using as his guide the one clear and very valuable portrait of Harry in uniform that had been given to me by Joyce Ashmore, Peter was able to go through his vast photo library and pinpoint images that almost certainly show Harry in Gallipoli.

Other snippets of information came from a variety of different sources. The archives at Harry's old school, which was mine too, yielded a little more of his story, and also offered a valuable explanation for the death of his brother Richard. Margie Sale, Harry's true love, emerged from the shadows thanks to some assiduous sleuthing that revealed that she had married after his death and that enabled contact to be made with her grandchildren. They provided a photo and a pen portrait of her, both of which immeasurably enriched her presence in the story.

Inevitably, some enquiries led nowhere. I still don't know for sure why Harry ended up on Ted Healy's farm in New Zealand. I don't know who his friends were when he worked in India. I don't know how he became acquainted with the Kohnstamms.

Ultimately, I felt I had to call a halt and go ahead without uncovering every single detail. But one thing I've learnt in this whole detective process is that the past is never as locked as it seems. There is always information hidden away somewhere, and none of it is insignificant. This book is not the end of a story, but part of the constantly evolving process of finding out more about how we live and how we die. And in Harry's case, giving those who've disappeared a voice, and a story to tell.

TIMELINE

1825	(21 September) Birth of Edward Palin
1843/4	Birth of Brita Gallagher
1864	Death of Edward's father, Richard Palin
1867	(2 October) Marriage of Edward and Brita
1884	(19 September) Birth of Harry Palin
1899–1901	Harry attends Shrewsbury School
1901	Edith's wedding
1903	(November) Death of Edward Palin
1905	Harry arrives in India as a Traffic Probationer, Great Indian Railway Company
1908	(November) Having resigned from his job on the railways, Harry starts work at the Teok Tea Estate, Assam
1911	Harry leaves India and arrives back in England
1912	(May) Harry emigrates to New Zealand and takes up a job on Ted Healy's farm in Canvastown
1914	(4 August) Britain (in alliance with Russia and France) declares war on Germany and Austro-Hungary
	(14 August) Harry enlists with the 12th Nelson Company of the Canterbury Infantry Battalion

(5 November) Britain and France declare war on
the Ottoman Empire

(2 December) Harry and the 12th Nelsons arrive
in Port Said

1915 (19 February) Allied fleet bombards Ottoman
positions in the Dardanelles

(25 April) New Zealand and Australian troops
land on the Gallipoli peninsula

(7 August) New Zealand troops attack Ottoman
position on Chunuk Bair

(December) New Zealand troops withdrawn
from Gallipoli; Harry arrives in Egypt

1916 (13 April) Harry and the 12th Nelsons arrive in
France

(5–13 May) Harry on leave in England

(20 May) Harry arrives in the trenches outside
Armentières

(1 July) Opening day of the Battle of the
Somme

(31 July) Harry promoted to rank of Lance
Corporal

(8 September) Harry and the 12th Nelsons move
to Fricourt, near Mametz Wood

(25 September) Battle of Morval begins

(27 September) Harry killed in action

1919 (30 July) Death of Brita Palin

FAMILY TREE

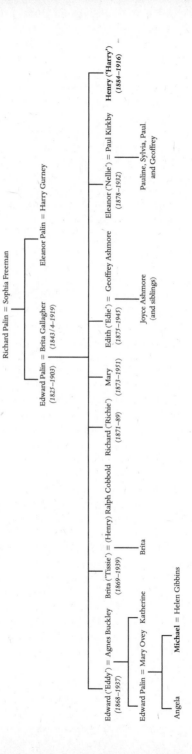

Richard Palin = Sophia Freeman

Edward Palin = Brita Gallagher
(1825–1903)

Eleanor Palin = Harry Gurney

Edward ('Eddy') = Agnes Buckley
(1868–1937)

Brita ('Tissie') = (Henry) Ralph Cobbold
(1869–1939)

Richard ('Richie')
(1871–89)

Mary
(1873–1951)

Edith ('Edie') = Geoffrey Ashmore
(1875–1945)

Eleanor ('Nellie') = Paul Kirkby
(1878–1932)

Henry ('Harry')
(1884–1916)

Brita

Edward Palin = Mary Ovey   Katherine

Angela

Michael = Helen Gibbins

Joyce Ashmore
(and siblings)

Pauline, Sylvia, Paul
and Geoffrey

ACKNOWLEDGEMENTS

Apart from his own war diaries, Great-Uncle Harry was the least recorded of all my Palin ancestors, so I owe a great debt of thanks to all those who gave their time and energy to unearthing evidence, hunting down clues and generally helping me piece together the jigsaw of his unheralded life.

The Reverend Allan Ricketts set the ball rolling with his comprehensive overview of Harry's father, Edward. On these foundations Roger Davies, with the help of the Linton and District History Society, built an extensive and invaluable structure of the Linton days, and he was never too busy to answer my queries, however small. Lynn and Clair Hodgson and Ben Casson, current occupants of Edward and Brita's vicarage, gave enthusiastic and informative help.

I owe a great debt of thanks to Michael Riordan, archivist at St John's College, for detail on Edward Palin's Oxford career, and particularly for finding totally unexpected photos of Edward as a young man. Katherine Kinrade at the Oxfordshire History Centre provided useful information about 7 Staverton Road.

Robin Brooke-Smith and his assistant Naomi furnished me with much new information about the various Palins at Shrewsbury School. As to Harry's time in India, Emma Jolly and Krutika Behrawala put together a comprehensive overview, Clare Patterson, of Glasgow University Archives, unearthed employment reports of Harry's time in the tea estates of Assam, and Richard Clifford gave me useful background information on his own family's experience as tea planters.

I owe a big thank you to Rosie Belton and her co-researchers Linden Armstrong and Joanne Pengelly for drawing up an invaluable portrait of Harry's time as a farmhand in New Zealand.

Once Harry joined the New Zealand Expeditionary Force, I had the combination of his diaries and Peter Jackson's encyclopaedic and generously shared knowledge to help me flesh out the extraordinary story of Harry's military career, first in Gallipoli and then on the Somme. Thanks, too, to Alan Ferris at the New Zealand Government Archive, Rob Cameron, who contacted me with vital information from the diaries of his grandfather Harry Dampier-Crossley, and Paul Reed, who kindly guided me round the battlefields of the Somme.

Thanks also to Malcolm 'Mo' Batters, for wonderful detail, both written and visual, on Harry's relationship with his best friend. Thanks in abundance to Sarah Paterson at the Imperial War Museum, Polly North at the Great Diary Project, Rachel Jobson for background to Caroline Watson in America, and Helen Melody and Dr Antonia Moon for help at the India collection at the British Library.

Acknowledgements

Thanks also to Clare Olssen, Judy Greenwood, Peter Attenborough, Madeleine Bunting, Andrew Tatham, Laura Brooke and John-Paul Davidson.

A special mention must go to Alison Sieff whose transcription of Harry's pencilled notebooks was a miraculous feat of concentration. The notebooks are delicate, the pencilled entries, often scribbled in the heat of battle, are often barely decipherable, yet not a word went missing.

Enormous thanks to my regular team at Mayday Management, Steve Abbott, Paul Bird and Mimi Robinson, who have encouraged me at every stage of the long search for my great-uncle.

The book would never have seen the light of day without the unwavering support and encouragement of my publisher, Nigel Wilcockson. His enthusiasm for the story was matched only by his obsessive dedication to the accuracy of the content. Unearthing the story of Harry's short life has been like living through a detective story. Nigel's eagle-eyed editing and forensic curiosity have provided the strongest possible foundation for this extraordinary story.

BIBLIOGRAPHY

Aitken, Alexander, *Gallipoli to the Somme: Recollections of a New Zealand Infantryman*, Oxford University Press, Wellington, 1963

Allen, Charles, *Plain Tales from the Raj: Images of British India in the Twentieth Century*, Andre Deutsch, London, 1975

Allen, Charles, *Raj: A Scrapbook of British India*, Andre Deutsch, London, 1977

Brereton, Cyprian, *Tales of Three Campaigns*, John Douglas Publishing, Christchurch, 2014 (first edition Selwyn & Blount, London, 1926)

Coke, Desmond, *The Bending of a Twig*, Chapman & Hall, London, 1907

Crawford, John, and McGibbon, Ian (editors), *New Zealand's Great War: New Zealand, the Allies and the First World War*, Exisle, New Zealand, 2014

Farrar, Ali Roff, 'What does your birth order mean?', *Psychologies* magazine, 2014

Gilbert, Martin, *Servant of India: A Study of Imperial Rule in India from 1905 to 1910*, Longmans, London, 1966

Gilmour, David, *The British in India: Three Centuries of Ambition and Experience*, Allen Lane, London, 2018

Harper, Glyn, *Johnny Enzed: The New Zealand Soldier in the First World War*, Exsile, New Zealand, 2016

Heffer, Simon, *High Minds: The Victorians and the Birth of Modern Britain*, Random House Books, London, 2013

Heffer, Simon, *The Age of Decadence: Britain 1880 to 1914*, Random House Books, London, 2017

Levine, Joshua, *Forgotten Voices of the Somme*, Ebury Press, London, 2008

Macdonald, Andrew, *On My Way to the Somme: New Zealanders and the Bloody Offensive of 1916*, HarperCollins, Auckland, 2005

Macdonald, Lyn, *Somme*, Michael Joseph, London, 1983

Macfarlane, Iris, *Daughters of the Empire: A Memoir of Life and Times in the British Raj*, Oxford University Press, Delhi, 2006

Malthus, Cecil, *Anzac: A Retrospect*, Reed Books, 2002 (first published Whitcombe and Tombs, Christchurch, 1965)

Malthus, Cecil, *Armentières and the Somme*, Reed Books, Auckland, 2002

Moore, Jenny, *45 Feet of Daughters*, self-published, 2011

Moorhouse, Geoffrey, *Calcutta*, Weidenfeld & Nicolson, London, 1971

Morris, Jan, *Pax Britannica: The Climax of Empire*, Faber & Faber, London, 1968

Pugsley, Christopher, *Gallipoli: The New Zealand Story*, Reed Books, Auckland, 1998

Pugsley, Christopher, *The Anzac Experience: New Zealand, Australia and Empire in the First World War*, Oratia Books, Auckland, 2016

Satow, Michael, and Desmond, Ray (foreword by Paul Theroux), *Railways of the Raj*, New York University Press, New York, 1980

Tolerton, Jane, *An Awfully Big Adventure: New Zealand World War One Veterans Tell Their Stories*, Penguin Books, Auckland, 2013

Wilson, A.N, *The Victorians*, Hutchinson, London, 2002

PICTURE ACKNOWLEDGEMENTS

Chapter openers: Chapter 1: reproduced by permission of the President and Fellows of St John's College, Oxford (059/ LG02). Chapter 2: Penta Springs Limited / Alamy Stock Photo. Chapter 4: reproduced by permission of Shrewsbury School. Chapter 6: © Look and Learn / Illustrated Papers Collection / Bridgeman Images. Chapter 7: Havelock Museum Collection, reproduced by permission of Linden Armstrong. Chapter 8: Nelson Provincial Museum (20232621) and Nelson Provincial Museum via Wikimedia Commons. Chapter 9: both images reproduced by permission of Malcolm Batters. Chapter 11: National Army Museum of New Zealand. Chapter 13: National Army Museum of New Zealand. Chapter 14: CBW / Alamy Stock Photo. Chapter 15: © Imperial War Museum, Q 4419.

Plate section: p. 1 (top and middle) reproduced by permission of the President and Fellows of St John's College, Oxford (Photos 15 and 163). p. 2 (bottom left and right) both images reproduced by permission of Roger Davies. p. 4 (top and middle) images reproduced by permission of Clair and Lynn Hodgson; (bottom) reproduced by permission of Roger Davies. p. 6 (top) The Print Collector via Getty Images; (middle) Pictorial Press Ltd / Alamy Stock Photo; (bottom) Royal Geographical Society via Getty Images. p. 7 (top) © Hulton-Deutsch Collection / CORBIS / Corbis via Getty Images; (bottom left) reproduced by permission of

Rosie Belton; (bottom middle) reproduced by permission of Jo Pengelly; (bottom right) reproduced by permission of Malcolm Batters. p. 8 (top) reproduced by permission of Jo Pengelly; (middle) reproduced by permission of Linden Armstrong; (bottom) reproduced by permission of Rosie Belton. p. 10 (top) reproduced by permission of WingNut Films, Wellington, New Zealand; (bottom) © Pen and Sword Books / UIG / Bridgeman Images. p. 11 (top left) Archives New Zealand via Wikimedia Commons; (top right) Historic Collection / Alamy Stock Photo; (bottom) by permission of the National Army Museum, London. p. 12 (top) Archives New Zealand via Wikimedia Commons; (middle) Argus Newspaper Collection of Photographs, State Library of Victoria; (bottom) Australian War Memorial collection. p. 13 (top) National Army Museum of New Zealand; (middle and bottom) Nelson Provincial Museum Collection, 300751 and 300749. p. 14 (top left) Archives New Zealand via Wikimedia Commons; (top right) National Army Museum of New Zealand; (right centre) Nelson Provincial Museum Collection, DT677; (bottom left) reproduced by permission of Margie Sale's grandchildren (the Orr family); (bottom right) Wikimedia Commons. p. 15 (top and bottom) © Imperial War Museum, Q 193 and Q 1243. p. 16 (top) © Imperial War Museum, Q 1312; (bottom) reproduced by permission of Paul Reed.

All other images from author's or publisher's collections.

The author and publisher gratefully acknowledge the permission granted to reproduce the copyright material in this book. Every effort has been made to trace copyright holders and to obtain their permission. The publisher apologises for any errors or omissions and, if notified of any corrections, will make suitable acknowledgement in future reprints or editions of this book.

INDEX

Index

Index